Living Letters
Daily Devotions for Busy Women

By Suzanne Chambers

Introduction

I have always wanted to write a book. For as long as I can remember, the desire to put my thoughts on printed page has lain dormant inside my heart. Not The Great American Novel, mind you. No, rather I have always longed to write a book that would teach and share, the truths that have shaped my life, helped me love God more, and follow Him better.

But the years passed and no such book got written. I was busy, yes, but I think I was just afraid I didn't really have enough worthy to put into print. The dream to write never would go away. I was pretty discouraged about it for a while. Was this going to be a failure in my life, an unfulfilled dream that would pester me forever? One day, the Lord revealed a great truth to me. I read this passage in 2 Corinthians 3:2 and I knew I WAS writing a book, *"You yourselves are our letter of recommendation, written on our hearts, to be known and read by all. And you show that you are a letter from Christ delivered by us, written not with ink but with the Spirit of the living God, not on tablets of stone but on tablets of human hearts."* Four books in fact, Living Letters that would one day be read in places I'd never go by people I'd never meet. The Chambers Chronicles, if you will! Raising these four kids that God entrusted me with–they are my life's books!

So I poured my energy into writing those books, knowing that I was merely the pen through which God would pour the indelible ink of His Word and His Spirit onto the pages of their lives. What a privilege! What a joy! The most exciting part of writing Living Letters is that they are just that: Living. They are dynamic, organic, growing, changing. These books will never be finished and the day eventually came when I was no longer a primary contributor, but because of God's generous grace, my imprint will always be on their lives. What a most wonderful opportunity!

As my little Living Letters grew, though, they came to be around less and less to hear my lectures, uh, teaching. They even got to the place of life where they moved out for good–can you imagine that? They weren't around to listen to me hardly ever, bless their hearts! Yet this urge to share my thoughts persisted, bless my heart. So I did what every woman with more words to say than there are folks around to listen does–I started a blog! Of course! That proved to be a healthy outlet for me to get all these thoughts out of my head and to share them in hopes that the same things God had taught me could also help someone else. My dream has been to write some lines into some other Living Letters, to be the pen that the ink of the Holy Spirit pours through and leaves beautiful and powerful imprints on the pages of their lives. So that they, too, will then write Living Letters of their own...for eternity.

The way we can do that effectively is through God's Word. To know it, obey it, love it, and share it–from one woman to another.

I really wish I could sit down over coffee (OK so I'd have TAB instead–but when I grow up, I am going to drink coffee!) and I could invest in your life. I would love nothing more than to be connected to you, to share things I've learned and struggles I've had and to walk through life with you. But time and space don't allow me to do that with every woman that wants to be a writer of Living Letters, an influencer for Christ.

That's why I wrote this devotional, sort of mini Bible studies that we can walk through together each day, to help other women impact their families, their communities, and their generation for the glory of God. God wants us to leave such a legacy.

The way we write these living letters–influence the world for Christ–is to get to know the Living God and to let His truth transform us, direct us, and sustain us. Most women that I know want to spend time in God's Word and prayer. They are acutely aware of their need for that and for the power God promises to unleash in response. It's not that we don't want to and it's not that we don't intend to–it's just that such desires get overrun by stomach virus epidemics, littles that rise unexpectedly early, or inexplicable noises coming from other parts of the house. So what are we to do, especially in these times when we most need to be fortified with His Word, not only for ourselves but also for those who depend on us for life, truth, and love?

I don't pretend to have a magic bullet that will give you the time you need to feast on Him. But He does! OK, maybe not a magic bullet, but certainly a desire to carve out that time, to commit to filling up your heart with truth, and the discipline to "just do it." I believe with all my heart that if you ask Him to help you invest time with Him, He will respond with overwhelming grace. In fact, I am confident that He who placed that desire within you (no matter how weak it may feel right now!) is just waiting for you to ask. So, right now, how 'bout you do just that? Confess your lack of discipline or failures or doubt. Take a step of faith, even if it's just to say you are willing to try and believe Him.

Then just do it.

This devotional is set up for you to read a passage of scripture and then provide you with a brief exploration of it. For five days. I am aware that there are seven days in each week but I set this up for five days intentionally. Because some days, the best we can do is a quick arrow prayer directed towards heaven, asking for help to not kill anybody on purpose! And, if you're like I am, if I miss several days, I feel behind and unable to "catch up"…and so I cave in and quit. I don't want you to do that so we have some margin built in to allow us to take seven days to cover five days' worth. God is aware of all on our plate–I believe He would rather we get in some good time with Him in for five days than to try hard for seven and give up after a month.

And by design, it is interactive. You will look up some passages on your own and answer some questions for yourself. There is great benefit to finding the treasures from scripture for yourself–check out Deuteronomy 29:29 to see what I mean! So let's resolve to dig into His Word together…

And to pray–specifically! I want you to get a journal–either a cute Lily Pulitzer blank book or a spiral notebook from CVS, it does not matter–and record prayer requests, personal thoughts, and new truths in it. I cannot overemphasize the importance of recording your petitions and dating them. Too many times we don't even recognize that God has answered our prayers because we didn't pray specifically or we didn't write down what we asked. And then we don't remember. What trophies in your faith case you will have as you periodically go back and see what God has done!

You may certainly pray according to whatever schedule you prefer but if you need some guidance, well, then I have a suggestion. Many years ago I became so overwhelmed by the thought of all I should be praying for that I practically quit, just from the feeling of "I cannot possibly do it all so I'll just not do anything." That was not successful, to say the least! Then God gave me the idea of addressing different needs on different days. Committing one day per week to each of the areas that I wanted to intercede for–how freeing it was to know I didn't need to cover everything every day! Word of caution, don't get legalistic about it. I don't fret if I am prompted to pray for a friend's needs on the day I have allocated to praying for the unsaved. And I don't fear that the world is "going to hell in a hand basket" because I forgot to pray for those in authority some Monday!

Here is what I do:

1. Monday: our nation and government/all in authority (list by name), read I Timothy 2:1-4

2. Tuesday: my family's financial needs and eternal investments, read Matthew 6:25-31

3. Wednesday: church (staff, leaders, their families, my involvement), read Titus 2:5-16

4. Thursday: unsaved and missions, read Acts 26:18

5. Friday: friends and their needs/requests, read Luke 5:17-20

6. Saturday: ministries we support, read Philippians1:3-5

7. Sunday: extended family, read Ephesians 3:14-21

EVERY day is "assigned" for my little tribe and our needs!

Also, you will notice an optional reading assignment at the very end. I'd like to challenge you to read through the entire Bible this year. If you've never done it, this will be a great accomplishment. If you've done it 15 times, this will still be a sweet treat. The optional reading is a schedule to enable you to do just that. Give it a try and see what you think.

One last thing before we jump in—more than a huge shout out to the more than fabulous Mandy Rice. Without her efficient expertise, her gentle proficiency, and her calming effect, this project would have been impossible. Mandy, I want to publicly thank you and praise God for how vital you are to me. May He bless you for eternity, dear friend!

And also, I want to thank my lifelong friend Tricia Bauman for her editing and proofreading extraordinaire! Her skills surpassed any professional editor and it gave me great confidence to know that this project earned a thumbs up from her. But, by far, the best gift she gave to me was not her grammar expertise. Not by a long shot. Had it not been for Tricia's influence in my life, not only would this devotional never have been written, the entire story of my life would have had a much different theme. For it was her life and her sharing Christ with me that brought me into a personal relationship with the creator of the universe. The words on all these pages, Tricia, came from the indelible ink you wrote into my life all those years ago. To say "thank you" will never be enough. But I know that He will reward you and on that day, and I get to have a front row seat and clap and cheer the loudest of all. I love you forever, my sister, my friend, my mentor.

Let's do this thing together. Just pray. Meditate on His Word. Influence the lives around us... and our nation...and the world. Let's do this thing!

Day 1

Therefore, be careful how you walk, not as unwise men, but as wise, making the most of your time because the days are evil. So then do not be foolish but understand what the will of the Lord is. Ephesians 5:15-17

Indeed we do live in days of evil! Not only do we see evil in the atrocities of Christians being martyred and persecuted, the corruption of corporate greed, and the pervasive wickedness of lusts and addictions, we must admit there is evil in our own hearts–jealousy, anger, laziness, pride, selfish ambition, fear, depression and the like. That's why scripture exhorts us to "*walk wise.*"

Unpacking this verse, we begin with the "therefore"–we must examine it to see what it's "there for!" The preceding verses tell us, "*But all things become visible when they are exposed by the light, for everything that becomes visible is light. For this reason it says 'Awake, sleeper, and rise from the dead. And Christ will shine on you.'*" (verses 13-14)

Because all things will one day be brought out into the open–even the secret thoughts, longings and hopes of our hearts–we must be careful: careful to live with wise intention, careful not to live foolishly or naively. Some translations of this passage use the word "*redeem*" for "making the most of" regarding how we use our time. It is helpful to think of our time as something that needs "redeeming" as a commodity that can be exchanged for something of value.

We have been allotted a certain number of days here on earth, days that can be spent, wasted or redeemed. Days that can be spent on our own dreams and agendas or redeemed–actually invested–for that which is of eternal value.

Today, let's pray that we will learn to "*walk wise.*" Verse 17 says it clearly–the word translated as "understand" here literally means "to put the pieces of the puzzle together." Let's start figuring out how to put our life's pieces together in such a way that the picture points the world to our incomparable Christ.

Day 2

The fear of the Lord is the beginning of wisdom; a good understanding have all those who do His commandments; His praise endures forever. Psalm 111:10

Yesterday we read about walking wisely., and putting the puzzle pieces together so that our lives are not foolish or wasted. Today's reading is the place we must begin in order to do just that. In order to be wise, we must first fear the Lord.

So what does it mean to fear the Lord? Doesn't the Bible tell me not to fear? This is confusing!

Some commentators say this means we are to respect the Lord. Others say we should be afraid because of His power. I am not a Hebrew scholar but I think that it's helpful to examine the word the psalmist used when the Holy Spirit inspired him to pen these words. The Hebrew word that we translate "fear" is "yirah" and it means abject terror, fear, awe, or reverence. Perhaps that doesn't help you much ☺ but let's unpack it together.

If you and I recognize God as omnipotent, omniscient, and omnipresent, then the way we live is bound to be affected. It causes us to respond in awe to His majesty in creation, to bow in humility and repentance that He knows our every thought, to rejoice in His presence that we are always loved and accepted, and to long to never displease Him because He is worthy of our devotion and affection and obedience.

That's how we begin our wise walk. And that "understanding what the will of God is" that we read about yesterday, the "putting together of the puzzle pieces?" Well, He tells us in His verse about that, too. That understanding–that "knowing which pieces go where"–hinges on obeying His commands.

Today let's pray this verse back to Him. Ask Him to show you His glory so you can worship Him. Ask Him to shine His light into your heart and reveal where you are falling short of what He desires for you. (Don't fear doing this–He is gentle and loving in His correction. He will not show us everything at once for we could not bear it. But when we confess and repent of whatever He shows us, He is faithful to cleanse us from all unrighteousness, even that which we are not aware of! I John 1:9-10) Then let His praises endure forever in your heart. Rejoice that He loves you faithfully and ask Him to show you specific things to obey.

Day 3

The wisest of women builds her house, but folly with her own hands tears it down. P[...]

If I weren't already motivated to gain wisdom, this verse would surely move me to [...] Knowing that my life impacts those I love is indeed great motivation. Nancy DeMoss Wogl[...] of Revive Our Hearts ministry says

"At any given moment, you and I are either wise or foolish women. Whether we realize[...] or not, we are either building our "house," or we are tearing it down. Every woman has a 'house,' an immediate sphere of influence. If you are married, if you have children, your family is your closest and most important circle of influence. Single women also have a "house;" it encompasses those lives they touch within their extended family, church, workplace, and community. A wise woman is actively involved in building her house on a daily basis, but the foolish woman tears down her house with her own hands."

As I meditate on this verse, I am prompted to consider my words, my actions, my priorities. Am I building up or tearing down? Pray with me that we will be women that build, not impressive physical structures, but rather lives that are monuments to the glory of God. Take a few minutes and write down some ways we can be wise builders...or foolish destroyers.

Wise builders:

Foolish destroyers:

Day 4

Therefore since we have so great a cloud of witnesses surrounding us, let us also lay aside every encumbrance, and the sin which so easily entangles us, and let us run with endurance the race that is set before (marked out for) us. Hebrews 12:1

Walking wisely–running our race–that's what we want to learn to do. This verse has so much for us to dig into! Let's get started...

1. Since we have *"so great a cloud of witnesses"*–whether that means those folks around us in this life or those who have gone on to glory but can still observe life here on earth- we can be motivated to press on well because we are being watched. Not like "Big Brother" in Orwell's *1984* but rather like Mike Mulligan and the Steam Shovel who worked harder, faster, and better when the crowd gathered around to watch.

2. Notice that two things can slow us down–*"encumbrances"* and *"sin which so easily entangles us."* *"Encumbrances"* are not sins–they can be good things like hobbies or priorities or even relationships that we put in a position of weighing us down instead of a proper place of enjoyment. We need wisdom to hear from the Lord about what things in our life are hindering us from running the race well.

3. *"Sin which so easily entangles us"*–clearly there are things that can ensnare us. Those things are sin. Ask the Lord to graciously shine His light on any place where sin is lurking.

4. *"Run with endurance"* –I once asked a most Godly woman who had raised five children to love and follow Christ wholeheartedly what the most important thing I could teach my kids was. I was expecting her to reply "Bible verses" or "obedience" or "respect." Know what she said? Perseverance. That's what endurance is. We are going to be tempted to give up or give in all along the way. We will become discouraged and weary and what we need is an injection of endurance. Lord, help us!

5. The last thing I see in this verse is *"the race marked out for us."* How tempting it is to look in the next lane at somebody else's race and think we'd rather be running that one! May God grant us grace to embrace with joy the race He chose specifically for us.

Day 5

He who walks with wise men will be wise but the companion of fools will suffer harm. Proverbs 13:20

I know we are called to be a light to this dark world, but in order to maintain our brightness we would do well to heed the counsel of this verse. Walking with wise men–that doesn't mean we never sit by a fool at our kid's soccer game! (Considering the behavior of most parents at kids' sports events...we would likely be in solitary confinement if that's what this verse intended!) Rather I believe it is calling us to choose carefully who we "do life with." Who are our close companions, whose company do we prefer, which people are the ones we rely on and turn to in times of need. It is of vital importance who those people are, that they are wise, or at least learning to be wise. Because hanging out with fools brings destruction–the phrase, *"will suffer harm,"* means to become evil, to be made worse, suddenly.

May God protect us from wanting to be with those who don't fear the Lord. Of course we should pray for them, share Christ with them, and show them love but there is inevitable inherent danger when we choose these kinds of folks to be our close friends. We can tell ourselves as many times as we want to that we are going to influence them for good, that we won't wind up like them, that these folks are more fun than other options. But mark my word, actually mark HIS Word, we will suffer harm. And it will come without warning.

I used to work for Truett Cathy at the corporate offices of Chick-fil-A and one of my many perks was to hear his homespun wisdom on a regular basis. My most favorite of his sayings was, "You'll be the same person a year from now as you are today except for the books you read and the people you associate yourself with. Friends will determine the quality and direction of your life. Choose wisely."

Amen, Truett, amen.

As we continue in our journey to walk wise, and put our puzzle together to the glory of God, are there some companions we need to back away from in order to avoid suffering harm? Ask God to reveal His desires for us.

Oh, and let's also pray fervently that we will be wise companions in the lives of those around us!

Living Letters

WEEK 2 - FEAR OF THE LORD

Day 1

"Am I a God who is near," declares the Lord, "and not a God who is far off? Can a man hide himself in hiding places, so I do not see him," declares the Lord. "Do I not fill the heavens and the earth?" declares the Lord. Jeremiah 23:23,24

Last week we began learning how to "walk wise" and the first step we learned is to fear the Lord. This week we will dig deeper into what that means by concentrating on the holiness of God. Obviously this topic cannot be exhausted in a lifetime much less in a week but my prayer is that the Holy Spirit will give us a glimpse into the character of our Holy God.

The verses from Jeremiah speak to His omnipresence–how mind-boggling is it to ponder on the fact that He is everywhere, all the time? (I don't know about you, but when my kids were preschoolers, that would have been a mighty awesome trait for Him to have imparted to me...Just sayin) What does that aspect of His character mean for us as His children? He is a God who is near; we cannot hide from Him? It brings us

1. Comfort: In Genesis 16:13, we see Abraham's servant Hagar comforted in her troubles by knowing that our God is *"a God who sees."* Many times we are tempted to feel that our lives are too unimportant for The Sovereign King but He assures us that He sees... and He cares (I Peter 5:7). He is not unaware of our pain or our problems because He is right there with us bearing them, comforting us and bringing peace and resolution.

2. Courage: The next way we benefit from His omnipresence is found in Romans 8:35-39. Yes, we will undoubtedly go through difficulties but we need not fear nor feel alone because of the promise in this passage: *"Who shall separate us from the love of Christ? Shall tribulation, or distress, or persecution, or famine, or nakedness, or danger, or sword? As it is written, 'For your sake we are being killed all the day long; we are regarded as sheep to be slaughtered.' No, in all these things we are more than conquerors through him who loved us. For I am sure that neither death nor life, nor angels nor rulers, nor things present nor things to come, nor powers, nor height nor depth, nor anything else in all creation, will be able to separate us from the love of God in Christ Jesus our Lord."*

3. Conviction: Knowing that we cannot escape His presence–even in hell! (Psalm 139:7-9, Revelation 14:10)–motivates us to live a life of holiness, for fearing of displeasing Him.

Day 2

For I know that the Lord is great, and that our Lord is above all gods; Whatever the Lord pleases, He does, in heaven and in earth, in the seas and in all the deeps. Psalm 135:5,6

Today our focus is on His omnipotence. Just to give us a glimpse of this attribute let's unpack this verse from Psalm 135.

- He is great: He is mighty and powerful. This truth has the potential to be absolutely terrifying were it not for the rest of Who He Is, which is found in verse 3 of this same passage, *"Praise the Lord for He is good; Sing praises to His name for it is lovely."* Indeed He is powerful but hallelujah He is not a despot but rather a benevolent ruler who loves His people!

- He is above all gods: Yes, there are other powers at work in this world, "gods" who wield influence and wreak destruction. That is true. But our God is above them all. The forces of evil cannot touch our lives without His permission (Job 1:6-12). Our God is sovereign; it is He who is in charge. We need not fear when things seem out of control because He is always in control. Even though we often cannot understand His plan, we can be confident that He is still on His throne, ruling with absolute power and love.

- Whatever the Lord pleases, He does: Sometimes it doesn't seem like He is in charge. Terrifying things happen all over, too close to home and in our own lives. Things we would not have chosen or even the things we fear the most. But this verse assures us that we can trust Him because He is accomplishing His plan. Job 42:2 tells us plainly, *"I know that You can do all things, And that no purpose of Yours can be thwarted."* And His purposes are good! Even if we are distressed for a time here, it is not without purpose and His plans for His people are good. All sorts of verses give us that confidence, especially Jeremiah 29:11, *"For I know the plans that I have for you, declares the Lord, plans for welfare and not for calamity, to give you a future and a hope."*

Today, let's bow before His throne, realizing He is sovereign...and we are not. Let us entrust our lives—and our families' lives—to Him, knowing that He is at work for His glory and our good.

Living Letters

Day 3 - The Preeminence of Christ

He is the image of the invisible God, the firstborn of all creation. For by Him all things were created, in heaven and on earth, visible and invisible, whether thrones or dominions or rulers or authorities—all things were created through Him and for Him. And He is before all things, and in Him all things hold together. Colossians 1:15-17

Not only is God all-powerful, and good and sovereign, so is Jesus. Because He is God! Before the earth was formed, in eternity Past, Christ existed alone with God the Father and the Holy Spirit. In perfect union and harmony, they fellowshipped together and created the world and all that is in it. And it is their existence that gives us life and holds all things together. Yes, this is a perplexing truth but praise God we worship one who is greater than our understanding! He alone is worthy of all our affection and our praise! Hallelujah that we belong to Him!

I believe that the reason Christians should study science is to discover the glory of God. I don't think that true science contradicts or threatens the truth of God's Word at all, but rather as we learn more and more about the world He created, we uncover glorious truths about Him. One of my favorite scientific truths stems from something very exciting that I learned about this verse, particularly the part about "*in Him all things hold together.*" Now, I don't need any "support" from the world to "prove" the truth of scripture but when something in science illustrates the truth of God's Word, it causes me to jump up and down with excitement over the glory of God. This is such a truth…

In all living cells, there is a molecule called laminin. This protein acts like glue, which keeps the parts of the cell from falling apart; it's the stuff that helps anchor cells to the membrane and is critical for the maintenance and survival of tissues. Well, that's all very interesting but what does that have to do with Jesus? This: If you and I could examine this "glue protein" under a microscope, we would see that its structure is the shape of a cross. For real! Check it out on Wikipedia and see for yourself. It is certainly no accident that our glorious creator chose to form this protein in the shape of a cross, knowing that one day technology would enable His creatures to discover Him even in the details of cells. Truly, by Him are all things are held together.

Today, let's rejoice that every aspect of our lives–down to the microscopic level of our cells, all things are held together by the one who loves us and gave Himself for us. To Him be the glory forever. Amen.

Day 4

"You are my witnesses," declares the Lord, "and my servant whom I have chosen, that you may know and believe me and understand that I am He. Before me no god was formed, nor shall there be any after me...I, I am the Lord, and besides me there is no savior. I declared and saved and proclaimed, when there was no strange god among you; and you are my witnesses," declares the Lord, "and I am God." Isaiah 43:10-12

We've had a few days to dwell on the glory of God, His power and sovereignty and love for us. Truly that causes us to respond in worship and praise.

But there needs to be more to our response.

To be His witnesses, to proclaim His marvelous truths to those around us, and to hear Him say to us as He did to the Apostle Paul:

But rise and stand upon your feet, for I have appeared to you for this purpose, to appoint you as a servant and witness to the things in which you have seen me and to those in which I will appear to you, delivering you from your people and from the Gentiles—to whom I am sending you to open their eyes, so that they may turn from darkness to light and from the power of Satan to God, that they may receive forgiveness of sins and a place among those who are sanctified by faith in me. Acts 26:16-18

He is worthy of our praise and our allegiance. He alone is worthy. And He desires that all should come to the knowledge of the truth (I Timothy 2:4, 2 Peter 3:9). Let's ask the Lord who He wants to send us to as His witness. It might be a family member or a stranger in the grocery store or it might be across the sea. How can we be witnesses of His glory today?

Day 5

For my thoughts are not your thoughts, neither are your ways my ways, declares the Lord. For as the heavens are higher than the earth, so are my ways higher than your ways and my thoughts than your thoughts. Isaiah 55:8-9

If you are anything like me, this verse is quite an understatement! I do not understand God's ways at all! Sometimes it looks as though this world is spinning out of control. Atrocities committed on innocent people. And then wretched people seem to prosper abundantly! Those in authority call evil "good" and good "evil." It makes no sense to me and actually makes me angry.

On the flip side, I cannot understand His goodness. The favor He shows to me and the blessings He bestows all around me are so undeserved, so unmerited.

All I know to do is to proclaim His worthiness, trust His goodness, and thank Him for His gracious gifts. Sometimes that's a tall order.

So here are some thoughts that help me and maybe they will be of benefit to you, too.

When evil seems to be winning in the world, I remind myself of His sovereignty and that He even uses calamity to reveal His glory (Isaiah 45:5-7).

When He permits things to happen that seem unfair and too hard to me, I remind myself that He is God and I am not. And that He is at work to accomplish His plan for not only my good but especially His glory. I'd best not argue with Him (Isaiah 45:9-10).

When He allows me to see Him at work or experience special blessings, I remind myself that He is indeed always kind and merciful and that He lavishes on those He loves just because He is a good, good Father. And I strive to ever be mindful that every good gift is from Him (James 1:17).

And I fall at His feet, rejoicing that I worship a God who is far greater than I, one that I cannot comprehend or explain. I can only respond to Him in love and praise. Hallelujah!

WEEK 3 - RESPONDING TO GOD'S HOLINESS

Day 1

Therefore, preparing your minds for action, and being sober-minded, set your hope fully on the grace that will be brought to you at the revelation of Jesus Christ. As obedient children, do not be conformed to the passions of your former ignorance, but as He who called you is holy, you also be holy in all your conduct, since it is written, "You shall be holy, for I am holy."
I Peter 1:13-16

Last week was a glimpse into God's holiness. While we cannot fully grasp that truth on this side of eternity, we can still respond in our attitude and actions with an attitude of awe and wonder that worships the one who is worthy, and with actions that reflect our desire to please Him and be like Him. Don't get confused and think that we have to work to receive His acceptance or that we have to earn enough "holy points" to merit His favor. Not only do we not have to–we couldn't do it even if we tried! But this verse explains that, as Christ is revealed to us, as we see Him for who He is, we receive grace. Grace…the desire and the power that God gives us so that we can obey Him.

As we begin to grasp the holiness of God, we see the need for action–if we are to be like Jesus, then we will have to change. If we are to be holy, then we can no longer live as we used to. Being holy means to be set apart for a special purpose–that of pleasing Him. I think of it like my wedding dress–it was set apart for a special purpose, indeed…it was "holy." I don't treat my wedding dress like any old pair of gym shorts, it is special and treasured and "holy." That's how we live, as we embrace the holiness of God. We are treasured, set apart, and we live for a higher purpose than just pleasing ourselves.

Today, take a moment and think about a wedding dress–your own, if you have one. Think about how lovely you feel in a wedding dress, how valued and treasured. Reflect on how your heart wanted to please your groom with how you looked on your wedding day. And then ask the Lord to transfer that earthly thought into spiritual action in your heart so that you and I can live set apart…holy…for Jesus, our Bridegroom!

Living Letters

Day 2

Search me, O God, and know my heart; Try me and know my anxious thoughts; and see if there be any hurtful way in me, and lead me in the everlasting way. Psalm 139:23-24

Pray that verse out loud for just a moment. Now let's look at it and see what we are asking God to do.

We are asking Him to search us…in order to know our heart. *"Know"* in the sense of intimately experiencing, not as in gaining knowledge. God already knows what's in our hearts! Here we are inviting Him in to fellowship with us, to uncover us…to reveal us to ourselves.

This passage leads us to a place of vulnerability with God. This vulnerability allows our anxious thoughts to be exposed and laid bare before Him. Then He can address our deepest needs. What are we worried about? What makes us fearful? Whatever it is prevents us from following Him fully and blocks our path in "the everlasting way."

The Hebrew word that is translated here as "hurtful" is "otseb." I have no idea how to pronounce that but its meaning is powerful. It comes from the word that means "idol." Wow. This passage is telling us that we become anxious, fearful, and worried when we have something in our heart that takes priority over God, an idol. It's something that we have allowed to control us, our thoughts, and our behavior.

And when that happens, we are off the everlasting path of peace and joy.

So we need to get back on it, and that's exactly where our God wants to lead us. That is why He beckons us to let Him know our hearts.

Spend some time today quiet before Him. Let Him show you the root of your anxiety; let Him lay bare any idols that are blocking your path. He is waiting to hear from you.

Day 3

Who can discern his errors? Declare me innocent from hidden faults. Keep back your servant also from presumptuous sins; let them not have dominion over me! Then I shall be blameless, and innocent of great transgression. Psalm 19:12-13

Psalm 19 is my husband's favorite chapter in scripture. I hope you'll take time to read all 14 verses, it is a perfect selection for this week as we focus on responding to God's holiness. The chapter begins with the glory of God, as seen in the heavens. Don't you love to stare at the sky and marvel at the greatness of the creator? I often ponder the fact that He could have made earth so bland and dull, without all the gorgeous aspects that we enjoy --- and we never would have known the difference! Instead, He displays His splendor in the skies and the flowers and the seas. Don't you just want to shout Hallelujah? Go ahead!

The psalm moves from God's glory to His law and how good it is, how it benefits us. God's law restores us, makes us wise, delights us, and keeps us from harm. These two verses at the end of the chapter show the response we have to seeing His glory and submitting to His law. We realize how far short we fall in our ability to keep His law and we cry out to Him for help. Apart from His Spirit, we are not even able to see where we are wrong!

So the psalmist asks the Lord to shine His light on the hidden things, areas of pride and presumption that can control us without our even realizing it.

Glory to God above all else–when we go to Him in this way, He responds with grace and forgiveness and declares us blameless before Him–hallelujah, what a Savior!

Spend some time asking Him to reveal hidden pride and presumptuous ways. Let Him show you so that you can then rejoice in His cleansing.

Day 4

Let no man deceive himself. If any man among you thinks that he is wise in this age, he must become foolish, so that he may become wise. I Corinthians 3:18

It has been several days of self-examination. I know that can be heavy, but don't despair or give up. Trust that God is working in your heart to bring you joy and peace and to equip you for the work He has for you to do.

Today will be brief. Ask Him to help you to not be deceived—by yourself. The danger of self-deception is so great. By definition, we don't know when we are deceiving ourselves because we are deceived! We can't see our blind spots because we can't see them!

But God has a remedy for that. Humility. When we come to Him and admit our vulnerability to being deceived, He opens up the floodgates of heaven and drenches us with His grace. He responds to us with light, light that shows us our need for wisdom. And then He lavishes upon us what we need to be wise—the ability to see life from His perspective.

Spend time today admitting your need for Him.

Day 5

Examine yourselves, to see whether you are in the faith. Test yourselves. Or do you not realize this about yourselves, that Jesus Christ is in you? Unless indeed you fail to meet the test! I hope you will find out that we have not failed the test. But we pray to God that you may not do wrong—not that we may appear to have met the test, but that you may do what is right, though we may seem to have failed. For we cannot do anything against the truth, but only for the truth. 2 Corinthians 13:5-8

Many of us struggle with assurance about our salvation. We wonder if we "did it right" when we trusted Christ way back when. It is very likely that I personally hold the record for accepting Jesus the most number of times–just to be sure it "took!" Knowing that propensity of most all of us, I am almost hesitant to ask us to go through this passage, because I don't want to create doubt and struggle where there need not be any.

But I must. This admonition is in scripture; therefore it is one we should heed. Are you in the faith? How do you know? Do you base your assurance on the fact that you "prayed a prayer" or "walked an aisle" many years ago?

If you are in the faith, then your life now will bear witness of that. No, not a perfectly sinless life, but there will be evidence of life–a hunger for His Word, a love for His church, a desire to please Him, fruit of His Spirit, a hatred of sin.

Please don't skip today's lesson. Examine yourself and see if indeed you are in the faith. If His Spirit assures you that you are, rejoice! If not, please contact me at chamfam@bellsouth.net or see a pastor or other Christian leader for help.

Day 1

He has made everything beautiful in its time. Also, He has put eternity into man's heart, yet so that he cannot find out what God has done from the beginning to the end. Ecclesiastes 3:11

Read this passage a couple of times. Let its truth sink into your soul. *"He has made everything beautiful in its time."* I don't know about you but there are more than a few things, or situations, that I just don't find beautiful at all–things that bring pain or destruction or angst. No, I don't think everything is beautiful at all.

Then I read the rest of that sentence…*"in its time."*

There is the key–*"in its time."*

How often do I come to a conclusion that something is wrong or awful or even irreparable when the problem is that I judged it too early? That broken relationship, that brutal disappointment, that bruised heart…nothing beautiful at all. And, yet, I need to trust that God's not done. *In its time* is not completed. God is still at work, unfolding His plan, fulfilling His purpose, and all will be beautiful, *in its time.*

The next sentence gives me the tool that helps me embrace this truth. Eternal perspective.

Often I cannot know what God is doing or how He intends to use the unbeautiful things in my life to make something glorious. I long for things like harmony and peace and fulfillment that seem to be elusive–at least on more than a temporary basis. That's because we were made for eternity. The longing I live with cannot be satisfied with the things of earth, and my heart groans at the insatiable yearnings.

What is to be our response?

Day 2

The years of our life are seventy, or even by reason of strength eighty; yet their span is but toil and trouble; they are soon gone, and we fly away. Who considers the power of your anger, and your wrath according to the fear of you? So teach us to number our days that we may get a heart of wisdom. Psalm 90:10-12

Yesterday we purposed our hearts to turn towards eternity, to consider the circumstances of our lives from a position of trusting God's eternal plan. How do you think this passage fits in with what we learned yesterday? In the space below, write out a brief summary of what these verses say.

Now ask the Lord to show you how to apply the truths in this passage in your life. What are specific ways to number our days? Are there things we would or would not do if we thought we only had a very brief time left on earth? Would our concerns be different? What about how we invest our time or gifts or money?

Day 3

And let us not grow weary of doing good, for in due season we will reap, if we do not give up. So then, as we have opportunity, let us do good to everyone, and especially to those who are of the household of faith. Galatians 6:9-10

Let's admit it—sometimes we just get plain tired of doing good. We've been at it for a while, serving others, ministering to their needs, not focusing on our own...and we just get tired. Weary is such a good word for it. It does mean fatigued and exhausted but it also can carry an element of dissatisfaction. I wonder if that is the connotation the Holy Spirit wants to convey here? To warn us that it's likely we will be doing good for a season and then become disillusioned. We might feel unappreciated or misunderstood. Maybe we even anticipate a tiny bit of reciprocation when it's our turn to be in need...and it doesn't happen. Weariness sets in. Another translation uses the term "lose heart." It can happen so easily, to all of us.

This passage encourages us not to give up because payday is coming. We are exhorted to have faith that fruit from our actions will come if we will but hang on. And we are reminded that the time will come when we won't have an opportunity to sow seeds of blessing. That season will be over and it will be time to harvest what has been planted.

So while we have the chance, let's do all the good we can to all the people we can... especially to those who belong to Christ. We will certainly one day reap the reward.

And remember that all those around us need every bit of goodness we can share.

Day 4

For we are his workmanship, created in Christ Jesus for good works, which God prepared beforehand, that we should walk in them. Ephesians 2:10

This verse follows the familiar passage that teaches us that we are saved by grace through faith and not of any good works that we might do. Yes, we are saved by grace, not by works. And our lives are to be displays of His workmanship, demonstrations of His glory and grace. Spiritual works of art and creations of His power that give evidence of His faithfulness.

No, we are surely not saved by works. Any good that we might try to do would be pathetic attempts to live up to His holy standards of perfection. We would always fall short. Always. So we cannot hope–nor should we even try–to be saved by good works.

But we are saved for good works! Changing that one little preposition changes everything! We do not save ourselves by good works. But make no mistake about it, He salvages our souls and sanctifies our lives so that we can display His glory by doing good works! In fact, He dreamed up good things for each of us to do before we were even saved and His desire is that we would live up to what He has planned.

Sometimes I wonder what He has for me to do. And then I ponder on the sobering truth that I am not doing all He fashioned me for, all that He planned out for me to do, because sometimes I grow weary.

Praise His name for His unconditional love, regardless of my performance. That is sure. But you know what? That doesn't make me feel "safe" about slacking off. Knowing that He loves me so freely–without my ever being able to earn it–makes me love Him back all the more. And it fans the flame of my desire to discover all He has for me to do. Works that He has prepared for me to walk in…works that He has uniquely gifted and positioned and beckoned me to do.

Let's ask Him to show us what He has for us today…

Day 5

For we must all appear before the judgment seat of Christ, so that each one may receive what is due for what he has done in the body, whether good or evil. 2 Corinthians 5:10

What is the judgment seat of Christ? Who is it for? Can I lose my salvation because of evil I have done?

There are two judgments. Every person who has ever lived will be called forth in one or the other. These judgments at the end of time are exclusive–no one will be part of both.

For those without Christ, there will be the great white throne of judgment where all will be called before the throne of God to give an account for themselves. There will be no excuse accepted for falling short of God's standards of holy perfection. All will be found guilty and will be doomed to eternal separation from God–eternity without life or light or love, eternity with regret and torment and pain. Eternity.

But for those who have trusted Christ's righteousness to satisfy God's demands of perfection, we will not stand before God to give an explanation of our lives. We will not have to try and justify our failures or argue for acceptance. Because of Jesus, God declares us "not guilty." As unbelievable as it seems, God willingly accepts Christ's perfection on our behalf. Amazing! Can I get an amen and hallelujah?

However, there will be a time of accounting. In the original Greek text of this verse, the phrase *"judgment seat"* was "bema." This word refers to a raised platform used in Greek athletic contests where judges sat to oversee the games and recognize the victors. At the conclusion of the contest, at the bema, laurel wreaths were placed on the heads of the winners as a symbol of victory. This verse gives us the picture of the believer as a competitor in a spiritual contest. Just like the ancient Greek athletes appeared before the bema to receive a perishable award, so we believers will appear before the bema–the judgment seat of Christ- to receive an imperishable reward.

This will not be a time of punishment where we receive judgment for our sins but there will be recriminations for not having run well enough to win. In other words, we will not lose our salvation for how we live after we trust Christ but we very well could suffer the loss of rewards that are given for good and faithful service.

Ask God to help you live with the reality of the bema ever before you. May we all live so that Jesus can one day place a wreath on our heads to His glory!

Day 1

When the Pharisees heard that He had put the Sadducees to silence, they gathered themselves together. And one of them, a lawyer, asked Him a question, testing Him, "Teacher, which is the great commandment in the Law?" And He said to him, "You shall love the Lord your God with all your heart, and with all your soul and with all your mind. This is the great and foremost commandment. The second is like it—You shall love your neighbor as yourself. On these two commandments depend the whole law and the prophets." Matthew 22:34-40

The Pharisees and Sadducees were the elite religious and political leaders of the day in New Testament times. The Sadducees were aristocrats, tending to be wealthy and holding powerful positions, including that of chief priests and high priest, and the majority of the 70 seats of the ruling council called the Sanhedrin. They seemed to be more concerned with politics than religion. Because they were accommodating to Roman leaders and were the wealthy upper class, they did not relate well to the common man and vice versa. The common man tended to prefer those who belonged to the party of the Pharisees who were mostly middle-class businessmen. This group believed that the written word (Old Testament) was inspired by God but they also gave equal authority to oral tradition, which is forbidden (Deuteronomy 4:2). The Pharisees sought to not only strictly obey these traditions themselves but also to hold such obedience as the standard for righteousness for everyone. This was their ticket to acceptance by God.

The two groups were largely opposed to one another...except in their desire to discredit and eventually destroy Jesus. Scripture shows us time and again how these people tried to trap Jesus by asking religious questions that would inflame Roman leaders or give them grounds to humiliate Him before the people.

The above passage is one of those attempts.

Instead of holding out one command or law as priority above all others, Jesus boils them all down to two principles. He says that everything scripture teaches us is based on the preeminence of these commands. Therefore, it will serve us well to see what He says...and to evaluate ourselves against His standard. This week, we will look at LOVE... and for today, ask the Holy Spirit to shine His light into your heart, and to speak to us about LOVE.

Day 2

And one of them, a lawyer, asked Him a question, testing Him, "Teacher, which is the great commandment in the Law?" And He said to him, "You shall love the Lord your God with all your heart, and with all your soul and with all your mind. This is the great and foremost commandment. The second is like it–You shall love your neighbor as yourself. On these two commandments depend the whole Law and the Prophets." Matthew 22:35-40

Let's read this passage again today, now that we know the background. The Pharisees wanted to know which commandment was most important, which one should they concentrate on primarily. Perhaps they had looked inside their own hearts enough to know they couldn't keep them all and hoped to justify themselves by at least keeping the most important one.

Jesus dashed those hopes.

He told them…and us…that all the commandments are rooted in one thing–love. Our most important task in life is not establishing a career or having a great marriage or raising responsible kids. It's not writing books or being famous or having laudable talent. It's not even faithful church service or self-sacrifice for others.

It's love.

It's loving God and loving others.

I Corinthians 13:1-3 demonstrates the preeminence of love and the futility of all else, *"If I speak in the tongues of men and of angels, but have not love, I am a noisy gong or a clanging cymbal. And if I have prophetic powers, and understand all mysteries and all knowledge, and if I have all faith, so as to remove mountains, but have not love, I am nothing. If I give away all I have, and if I deliver up my body to be burned, but have not love, I gain nothing."*

Let's ask the Lord to teach us what LOVE is this week….

Day 3

Love is patient and kind; love does not envy or boast; it is not arrogant or rude. It does not insist on its own way; it is not irritable or resentful; it does not rejoice at wrongdoing, but rejoices with the truth. Love bears all things, believes all things, hopes all things, and endures all things.
I Corinthians 13:4-7

This is such a familiar passage. If you've attended a wedding lately, you probably heard it quoted, a lovely passage indeed. But God wants it to be far more than words on a page or phrases read to inspire. He wants us to embody love! He wants LOVE to be what oozes out of our lives and splashes onto all those around us–near and far.

Read back through those verses. Wherever you see the word "love," substitute your own name.

How did that feel? Would our families applaud such substitution or does that thought make us cringe a bit? Can we be described this way? Can anyone?

The only way is by God's Spirit. Because God Himself is LOVE, when He takes residence within us through a personal relationship with Christ, it is His love living in us and through us that touches other people.

I can be quite dismayed when I consider how far short I fall of God's description of love. Only when I realize that He is in the process of transforming me to look like Him–and that the process is not complete–am I comforted.

Today, let's let the Holy Spirit focus on just one aspect of love's definition, see how we measure up, and ask Him to develop that in us more fully.

Patient. What does it mean to be patient? The word that we translate from the Greek as "patient" is "makrothumeo" and actually means "to suffer long." That is quite a bit deeper than "patient" I think! Instead of standing up for my "rights" or demanding my expectations be met or drawing upon hasty presumptions, this requires that I lay down my "rights" and willingly suffer because of the actions of another. It means that I am to exercise understanding towards another rather than being easily angered or offended. It means that love is costly.

Pray that He will open your eyes to opportunities to demonstrate patience, to suffer long...and to times you have failed to do so.

Day 4

Love is patient and kind; love does not envy or boast; it is not arrogant or rude. It does not insist on its own way; it is not irritable or resentful; it does not rejoice at wrongdoing, but rejoices with the truth. Love bears all things, believes all things, hopes all things, and endures all things. I Corinthians 13:4-7

Not only is love patient (willing to "suffer long") but it is also kind, does not envy others, or boast, or act in an arrogant or rude way. How well does that describe you or me?

Ask the Holy Spirit to teach us what kindness is. It is significant, I believe, that kindness is paired with not being jealous or envious and then followed up with not being arrogant or rude. Context aids in the understanding of what kindness is. The word used for "boasting" explains the idea of calling attention to what one has, an attempt to show oneself as above another. This can be done in all sorts of ways, can't it? We often deceive ourselves but rarely is anyone else deceived when we try to make ourselves look good in the eyes of others by drawing attention to some blessing in our lives. Certainly God is not fooled. And that is not kindness... that is not love.

Neither is it loving when we display arrogance or rudeness. Before we assume we are not guilty of unkind acts such as these, let our minds wander to things like how we spoke to a telemarketer or our own child. Or how we responded when the checkout clerk made a blunder or the deliveryman was late. Or whether or not we overlooked the opportunity to greet a guest at church or invite that lonely person to sit beside us. Or maybe even those times we meant to do something kind but busyness distracted us...and the deed never materialized. That, too, is rudeness.

Instead, kindness focuses on blessing others and lifting them up—with words and deeds, attitudes and actions, intentions and follow-through.

Every day, all day long, God places opportunities to display His love through kindness right before us. It need not be on a scale the world considers "grand"...in God's economy, a cup of cold water given in His name brings great reward. Let's ask Him right now to open our eyes that we might see...and grant us His grace to respond with His love.

Day 5

Love is patient and kind; love does not envy or boast; it is not arrogant or rude. It does not insist on its own way; it is not irritable or resentful; it does not rejoice at wrongdoing, but rejoices with the truth. Love bears all things, believes all things, hopes all things, and endures all things. I Corinthians 13:4-7

Yes, I realize that we are reading the same passage for days on end! That is by design. It is the Word of God that has the power to transform us (see I Thessalonians 2:13), and that is why we meditate on the same passage over and over–we need transforming in order to live a life of love.

Today let's look at *"love does not envy."* It occurs to me that we don't hear many messages preached on envy. There aren't too many books on this topic and I rarely hear myself or others confess this particular sin. And yet, it is a major problem among those of us who are alive. Major. If we dig down to discover root causes of many other sins, we often find envy lurking there.

Think about it–have you gossiped recently? Or criticized someone? Or treated someone unkindly? Resented a friend or complained about something you did not have? Is there envy underneath those things? Could it be that we covet what someone else has–be it a lovely home or thoughtful husband or successful children–and that causes us to react in unloving ways to someone…as if we can somehow even the score?

Love does not envy. Instead, love rejoices over God's blessings to others and trusts that He is doing good to us, as well. Rejecting envy requires that we embrace certain truths about God. First, that it is HE who gives good gifts. Good things do not come as a result of self-effort but rather are from His hand. He determines who has what. And we need to settle that in our hearts. Next we need to know beyond a shadow of a doubt that He is always good in what He does. Recipients of His gifts may distort and misuse His gifts but He is always loving in His giving, and in His withholding. Psalm 84:11 tells us, *"no good thing does He withhold from those who walk uprightly."* If we long for something that someone else has and wonder why we can't have it too, God wants us to trust Him. He does not have a quota on blessings. He is not going to run out of resources and He does not limit us to some certain amount of His goodness. If we don't have something we are longing for, let's trust Him. Keep asking and listening and keep on trusting. If His answer is "wait," then trust His timing. If His answer is "yes," then rejoice and know that He blesses us so that we can be a blessing to others. And if His answer is "no," then choose to trust Him rather than to envy others. He is good, all the time.

Day 1

Love is patient and kind; love does not envy or boast; it is not arrogant or rude. It does not insist on its own way; it is not irritable or resentful; it does not rejoice at wrongdoing, but rejoices with the truth. Love bears all things, believes all things, hopes all things, and endures all things. I Corinthians 13:4-7

Read the passage yet again. Ask the Holy Spirit to shine His light into your heart and show you truth. And ask for His love to fill you so that you can love like Jesus does.

What nugget does He have for us today?

Love does not boast.

If you have kids, then you've most likely had to teach them not to brag. Not to boast about personal accomplishments or attributes. "Not boasting" is NOT natural. (And lest we think this is limited to children, just take a look at the Facebook pages of adults!)

No, "not boasting" is not natural but since scripture tells us not to, we can be assured that it is SUPERnatural—only possible through His Spirit, His grace, His strength.

What does it mean to boast? What does it look like in our lives? It is possible that we are so accustomed to its presence, so familiar with this attitude, that we don't even recognize it as wrong.

"Boasting" means that we call attention to some achievement or acquisition in order to gain glory for ourselves. That is where it is different from sharing good news in order to give glory to God or to praise another person. Boasting is an attempt to exalt ourselves. I don't even need to give you examples because I'll bet each one of us is acutely aware of having done this very thing. Not in sharing good news…but rather attempts to elevate ourselves in others' eyes.

Why do we do this and how can we not? We boast because we are trying to fulfill a need in ourselves that only God can meet—our need for significance. When we feel our value is lacking, we make desperate attempts to remedy this. Often we tear others down and/or try to exalt ourselves before others. The positive effect is, at best, fleeting. The negative impact is much longer, on others and on ourselves. What's the remedy for boasting? Worship God. Rejoice that He is even mindful of us! Marvel at His goodness and be humbled before Him. Constant exposure to who He is gets the focus off who we want to be…and increases our desire for HIS glory instead of our own.

Day 2

Love is patient and kind; love does not envy or boast; it is not arrogant or rude. It does not insist on its own way; it is not irritable or resentful; it does not rejoice at wrongdoing, but rejoices with the truth. Love bears all things, believes all things, hopes all things, and endures all things.
I Corinthians 13:4-7

We are working our way through this passage, and now we come to this description of love:

Love is not arrogant or rude.

Some translations say, "*It is not arrogant and does not act unbecomingly.*" I like that explanation.

First, let's address the arrogance. Simply put, LOVE esteems others as more important than ourselves. When we love, we seek to lift others up, prioritize what is best for others, and not assume that our position/opinion/view is the right one. Now, just a word of caution–I do not think that scripture is advocating a miserable existence where we denigrate ourselves and consider our lives to be worthless. That is actually just another expression of arrogance, because arrogance is self-consumption and deflation of others! Love is, instead, self-forgetfulness and the valuing of others. Love is not arrogant because love does not focus on self.

That's why the "*love is not rude*" admonition follows–rudeness is a lack of consideration of others, plain and simple. From civility of manners to common courtesies to respectful public behavior (including social media...), love is not rude. It does not treat others in an impolite, thoughtless or mean way. Love is not coarse or indecent or inconsiderate. Love listens and seeks to understand. Love places value on other people.

I wonder how many relationships could be repaired if we just would choose to reject arrogance and rudeness. And I wonder how many relationships are fractured because we didn't...

I believe that Christians should place a high value on treating others with respect and courtesy. We need to train our children to do so too...and we need to model it ourselves. Ask God to show you if there is a relationship or a situation where you have displayed arrogance or rudeness. Then repent and be reconciled.

That's what love does.

Day 3

Love is patient and kind; love does not envy or boast; it is not arrogant or rude. It does not insist on its own way; it is not irritable or resentful; it does not rejoice at wrongdoing, but rejoices with the truth. Love bears all things, believes all things, hopes all things, and endures all things.
I Corinthians 13:4-7

I'll bet you've memorized this passage by now–I hope so!

And I'll bet the thought has crossed your mind at least once that LOVE is pretty nigh impossible. You would be right. This LOVE–this ascribing of value to another and acting accordingly–is only possible when God's Spirit supplies it to our heart and enables it to flow out to others.

The word for love in the original Greek of the New Testament is agape. It is used to describe God's love for us and also to explain the love we are to have for others. Much of scripture is an unpacking of the definition to help us understand what it means.

In addition to the extrapolation in the above verses, it is helpful to remember both that this agape love is only possible through the work of God's Spirit and also that it is not primarily an emotion that we feel. Rather, it is a choice that we make–the volition to do good to others. This frees us from being controlled by what we feel; instead we are free to choose to obey God and love others. The passage above (and the other references in scripture) is showing us that we are to be vessels of God's love pouring through our lives to others. In spite of what our emotions may try to dictate, we do not have to please our flesh but instead can trust that God is greater than our feelings and we can–by His Spirit–choose to love others in the practical attitudes and actions explained in this passage.

And when we do, we become "perfected" in love (I John 4:16-21). This passage speaks not of sinlessness, but of maturity, of completeness. This maturing of love–as only God can do–benefits the giver at least as much as the receiver. This maturing love casts fear out of our lives. Hallelujah and Amen!

Day 4

Love is patient and kind; love does not envy or boast; it is not arrogant or rude. It does not insist on its own way; it is not irritable or resentful; it does not rejoice at wrongdoing, but rejoices with the truth. Love bears all things, believes all things, hopes all things, and endures all things.
I Corinthians 13:4-7

Love does not insist on its own way.

In other words, love is not selfish. As we've seen in the other descriptions, there is not a particle of selfishness in love. It seeks the good of others above self. It's as though the inspired word of the Holy Spirit wants to underscore that thought for emphasis. In case we missed it before, we see it spelled out explicitly here—love does not insist on its own way...it is not selfish.

Being "not selfish" requires humility, not assertiveness. This flies in the face of much of what we are instructed by the world. Stand up for yourself. Claim your rights (even as a Christian!). Look out for yourself. At least, take care of yourself! But God instructs us differently.

In Philippians 2:3-8, He says, "*Do nothing from selfishness or empty conceit, but with humility of mind regard one another as more important than yourselves; do not merely look out for your own personal interests, but also for the interests of others. Have this attitude in yourselves, which was also in Christ Jesus, who, although He existed in the form of God, did not regard equality with God a thing to be grasped, but emptied Himself, taking the form of a bond-servant, and being made in the likeness of men. Being found in appearance as a man, He humbled Himself by becoming obedient to the point of death, even death on a cross.*"

Do nothing from selfishness or empty conceit. Wow. That's a tall order indeed! But that is what love does, it submits to God's way, gladly yielding to His will and obeys His Word. How can we begin to do that? It seems impossible!

It is only possible if we trust Him—if we know that He is our defense, that He is at work to accomplish that which is good for us, and that His ways are always good. Then we can abandon our own selfish agenda and entrust ourselves to Him, because He loves us and gave His Son for us... and freely gives us all things.

That's love worth trusting.

Day 5

Love is patient, love is kind and is not jealous; love does not brag and is not arrogant, does not act unbecomingly; it does not seek its own, is not provoked, does not take into account a wrong suffered, does not rejoice in unrighteousness, but rejoices with the truth; bears all things, believes all things, hopes all things, endures all things. I Corinthians 13:4-7

I chose a different translation for today in order to deepen our understanding of this facet of love. Some versions say, *"Love is not irritable or resentful."* While that is true and accurate, I like this one that says, *"Love is not provoked."* What a great concept!

A wise friend of mine shared with me that he and his wife pray to "not be offended." That gave me so much to ponder–I had not ever thought to pray that before, but what a wonderful thing to do! LOVE is not easily offended, does not get provoked, and does not become irritable or resentful. Let's unpack it further...

The Greek word that we translate as "provoked" or "irritable" or "offended" is *paroxuno*. It is defined as "sharpness of spirit, to be irritated or incensed." From this we see that love cannot be sharpened to react towards others with an irritation of spirit. In other words, love would never say "She makes me so mad!" or "He annoys me!" A characteristic of love is to be good-natured and peaceful, even when being mistreated. No spewing of temper, no outbursts of exasperation, no hyper-sensitivity, no taking offense, no resentment, no temper tantrum... regardless of the action of others.

When we are controlled by the Spirit, we will not be quick to take offense, to be "prickly." Instead, the disruptions and disappointments and disturbances of life are met with a confidence that God is always at work, causing all things to work together for His glory and for the good of those who love Him. This assurance enables us to meet all circumstances (and all peoples) with a sweetness of temper, a gentleness of attitude and a genuinely optimistic outlook.

Love. It is not easily provoked. It does not anger easily nor react with irritability nor take offense. Let's ask the Lord to produce that maturity of love within us as well.

Day 1

Love is patient, love is kind and is not jealous; love does not brag and is not arrogant, does not act unbecomingly; it does not seek its own, is not provoked, does not take into account a wrong suffered, does not rejoice in unrighteousness, but rejoices with the truth; bears all things, believes all things, hopes all things, endures all things. I Corinthians 13:4-7

Love does not take into account a wrong suffered.

Before diving into this verse, let's look at another verse that will set the stage for us. Romans 10:8 says, *"Owe nothing to anyone except to love one another."* So basically, we owe love to everyone–anything less than love means that we are in debt to them.

The Greek word used here in the Corinthians passage *(logizomai)* is a bookkeeper's term, the word used for entering an item into a ledger so that it can be accounted for and not forgotten. What great imagery! Is that not an accurate picture of how we respond to the offenses committed against us? We "write down" the debit transaction incurred by another so that we might deal with it later. Perhaps we do not react immediately to a trespass against us but we store it up in our heart, stew over it, take revenge or at least complain about–uh, "share"–it with others so that they, too, might make an entry in their ledger.

But that's not what LOVE does. Love does not ignore or deny the wrongdoing but, instead of recording it as a debt owed, love erases the debt...by paying it oneself. That's right. Love does not take revenge but rather love forgives. That does not mean that we pretend the wrong never occurred, that would actually be foolish and unhealthy! But love does not hold the offender responsible for paying the debt; love releases the offender and refuses to keep a record of their action. But since the lack of love resulted in a debt owed, love pays the debt for the offender. Just like Jesus did at Calvary.

How do we pay the debt that another person owes us? In God's amazing economy, that payment can be made in a thousand different ways. It can be the absence of wrong action (as in not "telling your story" or not treating them as they well deserve) and it can be the presence of right action (blessing the offender in some way, praying for them, showing kindness to them). And, what a delight that God's economy works just fine with the installment plan! He allows us to make these payments for others' debts a little at a time if we need to!

As you read through this today, did your heart remember a debt that you are owed? Are you willing to not take it into account...will you forgive that debt and pay it yourself?

Day 2

Love is patient, love is kind and is not jealous; love does not brag and is not arrogant, does not act unbecomingly; it does not seek its own, is not provoked, does not take into account a wrong suffered, does not rejoice in unrighteousness, but rejoices with the truth; bears all things, believes all things, hopes all things, endures all things. I Corinthians 13:4-7

Love does not rejoice in unrighteousness but rejoices with the truth.

This aspect of love is not referring to our actions but instead calls up our relationship with others. The description reveals that when we lack love, we are guilty of an attitude that is glad (secretly or otherwise) over the faults, failures or misfortunes of others. Love, on the other hand, is grieved by such and rather rejoices when others walk in truth and enjoy the blessings of that.

It can be described as the malicious pleasure when we hear something derogatory about someone else. Ouch. Does that prick your heart like it does mine? It brings to mind I Peter 4:8, *"Above all, keep fervent in your love for one another because love covers a multitude of sins."* Love does not want to expose the sins of others–it longs rather to protect, to shield, to redeem. When confrontation is necessary (Galatians 6:1, Matthew 18:15-17), it is done gently, privately, with restoration as the goal, not exposure. The "covering" is not a denial of sin but rather a protection, a desire to see the person walk uprightly and avoid the consequences of sin.

Love is glad for another's righteousness and finds pleasure in the blessings that brings. This reminds us of the basic nature of love–that of unselfishness and of delighting in the highest good of others.

Let's pause for a moment and let the light of His truth penetrate our hearts. Is it shining on any dark spots of wrongly rejoicing? Take a few moments and confess this, knowing that He is faithful and just to forgive us when we do.

Then ask Him for the gift of repentance so that we can walk forward in truth.

Day 3

Love is patient, love is kind and is not jealous; love does not brag and is not arrogant, does not act unbecomingly; it does not seek its own, is not provoked, does not take into account a wrong suffered, does not rejoice in unrighteousness, but rejoices with the truth; bears all things, believes all things, hopes all things, endures all things. I Corinthians 13:4-7

Love bears all things, believes all things, hopes all things, and endures all things.

The idea conveyed here is similar to what we ended with yesterday–that of love covering. Perhaps the best way to think of it is that love does not cave under the pressure of all things put upon it. Love is so strong that it will not collapse; it will not give up, no matter what. This is not saying that love is naive or gullible but it means that love does not despair or lose confidence in what God says is true. Love withstands failures and setbacks, trusting in God's ability to accomplish what He desires. Love is not an unrealistic "Pollyanna" but it does persist with a positive, persevering attitude regardless of what circumstances seem to dictate. Love refuses to be discouraged or dismayed but delights in finding joy in the Lord's truth.

This love is what enables us to remain in difficult situations and refuse to say, "I can't take it anymore." This love is what holds us in a marriage that others say is hopeless. This love places trust in what God says, not what we can see. One of my favorite sayings is that God's Word is truer than our circumstances–that's what love clings to.

Take some time today and ask the Lord to speak to you about places in your heart where you have given up, where you have succumbed to the pressure of difficulties, or where you are not hoping in Him but rather are walking by sight. He wants His children to be mighty in spirit, to not grow weary in well-doing, to remain courageous under pressure. He longs to answer these prayers for you. Run to Him, remain in His arms, and abide in His love. Endure.

Day 4

Love never fails...now abide in faith, hope, love, these three; but the greatest of these is love.
I Corinthians 13:8,13

As we have gone through these past several days delving into what it means to love as God loves, it is tempting to feel like a failure. In fact, we should feel like a failure, because we do fall way short of loving the way God wants us to!

So what are we to do? We see the power in love, the command to love and we long to love as God does, but we know we don't measure up. In fact, it can actually seem that we are not making any "progress" in growing to love this way. I am actually more aware of my sinfulness now than years ago when I first began to walk with Christ. Does that mean I am going backwards?

Actually, no, let me explain.

I am not a great housekeeper. My goal is to keep things fairly uncluttered and just clean enough to not require immunization checks when guests enter my home. Probably my worst area is the windows, I just don't get those darned things cleaned! But I don't get all that bothered about it because it is honestly not all that noticeable.

Until Christmastime.

That is when my dear husband positions a large floodlight in the front yard to shine upon the front door and illuminate the decor there. It's quite festive.

Except that it also illuminates the dirt on my dining room windows! Ugh!

Now, I ask you: did that dirt just appear on my windows in December? Of course not, it's been there all year long. But not until the light shines on it do I become uncomfortably aware of its presence. (And hopefully motivated enough to do something about it!)

It is the same with the lack of love in my life. My failure to love is not new and I am not regressing in my love for others. But the longer I walk with Jesus–the more His light shines in my life–the greater my awareness of my lack of love. So my "seeing the dirt" in my life is actually a good thing–it means there is more light there than before.

The question then becomes–what to do now? This greater sense of my inability, of my sin, is an opportunity for greater love for the one who has forgiven me–and a growing maturity in loving others.

So, won't you join me in praising God for His light, for His love and His grace to help us love too?

Day 5

Above all, keep loving one another earnestly, since love covers a multitude of sins. I Peter 4:8

Love covers, what a great truth. Love is willing to overlook an offense, to absorb being wronged, to pay the cost for someone else's sin. Wow.

I want to be loved like that, don't you? For my family and my friends to forgive me when I mess up, to give me the benefit of the doubt, to understand me and accept me.

I know what the opposite feels like, don't you? I've had friendships dissolve because I wasn't enough something for the other person, I've felt walls go up because conflicts weren't resolved and I've been shut out because of a perceived wrong. Whatever the reality may be, the bottom line was that there wasn't enough love to cover.

I'll bet you have similar stories of hurt. I understand; I hurt with you and for you.

We have a choice about what to do when love falls short of what we need.

We can act in retaliation, hoping that the best defense is a good offense. But unfortunately, what works in basketball doesn't apply in relationships.

We can react out of self-protection. But we need to know that keeping our hearts in a cage does more to keep love out than to protect us from harm.

We can reciprocate with pretense and denial, insisting that we don't care what happens and we are fine no matter what others do. But the only one who's fooled is ourselves. The wound still bleeds, whether we ignore it or not.

We can wallow in our pain, hoping someone will rescue us. Good luck with that one!

Or, we can respond in a way that is counter-intuitive and actually seems to invite more opportunity for offense, for wrong, for pain. We can let our love cover the other person's offenses.

I know I want to be loved like that.

I know I want to love others like that.

Like Jesus does.

Day 1

The 23rd Psalm is one of the most well-known and most beloved passages in all of scripture. It is one of the most read and most memorized sets of verses, but perhaps it is so familiar to us that we have fallen short of a deep understanding of it.

First, the Word: please read it, every verse. Don't skim over it, telling yourself you are already familiar with it. Let each verse seep into your soul.

The Lord is my shepherd; I shall not want. He makes me lie down in green pastures. He leads me beside still waters. He restores my soul. He leads me in paths of righteousness for his name's sake. Even though I walk through the valley of the shadow of death, I will fear no evil, for you are with me; your rod and your staff, they comfort me. You prepare a table before me in the presence of my enemies; you anoint my head with oil; my cup overflows. Surely goodness and mercy shall follow me all the days of my life, and I will dwell in the house of the Lord forever.

Next, the author – scripture tells us that this is a psalm of David. Before he was King David, he was David, the shepherd-boy. Therefore, when he gives us the word-picture of God's people as sheep and the Lord as our shepherd, he was drawing from knowledge and experiences that ensure his creditability. In other words, he knew what he was talking about!

Since David asserts that The Lord is a shepherd, we must deduce that we are sheep. Some of you may have farm or veterinary backgrounds so that you know what sheep are like. I don't. So I did some research on the characteristics of sheep, just to help me understand why God, through the psalmist, would call us sheep. (BTW, this is not the only time in scripture that God's people are referred to as "sheep," so it's safe to assume God is consistently sending us a message by using this metaphor.)

Starting tomorrow, we will begin the unpacking of these verses. Until then, read over this psalm and think of yourself as God's sheep. So very precious to the shepherd!

Day 2

The Lord is my shepherd; I shall not want. He makes me lie down in green pastures. He leads me beside still waters. He restores my soul. He leads me in paths of righteousness for his name's sake. Even though I walk through the valley of the shadow of death, I will fear no evil, for you are with me; your rod and your staff, they comfort me. You prepare a table before me in the presence of my enemies; you anoint my head with oil; my cup overflows. Surely goodness and mercy shall follow me all the days of my life, and I will dwell in the house of the Lord forever.
Psalm 23

Here are some of the things I learned about sheep from my research:

- Feeding: constantly need fresh water, fresh pasture; have very little discernment in choosing good food/water; early morning dew is prime source of water

- Traits: not very intelligent, gullible; very vulnerable to fear, frustration, hunger; easily agitated, especially by pests and easily panicked; stubborn, even to the point of eating poisonous plants or drinking dirty water; habitual creatures, will follow same habit even if it is not helpful; resistant to being sheared or cleaned; easily "cast" (flipped over on back, unable to right themselves, shepherd has to intervene); easily killed by enemies (running away is only means of self-defense); completely dependent on shepherd; needs most care of all livestock in order to survive; poor depth perception/reluctant to go where they cannot see; appetite is an indicator of health (a loss of appetite means the sheep is ill)

- Social characteristics: one sheep in flock is usually the "leader"; easily influenced by sheep-leader and by shepherd; stampede easily, vulnerable to mob psychology; jealous, competitive for dominant position; shepherd is most effective at calming flock

In other words, real sheep bear little resemblance to the cute little lambs pictured in nursery rhyme books. The most amazing thing to remember, though, is that sheep are infinitely precious to the shepherd.

Can you relate to any of this?

Living Letters

Day 3

The Lord is my shepherd. Psalm 23:1a

Let's jump right in and dissect these five simple words...

The LORD: In the Bible, the word "Lord" is used a couple of different ways in reference to God. When spelled "The Lord," it is a translation of the name "Adonai" and means "Lord." When it is written in all caps as "The LORD," it is a translation of the most sacred and holy name YHWH. Although it is pronounced "Yahweh," it was regarded by the Jews with such reverence that they would not even speak it, thus it is written without any vowels. (Note: The word Jehovah originated from an attempt to pronounce the consonants YHWH with the vowels from the word Adonai. In the oldest Hebrew texts there are no vowels. So it is easy to see how this would happen since whenever YHWH occurred in the text, the word Adonai was pronounced by the reverent Jew. *Note taken from writings of John Piper.)*

What does YHWH or Yahweh or Jehovah or The LORD mean? And why is it significant? When God called Himself YHWH, He explained to Moses "I AM WHO I AM." (Ex. 3:13-15) This conveys to us that God exists solely of Himself–He was not created. HE JUST IS. No, I cannot explain that. Which is wonderful. Who would want to worship a God that could be explained? Jehovah exists, has always existed and will always exist. And He is always the same. He doesn't change based on circumstances or opinions or whims. HE IS. This powerful preeminent LORD is my shepherd and He requires not only my worship but also my submission. The great I AM is my shepherd and my will yields to Him.

The Lord is my shepherd: That means that HE is the one in charge. He is the one responsible for my care, for attending to my needs, for my protection, for my guidance. Hopefully, that makes us take some pressure off pastors! They are not supposed to carry all our loads, make all our decisions, or see that we have all the spiritual food we need. This verse implies that our spiritual leaders are more like the "sheep-leaders" and the best thing they can do for us is to set the example of how to follow The Shepherd. This powerful, preeminent, Holy One–He personally–is my shepherd. He never sleeps or slumbers and He is intensely aware of my needs and my fears. He is always at work on my behalf, whether I can see that or not, He is. If I get lost or head towards dangerous pastures, He comes after me and brings me back. He loves me. Jesus links this idea in the Old Testament to Himself in the Gospel of John when He explains that HE is the GOOD SHEPHERD. He not only cares for His sheep, but He also lays down His life for them. Literally. The Lord is my shepherd–I am not my own shepherd, He is mine. I belong to Him. If we are indeed His sheep, then we recognize His voice and follow where He says to go and do what He says to do. Sometimes that is hard. Thanks be to God that He is so good that He protects me from my enemy–who sometimes is my own stubborn, gullible, dumb self.

Let's close today by proclaiming with the psalmist–The LORD is my shepherd. Hallelujah!

Day 4

I shall not want. Psalm 23:1b

This phrase follows "*The LORD is my shepherd*" and therefore communicates a consequential relationship. BECAUSE The LORD is my shepherd, I don't want for anything.

First, I want to show you a few other places where this same truth is conveyed:

- Philippians 4:19 - *And my God shall supply all your needs according to His riches in glory in Christ Jesus.*

- Psalm 84:11 - *For the Lord God is a sun and shield; the Lord bestows favor and honor. No good thing does he withhold from those who walk uprightly.*

- Romans 8:32 - *He who did not spare his own Son but gave him up for us all, how will he not also with him graciously give us all things?*

Scripture is crystal-clear–if He is our shepherd, we will not want. No exceptions. No parentheses. Complete confidence.

Next, how does that apply to you and me? Or, as I love to put it –what difference does it make on Monday morning when the pew hits the pavement? Well, the word "want" can be misleading. Most of us equate it with "desire," but that's not what it means here. A more apt translation would be "lack" or "be in want." The priority of a good shepherd is to not only protect but also provide for the needs of his sheep. You may recall that one of the characteristics of sheep is their inability to discern good water and good food. So the shepherd has to do that for his flock. He may lead them on a long, hard climb through rocks and briars in order to reach good water and pasture. He knows what they need...and where to find it.

It's the same for us. Our Good Shepherd has promised that we will not lack anything that we need, that He will give us all good things–graciously, not begrudgingly. Sometimes we might have to go on a long, hard climb through rocks and briars, to reach the good water and pasture that He has waiting for us. In those times, it is comforting to know we can trust our Shepherd, knowing that He will indeed provide all the good things we need. Actually, above and beyond what we can ask or imagine.

I want to address something you may be thinking. You might have something in mind that you want, but do not have. Something you feel you lack and you don't know how to square that with this truth. Of course I don't know your situation but I do know that God's Word is truer than your circumstances. Here's how I think it applies–what you are longing for may look like a "good thing" to you and it may even be a "good thing" for someone else. If the Good Shepherd hasn't given it to you, then one of two things must be true: one, you may be on the long hard climb right now and that "good thing" may be waiting for you just ahead; or, two, although it looks like a "good thing," seems like a "good thing," or even is a "good thing" for someone else, it must not be for you. He promises that He will not withhold good things from us and He boldly states that He will graciously give us all good things. He has riches untold at His disposal–our inheritance. All good things are promised to us. If He is withholding something from you, trust Him. He is protecting you from bad water and poisonous plants.

Living Letters

Day 5

The Lord is my shepherd; I shall not want. Psalm 23:1

I'll bet you thought we finished verse 1 yesterday! Uh, no, not yet. We dissected it and looked at each part but I have a bit more to share about the verse as a whole.

The Good Shepherd is always at work on our behalf, in "a thousand ways we cannot see," as John Piper likes to say. He owns all good things and has already promised them to us, undeserving as we are. That's grace. But, like sheep, we are often stubborn and resistant to His care. Sometimes we insist on our way, foolishly believing that we know what pastures and waters are good. As if we could somehow know better than He. And, just like the wanderings of an obstinate sheep can get it into difficult and dangerous places, so do we often suffer injury or experience hardship as a result of going our own way. When a shepherd finds his wayward sheep stuck in a hillside's crag or sick from the wrong kind of food, he doesn't beat it or scream at it in hopes of changing its ways. Instead, he gathers it up in his arms and nurtures it back to health. He keeps it close beside him so he can carefully tend it. Most likely, that once errant sheep becomes so accustomed to the gentle proximity of the shepherd that it doesn't want to stray again.

It reminds me of Isaiah 42:3, "*A bruised reed He will not break and a dimly burning wick He will not extinguish.*" That's mercy.

One last thought on contrary sheep. In my research, I learned that sometimes there will be a sheep that is stubborn on steroids. He (or she!) repeatedly runs into danger and risks injury. The bigger problem, though, is what such behavior does to the rest of the flock. Remember the "mob psychology" tendency of sheep? They get all stirred up by the "black sheep's" actions and join right along. In these cases, the shepherd has no choice but to remove the offending sheep from the others–often permanently.

That reminds me of chapter 5 in Paul's first letter to the Corinthians. Particularly verse 6, "*Do you not know that a little leaven leavens the whole lump?*"

Day 1

He makes me lie down in green pastures. Psalm 23:2

This seems reminiscent of naptime battles when I tried to make one of my children take a nap against their will. I wanted to make them lie down! But I don't think this is what the Psalmist means. Here's what I learned about sheep that helps explain this sentence:

Sheep are pretty skittish and nervous and unable to assuage their own fears. In order for them to lie down and rest, circumstances need to be "just so..." Apparently, their requirements for rest are in four general areas:

1. They must be assured of their own safety; their security cannot be threatened by predators or menacing weather conditions. Sheep are timid and fearful and they need frequent reassurance to feel safe.

2. Likewise, the sheep must not be agitated by unruly flock members. Animals respond to social order within their group, the sense of dominance or status. When a bossy old sheep provokes other flock members, there is tension. Not rest.

3. Sheep must not be pestered by pests. Particularly in the summer, sheep can be driven to extreme frustration by flies and parasites. When they are so tormented, they cannot think of lying down to rest; instead they are stamping their feet, shaking their heads, trying to rid themselves of these pests.

4. Finally, they must be free from hunger. They are unable to find good grass and water on their own. If hungry, they are unable to rest; instead they wander off in hopes of something to fill their bellies.

In order for sheep to be able to lie down and rest, they must feel a sense of peace and security, freedom from fear, tension, aggravation and hunger. The shepherd assumes the responsibility of ensuring that these conditions are met so that sheep feel secure enough to lie down and rest. He must be sure his sheep not only are safe but also feel safe. The quiet, calm, gentle presence of the shepherd is the best means to freedom from fear. Often times, a shepherd sleeps with his flock and lays himself at the door of their enclosure, protecting them from intruders. If a bossy sheep-leader is grating on the nerves of the flock, the shepherd must either quiet him or remove him. Additionally, the shepherd must protect his charges from pests. He does this by clearing the grazing area and/or by applying insecticide meticulously to his flock. (Interesting note: in Biblical times, oil was the primary protection against flies, ticks and other pests. Later in this Psalm, the Psalmist extols the Shepherd for "anointing his head with oil"–remember that for later.) Finally, the shepherd takes great pains to find and prepare good grazing land for his sheep. This does not happen by chance–it requires a great deal of work on the part of the shepherd.

You are probably already drawing all the parallels. We will list them together tomorrow but for now why don't you jot down your thoughts?

Day 2

He makes me lie down in green pastures. Psalm 23:2

1. One of the (and possibly THE) most repeated phrases in all of scripture is, *"Do not fear."* Over and over and over, God reassures us, comforts us and proves His protection for us: John 14:1 *"Let not your heart be troubled"* and John 16:33 *"In this world, you will have tribulation. But, take heart; I have overcome the world."* Jesus also tells us that He is the door, nothing can get through to us without His permission. He is also the "door" to the Father.

2. Jesus knows we need freedom, not only from fear, but also from tension in our relationships with other people. Therefore, He directs us to be at peace with one another. Consider Matthew 5:23-24, *"So if you are offering your gift at the altar and while there remember that your brother has something against you, leave your gift there before the altar and go. First be reconciled to your brother and then come and offer your gift."* Time and time again, scripture tells us that our relationship to God is compromised when we have strife with our brothers and sisters. Simply put, we are unable to rest in Him very well if there is something wrong between us and someone else. And if we have been bruised by the horns of an uncaring fellow-sheep or injured in a head-butting incident, the Good Shepherd wants to take us in His arms and tend our wounds. He will bind up the broken-hearted; He will hold us and not let us go. He invites us to cast our care on Him, because He cares about how we hurt.

3. Being bothered by pests parallels the attacks believers experience by Satan and his minions. The Good News is that the Good Shepherd has already triumphed over them. He has provided us armor to withstand the attacks (Ephesians 6:10-18), and we just have to submit to Him and resist the enemy–because the enemy will flee (James 4:7).

4. Jesus meets our physical needs (Matthew 6:25-34). He points out to us that, if God feeds the birds and clothes the flowers, then surely He will provide what we need. We don't have to worry. Even better than meeting our physical needs, though, He satisfies the deepest hunger of our souls. With Himself. *"I am the bread of life; whoever comes to me shall not hunger and whoever believes in me shall never thirst."* John 6:35,36

Scripture often exhorts us to "rest in Him." And we can indeed rest, because all the conditions necessary for us to lie down in green pastures are met.

One last thought to treasure about Jesus having us lie down in green pastures: the Hebrew word that is translated "pastures" is "Na'ah." It conveys the idea of home, habitation, a dwelling, a pleasant place. Isn't that a wonderful thought? Home. The word carries the feeling of belonging, acceptance, security and unconditional love. The place of rest in Christ isn't just any green pasture, it's where we belong, it's home.

And, one day, we'll go to the pasture that He has been preparing for us for 2000+ years–our Father's house. Home.

Day 3

He leads me beside quiet waters. Psalm 23:2b

A sheep will not drink from rushing waters or from a swirling stream. Other animals will, but not sheep. Sheep need calm, quiet sources of fresh water. Turbulent waters or even murmuring springs are frightening to sheep, they need quiet and fresh water sources. A shepherd takes great care to locate proper sources for drinking. Some streams are too agitating and some still water is stagnant. Sheep need a quiet but fresh supply of water. Oftentimes, there are no such bodies of water in the area of their grazing and in those times, the early morning dew soaking the pasture grasses are their best source of hydration.

Thoughts that result from this knowledge of sheep and meditation on verse 2b:

1. We need spiritual water. We are on a constant quest in hopes of getting that thirst satisfied.

2. Our thirst is not quenched from frantically paced lives. Trying to drink from a chaotic lifestyle puts us in turmoil. Nor is it quenched from temporary things like riches, fame, popularity or success. These things are stagnant waters, which give us an initial sense of refreshment but soon leave a sickening taste in our mouths and stomachs.

3. Early morning is a good time to get the spiritual hydration that we need.

4. Divine water is found in a quiet, still state, time in His presence and time in His Word.

5. Jesus tells us that He is the source of living water and that if we drink from Him, we won't be thirsty for lesser sources or things that don't satisfy.

6. This living water that Jesus offers His sheep comes from the throne of God and of the Lamb (Christ). It is His love and His joy, and available to us all if we come to His throne to drink. Here we are free from fear and worry, and full of joy and contentment.

Isaiah 40:11 promises us that Jesus is taking care of us and leading us to the living waters that we need. Check it out. It's even got a precious extra promise for Mommies.

Like a shepherd, He will tend His flock, in His arm, He will gather the lambs, and carry them in His bosom; He will gently lead the nursing ewes.

Spend some time thanking Him for the water He provides...

Living Letters

Day 4

He restores my soul. Psalm 23:3

Notice how the psalmist has switched from the imagery of a sheep (green pastures, still waters) to that of a person in need–soul in need of restoration, a soul that has been worn out, messed up, marred and incapacitated. The Shepherd restores it. Let's unpack this passage...

In researching sheep, I learned where the term "cast down" comes from. You know how we use that phrase to describe someone whose expression is sad or dejected? Or we use it when referring to an action of getting rid of something we no longer want–"a castaway." Sheep can find themselves in a "cast" position. Now, don't think I am talking broken limbs here! A "cast" position means that the sheep has somehow gotten itself on its back, four legs in the air...and it is unable to right itself. It will flail and bleat and try to wiggle but it cannot get back on its feet. This kind of activity actually exacerbates the situation! A cast sheep is not only easy prey for wolves and coyotes; it can also starve to death flat on its back. Unless the shepherd intervenes, the sheep will die in that position because it alone cannot restore itself to standing upright.

That is apparently what David had in mind when he penned this phrase. Surely he had repeatedly been the one to find a sheep "cast" and then pulled and pushed until he got it right side up. How does a sheep get cast? It seems there are three general areas that get sheep into trouble. First, being too fat. A fat sheep can meander down into a comfy little hollow to lie down. It might then stretch out and turn slightly on one side to relax and its body's center of gravity can then shift so that its feet are no longer touching the ground. This probably generates a sense of panic so that the sheep paws its legs in the air. Such action, of course, only makes things worse. This causes the sheep to roll over even further until it is on its back... cast. Its fat belly makes it impossible to get upright.

Another way sheep get cast is by stepping off the path and into a hole or crevice. This causes them to lose their balance and they cannot easily regain equilibrium.

One other factor that seems to contribute to a sheep being cast is having too much wool. When its fleece becomes too long, it will easily get matted with mud, brush and other debris. This extra weight weighs down the sheep, just like extra fat, making it unable to move as easily. Thus, the shepherd is constantly watching out for ways to guard against his sheep being vulnerable to being cast. He sees to it that they don't gorge themselves too much; he keeps them on safe paths; he shears them not only for the benefit of having wool but also for the good of the sheep.

I am sure you see the parallels to us as Jesus's sheep. We, too, can become downcast through defeat or discouragement or daily cares. In spite of how much we bleat and flail our legs, we cannot get ourselves upright. No matter how much we think we can, we need Him to pick us up: to put us on the right path, to get us to good pastures and to get rid of our excess wool, because downcast sheep are easy targets for predators.

He restores my soul.

Day 5

He leads me in paths of righteousness for his name's sake. Psalm 23:3b

In Bible times, he position of "shepherd" was a lowly one. It was not one that people looked up to, aspired to or admired. Even in this humble spot, though, a shepherd took pride in the health and appearance of his flock. He didn't want sickly, weak, feeble sheep that would prove detrimental to his reputation.

So, what does it mean that He leads us in paths of righteousness for His name's sake?

First, let's look at "paths." The route to grazing places was often difficult for the sheep and these paths needed to have adequate food and water. A shepherd needs to find not only good grazing places but also good routes to get to these places. Sheep, if left to themselves, will follow the same path until it becomes a rut. The path becomes not only void of grass to eat but also polluted with disease and parasites. Sheep cannot be left to themselves. The shepherd must keep his flock on the move, shifting periodically from pasture to pasture, which protects not only the sheep but also the landscape! Such careful direction prevents overgrazing of the land and parasite infestation of the sheep.

So it is with our Good Shepherd. He shows us how to live successfully ("walk in paths of righteousness"), and He shows us that the paths of righteousness ("right living") are not to restrict us from having fun–in fact, the complete opposite is true! The paths our Shepherd directs us to lead to blessings and fullness of joy! Walking His way keeps us from being slaughtered by the enemy of our souls and keeps us from feasting on things that look good to us but are actually sources of poison and destruction. I have found the primary source of such leading is through His Word. It is there that He teaches us the principles we need to live victoriously in this life: principles about finance, marriage, parenting, work, decision making, reconciliation, restoring our souls and more. We need to walk in the paths of righteousness because otherwise, we get ourselves in messes through UNrighteousness. Notice that this phrase follows *"He restores my soul."* The way to restoration is via the paths of righteousness.

Two final thoughts about "paths of righteousness." First, I need reminding frequently that MY righteousness is unacceptable and is ineffective for soul-restoration. My efforts to make myself happy or whole or good flat out do not produce the benefits I am striving for. God actually describes the best I can do or be as "filthy rags." Ugh. I need, instead, the righteousness of Christ living in me and working through me. That's what restores me to wholeness, brings beauty out of ashes and sets me in the place of victory.

Finally, we must remember that our restoration, the process of His righteousness working in our lives to produce right-living, is not merely for our joy. It is first and foremost for His glory, for HIS NAME'S SAKE. He has chosen to entrust to us, His fallible, dumb, errant...and treasured sheep, with His reputation in the world. Our lives are a reflection of who He Is. He leads us in paths of righteousness...for HIS NAME'S SAKE.

Living Letters

Day 1

Even though I walk through the valley of the shadow of death, I will fear no evil, for you are with me. Psalm23:4

Notice first that the psalmist changes from speaking about the Lord as his shepherd to speaking to Him. Perhaps the truth conveyed there is that when we are personally acquainted with our Shepherd, we can't go long talking about Him without soon talking to Him! Or it may be that the topic, the valley of the shadow of death, requires a more intimate approach. The psalmist is responding to the need to have close and direct communication with the Shepherd when walking through the valley.

Next, what are the valleys that shepherds traverse and why? In hill country, where sheep are most common, mountaintops often offer the best grazing land. Getting to those spots requires taking routes through deep ravines and valleys. These places are often narrow and dark, shaded by rocks and crags. It is a difficult journey to pass this way but these paths are often the most well-watered routes, the gentlest grade (which makes for better climbing) and provide choice grazing spots along the way.

What about the "shadow of death" reference? Valleys are usually flanked by cliffs on either side, which prevents the sun from reaching there except for a few brief hours. This creates a cold and gloomy atmosphere of shadows. In the shadows and darkness, it is easy for predators (bears, wolves, coyotes, etc.) to hide and wait for a sheep to stray off from its shepherd. Other dangers such as rockslides, mud or snow avalanches are more catastrophic in a valley than in an open field because there is no way of escape. Thus, for the shepherd, "shadows" and "death" are linked with the paths through valleys.

Yet, in the face of such gloom and danger, the psalmist says he doesn't fear...because the Shepherd is with him. Through these valleys, these paths to the mountaintop, the sheep are cared for vigilantly and protected with the shepherd's very life. A good shepherd is aware of the potential danger and keeps constant watch over each member of his flock. So it is with our Good Shepherd....

Tomorrow we will look more deeply at this on a personal level. Today, let's close with thanksgiving for our Good Shepherd and His care for us.

Day 2

Even though I walk through the valley of the shadow of death, I will fear no evil, for you are with me. Psalm 23:4

Yesterday we looked at this verse as a shepherd might, thinking of his sheep. Today, let's take it home...

Every life has valleys. And in those valleys, there is the threat of evil, lots of different kinds. Sometimes evil comes in the form of rejection or discouragement or depression. Other times it appears as condemnation or even physical danger. Yes, most of the time, the presence of evil lurks in these valleys. Sometimes we get in these valleys through our own errant wanderings but other times, the Shepherd leads us right into them on purpose...and with purpose. He wants to get us to the mountaintop. And the valley, though seeming gloomy and dangerous, is full of the choicest grazing spots and the best water sources. It is in the valleys—not just through them—that we have the closest intimacy with THE shepherd and the best access to Him as our source of living water and bread of life. The most valuable treasures are those that are hidden in the cold shadows. Unless we go there, we never obtain them.

During one such "valley season" of my own, the Lord gave me a truth that was of great comfort to me and provided some answers for me. In this time I felt so alone. I wanted friends to minister to me but it seemed as though they either didn't understand or perhaps didn't care. This deepened the valley. It was during this time that He spoke to me with this: "The path through the valley of suffering is ultimately single file." He taught me that He intends for the valleys to be so narrow in certain points that no one can walk beside us. While we are called to bear one another's burdens and to care for each other sacrificially, what He requires ultimately is that we learn to lean not on others but only on Him. When we get to the tightest spots in our valley, no friend can pass through with us—we walk single file behind our shepherd, holding tight to His hand...or He gathers us up in His arms and carries us Himself.

Yes, there are shadows in the valley. It is rocky and narrow and difficult. And there are ever-present dangers there. But if we let those shadows and difficulties and dangers press us close to the Shepherd, we will have good grazing, fresh water and intimate security. And, for those of us in Christ, we do not fear evil in any form, even Death. It is only a shadow and it has no hope of victory in our lives, because we have eternal Life.

You may be in a valley right now. It is my prayer that you will trust the choice of our Good Shepherd to lead you to it, in it and through it. Don't miss what He has for you in this valley. Cling to His hand and know that, even in the valley of the shadow of death, you need fear no evil...He is with you.

Living Letters

Day 3

Your rod and your staff, they comfort me. Psalm 23:4b

I don't know about you, but *"rod and staff"* don't strike me as comforting. When I am afraid or in need of comfort, what I want is someone by my side who knows how to accurately shoot a rifle, a place to hide and a big pile of chocolate. The psalmist prefers a rod and staff...

Since these two items don't appear on my top 10 list of comfort-providers, the problem could lie in me not understanding what they are and how they are used (ya think?). A rod and a staff were the instruments of choice for primitive shepherds. The reference to these two items would have struck a very familiar cord with the earliest audience of this psalm. Modern readers need a little bit of explanation to understand. Let's explore that...

The rod was the primary means of protection for the shepherd and his flock. It was a long, sturdy stick that the shepherd had selected and crafted to fit him perfectly. The rod was so customized to its owner, in fact, that it was seen as an extension of his arm, a symbol of his strength, power, and authority. With the rod, the shepherd could club would-be predators to death. We recall from Bible stories how David the shepherd-boy killed ferocious animals to protect his sheep. His rod would have been his ally. Interesting to note is that "rod" is a slang term applied in more modern times to the pistols carried by cowboys!

Other than protection, the rod could be used for discipline. The primary disciplinary use of the club, however, was not to beat the wayward sheep. Instead, if the shepherd observed one of his flock wandering away or approaching poisonous weeds or getting close to danger, the club would be sent sailing through the air to send the erring animal scurrying back to the group.

One final mention of how the rod was used by the shepherd was to count and examine the sheep. The rod would be held out and laid onto each sheep, one by one. This gave the shepherd the chance not only to account for each sheep, but also to carefully examine them for disease, defects or wounds. A conscientious shepherd would use the rod to open the fleece with his rod, scrutinizing the condition of the skin and looking for parasites or open wounds.

Protection from predators, sounding an alarm of danger, providing close inspection for detecting problems—in these ways, the rod would indeed be a source of comfort to a sheep.

What about the staff?

We will look at that tomorrow and draw the parallels to our Shepherd and His sheep. Until then, rehearse the truth that The LORD is our shepherd, we shall not want.

Day 4

Your rod and your staff, they comfort me. Psalm 23:4b

Perhaps no other piece of equipment identifies one as a shepherd more than a staff—the long, slender stick with the crook on one end. Think of all the Christmas pageants, the shepherds had to have a staff so we would know they were shepherds! A shepherd's staff is designed and shaped especially for the needs of sheep, not for cattle or horses or other animals.

Here's how a shepherd utilizes his staff...

- To reach out and "catch" individual sheep and draw them close to him for examination. Little lambs or timid sheep often keep their distance from the shepherd but his staff can pull them in close.

- To guide sheep, such as through a gate or along a difficult path. The shepherd doesn't use it to beat the sheep but rather to gently pressure it into the direction it needs to go.

- To rescue sheep. Sometimes sheep get themselves into places where only a staff can reach. The shepherd can manipulate his staff into crevices, amidst entanglements, along precipices or even into water to rescue the sheep and set it back on safe ground.

- To draw sheep into intimate relationships with another. If a newborn lamb becomes parted from its mother, the shepherd uses the staff to bring them together rather than putting the scent of his hands on the little lamb and risk rejection by the mother.

While the rod is an instrument primarily of protection, the staff is mostly an instrument of compassion and care.

Now I can understand why the writer of Psalm 23 proclaims that the *"rod and staff"* of the Good Shepherd are a source of comfort. We are protected by the strength and power of the Lord. He guards us against the enemy of our souls and provides us with His Word as our weapon against the defeated one. Likewise, through His Word He warns us of dangerous thoughts, habits and actions, so as to prevent our falling into harm's way. And, finally, He exhorts us to use His living and active word to examine our hearts and lives...His Word, which is sharper than any two edged sword and is able to pierce even to the division of soul and spirit, joints and marrow, discerning the very thoughts and intentions of our heart. Comfort, yes, in being protected by enemies without...and within.

We are comforted, too, by the compassion of His staff. Sometimes His Word acts like a staff, pulling us close to the Shepherd so He can examine our hearts and ways for things that would hurt us. Other times we need His Word to guide us, to gently press us when we are headed in the wrong direction and then show us which way we should go. And many many times, His Word is a source of comfort to help us reconcile relationships, heal our wounds and restore us to fellowship with one another and with Him.

Like David, I can surely say, "Thank you, Lord; Your rod and staff, they comfort me." Amen

Living Letters

Day 5

You prepare a table before me in the presence of my enemies. Psalm 23:5a

What picture does this create for you? Seems a little odd to me. Like sitting down to eat lobster and steak on the battlefront while the enemy is launching grenades at my head. Not sure I get the picture the psalmist intends, so let's get some background...In some of the world's best sheep country, the high plateaus for ranging are referred to as "mesas," which is the Spanish and African word for "tables." Apparently, the picture David is trying to evoke for us is one of these high, flat-topped plateaus where the choicest grazing was to be found. These spots were remote and difficult to reach but the shepherd would go ahead of his sheep to locate them and prepare them for his flock's arrival.

To get the mesa, or table, ready for his sheep, the shepherd would rid the area of any poisonous weeds or entangling briars. He would often distribute salt and other minerals that would be pleasing and beneficial to his flock in strategic spots throughout the area. The shepherd would also clean out the watering holes and springs, making sure that his sheep would have a sufficient supply of fresh, quiet waters. Another responsibility of the shepherd would be to look for signs of wolves or bears or other predators. He would be increasingly vigilant once his sheep were grazing there, ever ready to protect them from attack. So, there, in the presence of sheep's enemies, the shepherd prepares a mesa, a table, for his sheep. And because the shepherd provides such security for them, the sheep are able to eat and rest without agitation or fear.

What comfort and confidence that gives us as Jesus's sheep! We don't need to fear because He has gone before us and prepared just what we need. Since God knows what we are going to face up ahead (because He is I AM, which means He lives in eternity past and eternity future and the present...all at the same time!), He gives us just what we need in order to not only "face the problem" but to actually experience blessing and victory in the midst of it–to feast at the table He has so abundantly prepared in spite of the fact that our enemies are trying to get to us. So many times, I have feared a potential situation knowing I could not handle "such and such." I can get all worked up just anticipating the "what if's " and "might happens." What a waste of energy! I have no need to worry or to fear because Christ has prepared the place I am to go and will provide for me just what I need when He leads me there. I can feast on His Word and find the strength and grace and victory needed for everything He allows in my life, a feast that would not be possible in the lowlands.

Just a couple of thoughts to bring this home, close out this passage: First, let's all remember that the "*enemies*" in our lives are not people. No matter who is attacking you or threatening you or frightening you, they are not your enemy. Ephesians 6:12 proclaims, "*For we do not wrestle against flesh and blood, but against the rulers, against the authorities, against the cosmic powers over this present darkness, against the spiritual forces of evil in the heavenly places.*" Don't mistake the vehicle of your danger for the danger itself, and do your battle in the spiritual realm, not the physical one. Pray!

When you ARE in the presence of those enemies, feast at His table. Find abundant satisfaction in His Word, knowing you are safe because of His protection. Even in the midst of pain and attack, actually especially in the midst of pain and attack, feast at His table. Don't fret at what is happening around you or to you because in the midst of it all, He has a table prepared for you–a table of the choicest foods, selected and prepared just for you. Do not let the enemy prevent you from sitting at the table with Him in sweet fellowship. He has prepared it for you to enjoy together.

Day 1

You anoint my head with oil. Psalm 23:5b

Does this conjure up for you scenes from the teenage years when we needed to wash our hair twice a day to get rid of the flat greasy look? We seemed to have had our heads anointed with oil! Somehow I don't think that's what the psalmist meant...

He is referencing something positive and desirable here so let's find out what he means.

A little background–sheep are often plagued by little flies called nasal flies. These creatures buzz around the sheep's nose and try to deposit their eggs in the moist membranes there. Once deposited, the eggs hatch in a few days into wormy larvae that wiggle up into the sheep's head and burrow in. This is obviously intensely agonizing to the sheep. Infestations can even lead to blindness in extreme cases, but even in the least cases, it is extremely painful and the sheep wants relief. In an attempt to get rid of these internal pests, the poor sheep will rub its head in the soil, beat it against trees or rocks or throw itself on the ground in desperation. Such frantic behavior disrupts the entire flock and can send them all into a frenzy. Apparently, sheep are smart enough to recognize that these flies are potentially hazardous; whenever they detect some anywhere near the flock, they become exceedingly agitated, running, bleating and disrupting even the sheep not infected.

Oil is the medicinal remedy the shepherd chooses. When he first spots flies among the flock, he smears oil over the head and nose of each sheep. The sources I consulted said that this produces an immediate change for the flock; the sheep quiet down, graze quietly and even lie down to sleep in peace. Somehow they sense the ability of the oil to protect them from the dreaded flies.

In addition to the flies, there is another unwelcome parasite that shepherds have to guard against. A microscopic critter can create a condition called "scab" on its host. This is an irritating and highly contagious disease common to sheep, particularly in warm weather. It is most often found around the head area and spreads by contact. Since sheep love to rub heads with other flock-fellows, this infection spreads easily and quickly. As with the flies, oil is an effective antidote to scab. Sometimes, the sheep's head is doused with oil and other times, the entire animal is plunged into a vat of oil so as to ensure the scab will be eradicated.

One last interesting use of oil on sheep–in mating season, rams vie for the favors of the ewes. They will butt and crash and collide with one another, often causing serious injury. In anticipation of such rowdy contests, a shepherd will spread thick oil or grease on the heads of his rams. Then, when they slam into one another, their heads are so slick that they slide against one another instead of doing damage.

Tomorrow we will delve into application. For today, mediate on the fact that the Shepherd is so good to us and give Him praise!

Day 2

You anoint my head with oil. Psalm 23:5b

So, what does this verse mean for us? How and why does God anoint our heads with oil? I am not sure I have it all figured out but here are some thoughts to ponder:

- Oil is used in scripture oftentimes to refer to the Holy Spirit. Remember that his phrase follows, *"You prepare a table for me in the presence of my enemies."* Perhaps the truth conveyed here is that God abundantly supplies us with His Holy Spirit so that we are equipped for what He allows into our lives. His Holy Spirit is our strength for the battle; and the fruit of His Spirit in our lives comes forth as love, joy, peace, patience, kindness, goodness, faithfulness, gentleness and self-control.

- Oil is also used specifically in conjunction with JOY. Again, fruit of His Holy Spirit in us. When we are filled with His Joy, we are not tempted to fill ourselves up with lesser things...things which can often become an enemy to our soul.

- Oil was used in Bible times to anoint priests and kings. To "anoint" something is to make it sacred, to set it apart for God's use. This phrase of Psalm 23 could be reminding us that we are holy and set apart for God's plans and purposes. Jesus is called both High Priest and King of Kings–scripture also refers to our position in Him as the "priesthood of the believer" and our role as reigning with Him.

- In scripture, oil is seen to have medicinal uses as well as for burial preparation of the dead. We can infer that God's Holy Spirit has healing powers–sometimes physically but especially spiritually. And, the use of oil for the dead can also refer to us who have died to ourselves but live in Christ.

- When I think about the shepherd's use of oil to reduce the sting of the head-butting, I can't help but think about how the Holy Spirit often softens the blows we inflict on one another. Sometimes our interactions with fellow believers leave much to be desired. We need to be "greased with the Holy Spirit" so as to slide past the bang and not return "head butt for head butt."

- Jesus anoints our heads with oil. I pray that we are running to Him regularly for the oil bath!

In summary, Christ anoints us with oil, and sets us apart for God's purpose and our blessing–oil of gladness, oil of power, oil of healing and oil of reconciliation. Wow. Powerful.

Let's spend some time today asking Him to anoint us...and bowing before Him in submission.

Day 3

My cup overflows. Psalm 23:5c

The psalmist just told us about the table the shepherd has prepared and the oil that anoints the head. Now we read about the cup. Why a cup? Why not a platter or a bowl or a pitcher? Hmm, let's see...

First, let's notice the pronoun "*my.*" Not "the" or "a" but the personal pronoun "*my.*" The point conveyed here is that of individual attention from the shepherd–personal, not corporate. The shepherd deals with us intimately, according to our individual needs and bents. That's how He blesses us: specifically, individually, personally. Not en masse.

Now, "*cup.*" In scripture, "cup" is often a metaphor for an individual's lot in life, his fate, so to speak. In Bible times, when a host wished to welcome his guests and express his desire to share abundantly with them, he offered them a cup of choice wine and carefully filled it up till it ran over. The over-full glass of wine implied that while they remained there, they should have an abundance of everything. This verse tells us that the Good Shepherd fills our "cup," not partially nor even to the brim, but rather abundantly overflowing. Get the picture...a cup with liquid spilling over, gushing down the sides, continuously...life with Jesus is extravagant!

Here is some of what fills us to overflowing:

1. Salvation: "*The cup of salvation,*" (Ps. 116:13). Jesus' blood abundantly satisfies the wrath of God.

2. Satisfaction: "*Filled the hungry with good things,*" (Luke 1:53). He alone satisfies our deepest longings.

3. Happiness: "*Filled our hearts with...gladness,*" (Acts 14:17). He fills us up, over and over, forever!

4. Peace: "*Filled you with joy and peace,*" (Romans 15:13). God is the overflowing fountain, the river of life and peace and joy.

5. Holy Spirit: "*Be filled with the Spirit,*" (Eph. 5:18).

6. Suffering: (Phil. 3:10) The cup of suffering is one all of us must taste. It is a part of life and it's inescapable. Our suffering may differ. For some people it is physical pain–hard, unrelenting, pain. For some people it is mental suffering–What decision will I make? Which road shall I take? For others it is the suffering we call heartache–that deep pain that goes to the innermost part of our being. The kind of suffering may differ, but every one of us must taste the cup of suffering. And when we do, we find precious fellowship that is only possible through pain.

In Matthew 26:29, Jesus speaks of a cup that He will not drink until He drinks it with us in heaven. I asked my friend Susan about it because she is an expert on all things Jewish. This cup is one of the four cups of the Passover observance. The fourth cup is the cup of praise. Sounds to me like Jesus is telling us His joy won't be complete until we are all with Him for eternity in heaven. Only then will He drink the cup of praise for our salvation perfected. Completed. Joy in abundance and our cups running over. Amen and amen!

Living Letters

Day 4

Surely goodness and mercy shall follow me all the days of my life, and I shall dwell in the house of the LORD forever. Psalm 23:6

We have come to the end of Psalm 23. This last verse is so very familiar and so very comforting. It is our promise that all will end well and will last forever. Some of the research about sheep shed a new light of possibility on what God means by this. Let's unpack it...

First, we embrace the glad truth that goodness and mercy are forever with those who follow Christ. Goodness–that is just what it sounds like–good deeds. That same thought shows up in Paul's letter to the Galatians when he explains that the result of God's Spirit in us is fruit...like goodness. Mercy–plain and simple–not giving people what they deserve. Just like Jesus treats us. He protects us, provides for us and promises us abundant life with immeasurable blessing.

True. All true. But there is another dimension that we should consider. The word *"follow"*–why did God choose that particular word? Why not "accompany"? Or "surround"? Hmm...follow means to come after.

Here's some info on sheep. If the flock is neglected or not managed well, the sheep can be quite destructive to the landscape. They will overgraze and ravage the land almost beyond repair. However, under careful supervision and guidance, they can be the most beneficial of all livestock to the land they pasture. Sometimes sheep are even referred to as "the golden hooves" because of the benefits to the soil from their manure. Sheep rid their grazing lands of all sorts of undesirable plants and herbage that would otherwise ruin the landscape. When the shepherd leads the flock to high pasture for resting, the fertility from the rich low lands is deposited on these less productive grounds. A flock of sheep under the care of a wise shepherd can clean up and restore pasturelands as no other livestock can. One shepherd writes that because of sheep, "I have, in just a few years, seen two derelict ranches restored to high productivity and usefulness. More than this, what before appeared as depressing eyesores became beautiful, park-like properties of immense worth."

Sounds like goodness and mercy followed those flocks. The places they grazed were better because the sheep had been there, more productive, more beautiful and more beneficial. Can this be part of the meaning the psalmist has for us?

Tomorrow we will look at what that might mean for us. For today, ruminate on what we've just learned about sheep and see if you can draw the parallels yourself...

Day 5

Surely goodness and mercy shall follow me all the days of my life, and I shall dwell in the house of the LORD forever. Psalm 23:6

Surely we have all witnessed (or perhaps participated in) scenarios where Christians leave behind shipwrecks instead of a restored field. We can recall all too vividly being hurt or wronged by fellow believers. We have all seen the damage done by a critical spirit or a gossipy tongue or a vengeful heart. We've probably all done some damage-inflicting ourselves. But I think that maybe, just maybe, the point of verse 6 is a plea, a call and a prayer that "surely" this won't be true for us. "*Surely*" we will be those who leave things behind us better than when we arrived.

Numerous examples of this truth come to mind. I think about some college kids I know who have built authentic relationships with scores of homeless folks, faithfully loving on them and ministering to more than just their physical needs. I think about a relative of mine who consistently invests herself in folks who need some help in all sorts of ways, and about a friend of mine who brightens up a room when she walks in, leaving a trail of encouragement and cheerfulness. I think about a few men who addressed the medical needs of the poor in our community...and a free Christian medical clinic named Mercy Health Center followed. About a young woman at my church who responded to a crisis in her own family by birthing a ministry of compassion to others who face similar situations–Bryan's Blankies. And a missionary friend who plants seeds of grace and truth in my heart every time I have the blessing to speak with her.

May the desire of our hearts be that goodness and mercy will be the trail that we leave. May our lives be so lived that the places we travel will be better off because we stopped by. May those that watch us learn about the goodness and mercy of our shepherd...through the fragrance of our lives.

For today, let's ask the Lord to help us sow seeds of goodness and mercy right where we are. Ask Him to open our eyes to see the needs of the people we meet and then guide us as to our role in meeting those needs. May He grant us grace so that the trail we blaze today will be better because we walked it.

And then, we will surely dwell in the house of the Lord...of our Shepherd...forever. Because of His mercy, goodness will be ours. Unendingly. Abundantly. Amen.

Day 1

An excellent wife who can find? She is far more precious than jewels. The heart of her husband trusts in her, and he will have no lack of gain. She does him good, and not harm, all the days of her life. She seeks wool and flax, and works with willing hands. She is like the ships of the merchant; she brings her food from afar. She rises while it is yet night and provides food for her household and portions for her maidens. She considers a field and buys it; with the fruit of her hands she plants a vineyard. She dresses herself5 with strength and makes her arms strong. She perceives that her gain is profitable. Her lamp does not go out at night. She puts her hands to the distaff and her hands hold the spindle. She opens her hand to the poor and reaches out her hands to the needy. She is not afraid of snow for her household, for all her household are clothed in scarlet. She makes bed coverings for herself; her clothing is fine linen and purple. Her husband is known in the gates when he sits among the elders of the land. She makes linen garments and sells them; she delivers sashes to the merchant. Strength and dignity are her clothing, and she smiles at the time to come. She opens her mouth with wisdom, and the teaching of kindness is on her tongue. She looks well to the ways of her household and does not eat the bread of idleness. Her children rise up and call her blessed; her husband also, and he praises her: "Many women have done excellently, but you surpass them all." Charm is deceitful, and beauty is vain, but a woman who fears the Lord is to be praised. Give her of the fruit of her hands, and let her works praise her in the gates. Proverbs 31:10-31

This passage is a poem, an acrostic with each phrase beginning with a successive letter of the Hebrew alphabet. Here we find the heart of a mother extolling the characteristics of the wife her son should look for and the description of what each woman can uniquely be as an outgrowth of her love relationship with Jesus, her Heavenly Bridegroom. When we read through these verses, instead of throwing up our arms in despair, let's fall on our knees in our need to ask Him to grow us into the Spirit-filled woman He uniquely created us to be. When we see ourselves as HIS BRIDE and seek to please Him as our husband, the attributes of the P31 Woman are manifested in our lives. He does not intend for us to fit a rigid mold conceived by someone else's ideas but rather that our lives would reflect His glory in a personal, individualized way.

Read through the passage again and ask Him to speak to you in a personal way as we unpack these verses over the next few days. Ask Him to help you discard any preconceived notions you might have towards the idea of a P31 Woman and trust Him to show you how to apply it in a way that brings joy and excitement, not dread or legalism.

Day 2

An excellent wife who can find? She is far more precious than jewels. The heart of her husband trusts in her, and he will have no lack of gain. She does him good, and not harm, all the days of her life. Proverbs 31:10-12

The word that we translate as *"excellent"* derives from the Hebrew word "chayll" and its meaning includes might, strength, power, valor, virtue, riches, substance, and even army! Talk about a catchall! It seems that the writer wants to convey a woman that defies description; a weak, dependent, incapable, clinging vine is definitely not the P31 idea.

This depth of strength and character is what makes her so valuable, *"more precious than jewels."* Instead of an enviable dowry, this husband is seeking a woman who is stable and strong, capable and secure, dependable and diligent. This is what enables him to trust her. Her character gives him a firm expectation of confidence and a secure sense of well-being.

This woman will not cause him to fear, even as he shares his deepest concerns or his changing circumstances. When he loses his job or fails at his latest endeavor, he knows she is "safe" to confide in. She will not fall apart nor rip him to shreds. A man's greatest fear is that of failing, of losing respect, and in perilous times, he needs a woman who will build him up and supply generous encouragement to his wounds and gracious assurances to his fears.

How can a woman possibly live up to this ideal? How can we exhibit confidence when faced with uncertainty? Or strength in the face of adversity? Or joy in the midst of heart-wrenching disappointment, even devastation?

We are only able to by the assurance that, underneath all that threatens our security, are the Everlasting Arms. Only by the knowledge that He, and He alone, is the source of our stability and joy and that the Prince of Peace is our supply–not pleasant circumstances or even wonderful husbands.

When we operate with this confidence, indeed we will be enabled to live so securely that we live trustworthy, benevolent lives for as long as He leaves us on earth. And that is why the writer of this passage says it is difficult to find a woman like this...so different from the rest of the world.

Day 3

The heart of her husband trusts in her; and he will have no lack of gain. She does him good, and not harm, all the days of her life. Proverbs 31:11-12

We learned earlier that this passage of scripture is an acrostic, a poem whose lines begin with each successive letter of the alphabet. Let's make an acrostic of our own for the P31 Woman, based on the truths of these verses.

The verses describe a woman who is referred to in verse 28 as "*blessed,*" so our acrostic will spell out B-L-E-S-S-E-D, each letter representing a principle for us to follow. The first phrase in our acrostic is "Builds her marriage." And although we touched on this yesterday, we are camping out here again today.

What makes the heart of her husband trust her? What assures him that this woman will be an asset rather than a liability (or an albatross)? What will make our husband's heart trust us?

The remainder of the passage reveals much about this type of woman and we will dig into it over the next few days. But for now, we will ponder some characteristics that make a woman worthy of a man's trust…

1. Capable: We do not have to be the most beautiful or talented or brilliant woman in the universe–we just need to be capable. To be aware of the gifts and abilities the Lord has given us, to develop them continuously and to employ them for the good of others and the glory of God.

2. Dependable: Can we be counted on to do what needs to be done? Are we faithful and sturdy and trustworthy?

3. Loyal: Does my husband know I will always be loyal to him, especially in times of doubt or difficulty or failure? Do I protect his reputation with our children, his family, and our friends?

4. "*No lack of gain*": what does a husband need?

5. Respect: This cannot be overestimated. Women need love and men need respect. And we need to give it.

6. "*She does him good, not evil, all the days of her life*": Good–pleasant, beautiful, excellent, lively, delightful, joyful, fruitful, cheerful, happiness. Evil–inferior quality, malignant, noxious, injurious words of thoughts, giving pain or causing unhappiness

Which best describes your actions towards your husband? If you are unmarried, then remember you have a Heavenly Bridegroom. We all do! Would He say we treat Him this way?

Day 4

She seeks wool and flax, and works with willing hands. She is like the ships of the merchant; she brings her food from afar. She rises while it is yet night and provides food for her household and portions for her maidens (servants). She considers a field and buys it; from her earnings she plants a vineyard. She girds herself with strength and makes her arms strong. She senses that her gain is good. Proverbs 31:13-18a

B is for Builds her marriage and from these four verses we see that the P31 woman also labors with delight.

God intends that we work, girlfriends! And work hard! Although the focal point of energy is for the home, it is clear that working outside the home is not excluded. But keep in mind that, as a wife, the home is our primary priority and primary responsibility. (Caution, do not demand or expect that your hubby will be your helper! You are designed to help him!)

When this passage says that the P31 woman "*works,*" the word here literally means "creatively works to improve." That is such an apt description of us females! We walk in a situation, size it up and our brains immediately begin assessing how we can make things better! Whether it is a house to purchase and renovate, an impoverished village needing the basic necessities of life or a grief stricken family without hope. We girls are all about making things better...and with willing hands, not begrudgingly.

The reference to "*merchant ships*" means going to great lengths to serve our families–especially when it comes to feeding them! And that rising while it is still night to provide that food...well, that could range from nighttime nursing sessions to getting up early enough to prepare a cheerful and peaceful breakfast...instead of a consistently frantic and chaotic race out the door!

Yes, this woman is diligent and efficient and don't think it's impossible for us because we don't have servants. If you have a washing machine, an oven or a dishwasher, then you have household servants!

The last phrase in these verses indicates that this woman is equipped with business sense and that she possesses stamina. "*Girding herself with strength*" conveys the picture of being prepared and qualified to face life's demands.

Reading this passage alone is enough to tempt us towards discouragement, the feeling of never being able to measure up. Let's not view it like that. Instead of a list of requirements we have to meet, let's see this as the path to blessing. When we are letting God develop us into the woman He has called us to be–developing and using His gifts to fulfill His unique purpose for our lives–we will find ourselves blessed instead of frustrated and content rather than overwhelmed.

What is one aspect of this passage He wants you to focus on today?

Day 5

Her lamp does not go out at night. Proverbs 31: 18b

With all that we've uncovered so far about this woman, we are likely to think this means she stays up all night to get everything done! But that is not it at all. Far more meaningful and encouraging than that:

B - Builds her marriage
L - Labors with delight
E - this woman exudes the Light

"Lamp" does not mean a physical light; the word in the original Hebrew text instead means influence, instruction and the light of the soul.

There are many "nights" in the life of every woman: times when financial security is stripped away, or relational stability is shattered by unfaithfulness, or death, times when she is plagued by fears, not only about the future, but also about the very moment of now, times when the condemning voice of parenting failure echoes incessantly or when the shakiness of her own emotions threatens to be her undoing. Darkness. Night.

During those times lots of lamps flicker and some even go out completely.

But some continue to shine, even brighter, illuminating the surrounding night.

A lamp that shines in the night is possible, not just for the Proverbs 31 woman, but also for all of us who trust in the Light of the World. We know that He cares for us in the night, that He is still sovereign over the night and that all His ways are good. We know that He is faithful and compassionate and at work on our behalf in a thousand ways we cannot see, and that He is our greatest treasure, the object of our heart's desire.

Our lamp-light can get clouded by busy schedules that crowd out the seeking of The Light or too many voices that dull the ability to hear truth. Unconfessed sin, relationships in disrepair, unforgiveness and disobedience all dim the visibility of the Light in us.

This lamp, scripture tells us, is our eye. If our eye is clear, our life is full of light. If instead, our eye is bad, then our life is full of darkness. And if the light that is in us is darkness, how great is the darkness (Matthew 6:22-23)!

What our eye is focused on determines the brightness of our light.

Focus on the goodness of God, the treasure of Christ...and our lamp will not go out at night.

But if we focus instead on what this world has to offer...darkness.

Day 1

She puts her hands to the distaff and her hands hold the spindle. She opens her hand to the poor and reaches out her hands to the needy. Proverbs 31:19-20

Remember that this is the path of blessing, not a spiritual laundry list of things for us to do. Here we see a most critical component of living a blessed life...serving the Lord by serving others.

B - Builds her marriage
L - Labors with delight
E - Exudes the light
S - Serves

We know that serving is the heart of God. Look up Mark 10:45 and record what we see about Jesus there:

Serving others–that is how we serve the Lord.

These verses illustrate two different areas of service shown by the two different Hebrew words used that are both translated as "hands." The first, "yad," used with "distaff" and "spindle" actually means "woman's work." We get the picture of working in the home, serving others by preparing meals, doing laundry, etc. What we might think of as "menial work" is being extolled by the speaker in this passage–the Mother of the King–as lovely, desirable and important. Food for thought indeed.

Another thought on this aspect of service is in Revelation 5:14 and 19:4. What do you see the elders doing here?

If you wrote "worshipping the Lord" then you are correct. The work of the elders in heaven is to worship, which helps us understand that our work here on earth should be an act of worship to the Lord. That is what Colossians 3:23 is telling us when we read, *"Whatever you do, do your work heartily, as for the Lord, rather than for men."*

The word used for *"hand"* in verse 20 is "kaph" which literally means "hand." (That's handy. Sorry–couldn't resist!) This tells us that she gives of herself. She gives of herself to the poor and needy, to those who cannot repay her nor return benefit to her. There are lots of areas in which to be poor or needy: certainly financially, but also relationally, emotionally or physically. God places the poor and needy in our lives so that we can bless them by meeting their needs... and so that we can receive the greater blessing by being the one to give.

The last thought for today–the phrase "extends her hand"–gives a specific picture of hands being folded in prayer. Perhaps the greatest way we meet the needs of others is to pray for them. Let's close out today by praying for a specific situation where someone is needy and ask the Lord how He wants you to meet that need.

Living Letters

Day 2

She is not afraid of snow for her household, for all her household are clothed in scarlet. She makes bed coverings for herself; her clothing is fine linen and purple. Her husband is known in the gates when he sits among the elders of the land. She makes linen garments and sells them; she delivers sashes to the merchant. Strength and dignity are her clothing, and she smiles at the time to come. Proverbs 31:21-25

B - Builds her marriage
L - Labors with delight
E - Exudes the light
S - Serves the Lord by serving others
S - Smiles at the future

There are three possible reactions to the future:

1. Seek it because we are discontent with the present

2. Scared of it because we distrust God's plan

3. Smile at it because we know God is loving and sovereign over all of our ways

How can we be women who smile at the future? Verses 21-25 help us understand.

Sometimes we cannot smile at the future because we are held captive to our past. When we read the activities of this woman (verses 21-22), we not only see her work of preparation but we get a glimpse into how she views herself. Scarlet, fine linen and purple materials let us know that this woman did not see herself as a pitiful bag lady who had to take whatever came her way. Regardless of her past situation, she now sees herself as royalty...and the same is true of us who are daughters of the King of Kings. We are secure in our position in Christ, knowing our past has been redeemed and we are clothed in His righteousness!

Also, she is not afraid of the future because she has prepared for it in the present. Her priority is not only in seeing that the future needs of her family are met but also in living a life that distinguishes her family. The phrase *"her husband is known in the gates"* could be better understood as "her reputation enhances the role of her husband among the elders." Sounds to me as though her name is equated with integrity and excellence for the work she does!

Lastly, this woman is able to smile at the future because she is calm and secure about who holds it. She is not fretting nor fearful, anxious or alarmed because her strength is in the plan of God. Such trust gives her not only strength but also dignity.

Close out today by reading Jeremiah 29:11 and asking the Lord for grace to trust Him with your future.

Day 3

She opens her mouth with wisdom, and the teaching of kindness is on her tongue. She looks well to the ways of her household and does not eat the bread of idleness. Proverbs 31:26-27

B - Builds her marriage
L - Labors with delight
E - Exudes the light
S - Serves the Lord by serving others
S - Smiles at the future
E - Exemplifies wisdom, kindness, and diligence

Here we see a characteristic that perhaps sets this woman apart more than any other–the way she uses her tongue. With it, she speaks wisdom and she teaches kindness. That is powerful. How can the same be true of us?

Take a look at Luke 6:45. Does that give you a hint? *"Out of the abundance of the heart, the mouth speaks,"* Luke tells us. We might say it this way–what's inside is what will come out!

The way to have wisdom and kindness come out of our mouth is to be careful about what goes into our heart. We must fill our hearts with the truth of God's Word, renewing our mind to become transformed into the image of Christ. If instead, we allow the UNtruths from the world to permeate our minds, we will hear foolishness, not wisdom, spoken from our lips. And we won't be able to teach kindness or grace because our lives will speak way louder than what we try to preach.

That last phrase about not being idle perhaps helps explain a wise and kind tongue. This woman keeps herself occupied with the right priorities and that leaves no time for idle gossip!

As we close today, let's let the Holy Spirit speak to us individually through His Word. Read these verses and ask the Lord what He has for you today.

Proverbs 4:24
Proverbs 10:11
Proverbs 10:32
Proverbs 12:25
Proverbs 15:1-2
Proverbs 16:21
Proverbs 17:9
Proverbs 19:13-14

Day 4

Her children rise up and call her blessed; her husband also, and he praises her: "Many women have done excellently, but you surpass them all." Charm is deceitful, and beauty is vain, but a woman who fears the Lord is to be praised. Give her of the fruit of her hands, and let her works praise her in the gates. Proverbs 31:29-31

BLESSED

B - Builds her marriage
L - Labors with delight
E - Exudes the light
S - Serves the Lord by serving others
S - Smiles at the future
E - Exemplifies wisdom, kindness, and diligence
D - Does get her reward!

If we are honest, there has probably been a whisper in our soul as we've unpacked the truths about the P31 Woman of "what's in it for me?" After all, this gal gives, serves, works and pours out her life continuously. How can she keep going?

Because God is far more generous than we can ever imagine.

These last verses assure us that we indeed will be rewarded. There will likely be a time lag between our endeavors and the results longed for. Maybe such a long lag that we wonder if it will ever happen! But it will. Those little people that you lay down your life for day after day will one day grow up. (That is what "rise up" means–not that they get themselves off the sofa where they've been eating chips and watching TV!) And when they do, they will supernaturally acquire an awareness of what you've done for them, and they will bless you in return. Your investment in their lives will return not merely in the form of gratitude and praise but more so in the fruit of their character. It will be worth it. And even if you never experience the praise of an earthly husband, remember that this passage means far more than what we see here and now. One day, Lord willing, our Heavenly Bridegroom will speak the words we long to hear.

Read these verses and write out your own prayer to the Lord:

Proverbs 11:25
Matthew 19:27-30, 20:25-28, 25:14-30
Revelation 22:12

Amen.

Day 5

As a ring of gold in a swine's snout, so is a beautiful woman who lacks discretion. Proverbs 11:22

Women, all women, desire to be beautiful. Personally, I believe God wired us up this way. It's not only not a sin to be beautiful, I believe that doing the best with what we have to work with can honor God. After all, He created beauty!

What spoils God's design for beauty is a lack of discretion.

So what is discretion? Webster defines it as "the quality of being discreet, especially with reference to one's own actions or speech; prudence or decorum." Umm, what's discreet? "Modestly unobtrusive; unostentatious."

Hmm. Apparently the litmus test of gold rings for pigs is how much attention we are trying to attract by our dress or our make-up or our actions. Or—I just gotta say this—our lack of dress. Lots of noise lately about our "right" to dress like we want to and our "right" to look attractive. Let's us girls be careful. Gold rings are pretty...but not on pigs. What a waste of treasure!

As you get dressed today, ask the Holy Spirit to help you choose clothes and makeup and a hairstyle that reflects the beauty that comes from within rather than attempting to draw attention to the shell that houses this beauty.

Amen.

Day 1

He will guard the steps of His saints. I Samuel 2:9a

How does He guard the steps of the saints?

1. Literally. I am convinced of the presence of angels that guide our steps, often protecting us from physical harm and preventing many casualties. Perhaps when we get to heaven, God will pop in a DVD of our lives and allow us to view what was going on behind the scenes. Maybe we will be able to see what is unseen now, the activity of angels in our lives. (When I get there, my guardian angel will surely heave a sigh of relief that this particular tour of duty is over!)

2. Symbolically. I believe He often intervenes to keep us from heading in harmful directions. What we might initially see as a disappointment, oftentimes in hindsight turns out to be His protection from a place or a relationship that would have spelled sure disaster.

3. Directionally. He guards our steps by guiding them and providing wisdom about which path to choose or which direction to take. If we ask...

4. Protectively. Sometimes we stumble in our walk. Simply put, we just mess up and figuratively fall on our faces. He is the one who wants to pick us up, dust us off, and show us how to fix the mess. To try again. To avoid the same mistake later.

5. Provisionally. Psalm 37:23 further explains that, "*the steps of a righteous man are ordered by the Lord.*" We can trust that, for those of us who are in Christ, He is in loving sovereign control of our lives. That is great comfort and assurance!

Close out your time with Him today by thanking Him for how He guards your steps. Tomorrow we will look at our part...

Day 2

He will guard the steps of His saints. I Samuel 2:9a

What is our part? If this is what God is doing on our behalf, what do we do?

Maybe a million things, but here is a more manageable list:

1. Ephesians 4:1 tells us to "*walk in a manner worthy of your calling*": Paul's instruction to so walk includes "*all humility and gentleness, with patience, showing tolerance for one another in love, being diligent to preserve the unity of the Spirit in the bond of peace.*" There are six things right there.

2. Ask for His help: Many times He blesses us without our even asking. (As in, causing the sun to shine and the rain to fall on the just and the unjust). But there are blessings we forfeit, help we don't receive, and guidance we never get just because we fail to ask, not because He doesn't want to give it. Often He is waiting for us to recognize our need for Him before He gives His help.

3. Walk right: Yes, God often intervenes to protect us and to guide us, but He also commands us to avoid evil. In fact, He goes so far as to tells us to, "*Avoid all appearance of evil,*" in 1 Thessalonians 5:22. Don't step into places you are not supposed to be.

4. Trust Him: Trust that He is good and worthy of your desire to please Him. Trust that, because He is good, not because we merit His favor, He is guiding and guarding your steps for your good. Colossians 1:10 says to, "*Walk worthy of the Lord, to please him.*" And in Hebrews 11:6 we are instructed that, "*Without faith it is impossible to please him.*" So the command to walk "*worthy of the Lord*" is a walk of faith.

Next time you go for a walk, remember that He is guarding your steps—on that walk and in your life. Thank Him, always remember to thank Him.

Living Letters

Day 3

In everything give thanks; for this is God's will for you in Christ Jesus. I Thessalonians 5:18

I can easily understand and deliver on the command when things are "good," aka, the way I want things to turn out, but what about those things that we interpret as "bad"? What about those things that make our life uncomfortable or painful or downright tragic? Surely God has an exception clause that permits us to skip the thanksgiving in those things!

Not at all, He is very clear about the *"in all things"* part. Give thanks. Whoa. How can He expect us to do that? When that red light makes us late for an appointment? Or the promotion goes to someone else? Or we are betrayed, mistreated, persecuted? Or we realize that our dream of parenthood is never going to come true? Or someone we love with all our heart is gone? Or all of the above?

Maybe we could choke out the thanks more easily if we thought "these things just happen." If we cut God some slack, so to speak, and accept that this is "life" and we have to take our lumps like everybody else, it wouldn't be easy, but it seems as if we could learn to accept bad things if we viewed them as an unfortunate twist of fate. Then we could make the best of it.

But God clearly doesn't want to leave that as an option. He tells us not only the "what" and the "when" but also the "why." Give thanks. In all things...for this is God's will for you in Christ Jesus.

Stops us in our tracks, doesn't it? Those things that are not what we prayed for. Those things that complicate our lives, that hurt us, that inconvenience us, and that seem to go against all we would consider good and blessed and right. He wants us to thank Him for those things because they are from Him.

Wait! No! Surely I don't mean that cancer and infertility and divorce and tragedies are from God! Well, while He is not the author of evil and He only gives good gifts, He alone is sovereign. He has the power to stop or remove any and everything from our lives. So if something comes into the life of a Christian, it only got there after being filtered through His hands–His loving, sovereign, and omnipotent hands.

Not only allowed through His hands, but especially designed for my benefit and for His glory. Gulp, that's hard, but that's where faith comes in and the giving of thanks in all things. He wants me to trust Him and His Word. He tells me that all things work together for my good and His glory. He assures me that all His ways are loving and faithful, and He promises that He doesn't withhold anything good from those that walk in Him.

So, that's how I can thank Him. No matter what it looks like from my perspective, I can trust His perspective and thank Him because He is always working for my good and His glory. No matter what it looks like to me.

In all things, give thanks, for this is the will of God for you in Christ Jesus.

Day 4

And for this reason we also constantly thank God that when you received from us the Word of God's message, you accepted it not as the word of men, but for what it really is, the Word of God, which also performs its work in you who believe. I Thessalonians 2:13

I don't think I could ever single out one verse out of all of scripture as my favorite but this certainly has to be ONE of them!

That one little phrase, *"performs its work in you who believe,"* is what makes it a treasure to me. The Greek word for *"performs its work"* is "energeo," which means active and energetic, accomplishing action, and proving strong. We get our word "energy" from it. This is what God's Word does in us–it is active (living and active, Hebrews 4:12 tells us) in our lives, not static. It is always at work in us, accomplishing what God wants to do in us. God calls the process "sanctification." Making saints out of sinners, transforming us, working our salvation out from our spirit to our behavior and changing how we think, how we act, how we feel, and who we are.

So, how do we tap into this energy, this active and accomplishing power? Can we just "claim" a few lines from the Bible each day and expect God to work His magic? Can we recite a bunch of verses from time to time and watch ourselves turn into superheroes? No. That's where the remainder of the phrase comes in, *"in you who believe."* God's Word does indeed perform its work...in you who believe.

What is belief? Faith. And what is faith? Mental assent? God says, *"By faith, Abraham...obeyed,"* in Hebrews 11:8. So, *"you who believe"* means "you who obey," because if we believe what God's Word says, we will obey it. And when we obey it, we are demonstrating faith, and faith pleases God. In fact, without it, it is impossible to please God. And it is His pleasure that works in us to transform us.

If I want to see more of God's energy, power, and transformation in my life, I need to get His Word in me. I need to read it regularly and to meditate on it, memorize it, treasure it, and then I need to believe it, obey it, live by it, and arrange my life around it.

And watch it perform its work.

Day 5

And for this reason we also constantly thank God that when you received from us the Word of God's message, you accepted it not as the word of men, but for what it really is, the Word of God, which also performs its work in you who believe. I Thessalonians 2:13

If we really believe this is true, let's take God at His Word. Select one of these verses and memorize it. Today.

Write it out in the space below five, six, seven times, reading it aloud as you do. See if you can memorize it by the end of the day, and if you do, email me at chamfam@bellsouth.net and let me know!

- Galatians 2:20

- Galatians 6:7-8

- Hebrews 11:6

- Hebrews 12:12

- James 1:20-21

- I Peter 1:14-15

Day 1

Death and life are in the power of the tongue and those who love it will eat its fruit. Proverbs 18:21

The power of life and the power of death–the power is in the tongue. The choice of which to employ resides in our hearts.

The power of life: one such example is found in Proverbs 15:1a, "*A gentle answer turns away wrath.*"

A gentle answer…but notice that scripture doesn't say "a correct answer." Being "right" isn't always best, being gentle is.

A gentle answer…I think that God is helping us understand that ignoring another's wrath isn't an option. Answer it, just do it gently. "No response" isn't a gentle answer, and it can actually sound like harsh words.

A gentle answer…the power to diffuse anger, to change a situation from frazzled to peaceful, and to bring life.

"*But a harsh word stirs up anger.*" Proverbs 18:21b

Just as a gentle answer gives life, a harsh one has the power of death.

Anger is an emotion that results when some goal of ours is blocked or some desire is unfulfilled. This might be minor, like missing out on a good parking place, or quite major such as parental rejection. Most all of us have pockets of unresolved anger submerged somewhere in our hearts, and harsh words from another person can draw it out and stir it up. Have you ever had the experience of someone reacting to something you said in a seemingly disproportionate way? You know what I mean–you are having a conversation with your spouse and it turns into a "discussion." (As in, "we aren't arguing–we are having a discussion.") One of you slips in a "small" jab and the other person erupts, seemingly disproportionately. Now you know why–that harsh word was like a drone missile that zeroed in on a hidden pocket of anger, and it found its target and stirred it up.

So don't use harsh words, they carry the power of death. Seriously. Jesus connects the dots for us between anger and murder in Matthew 5. Don't be the source of harsh words–it's a revelation of what's in your heart. Later in that same book of the Bible, Jesus says, "*For the mouth speaks out of what fills the heart.*" (Matthew 12:34) Our problem probably isn't that we don't know how to communicate, it's that we have a heart problem instead. If you use or have used harsh words, go to the ones who have heard them and make it right. That will carry the power of life. Last, if you hear those harsh words from someone else, realize that those words (and that person) are not the cause of your anger. They're just the pot-stirrer. Don't react to the one stirring the pot–instead, deal with what's inside.

Living Letters

Day 2

A word fitly spoken is like apples of gold in a setting of silver. Proverbs 25:11

Doesn't this conjure up a beautiful picture for you? Golden apples encased in silver settings that are beautiful, valuable, and rare.

"*A word fitly spoken.*" Notice it's not "a word spoken in a fit," but rather, a word fitly spoken! A word that is appropriate in its message and delivery...and timing.

What's a "fit" message? It is one that meets the need of the moment...in TRUTH, and is one without assumption or presumption. TRUTH. It might be words of affirming praise or it might be difficult precepts but if it is TRUTH, it can still be valuable to the hearer. Not flattery, for that is a word spoken in order to send benefit back to the speaker. Nor is it true words misapplied. (Been there. Said that. Heard that, too. UGH) Instead, it is truth appropriate for the moment... apples of gold.

A word fit in delivery, even if the message is truth, is not beautiful or valuable to the hearer if we don't deliver it in love. "*Fitly spoken*" includes the tone of voice, the words chosen, the facial expression (gulp), and the body language. Some studies indicate that up to 93 percent of communication effectiveness is determined by nonverbal cues. Delivery matters...settings of silver.

The timing is as important as the message and the delivery. Oh how important is the timing! Too many times I have delivered the message of truth to one of my children...at the wrong time. There have probably been times I have delivered too late, but mostly I'm too early. Giving them what they need to hear when they are not prepared to hear it is counterproductive. Learning to wait until the time is right requires patience, self-control, and wisdom.

But when the message is true, delivered with love, and at the right time, oh what a treasure for the hearer! Words fitly spoken can shape a life. My husband will never forget an uncle's specific compliments about his public speaking abilities...from over 40 years ago. Little wonder that he chose a career that capitalizes on that talent. I can recall with delight apples of gold that were delivered to me in settings of silver...and some specific ones that kept me teaching, or parenting, or walking with Jesus...even words from strangers.

A word fitly spoken, in message, in delivery, and in timing are apples of gold in settings of silver. Let's plant some apple seeds today!

Day 3

There are six things the Lord hates–no, seven things he detests: haughty eyes, a lying tongue, hands that kill the innocent, a heart that plots evil, feet that race to do wrong, a false witness who pours out lies, a person who sows discord among brothers. Proverbs 6:16-19

When I was a little girl, a popular TV show had a segment where a group of girls sang a song that went something like this, "You'll never catch one of us repeating gossip...so you'd better be sure and listen close the first time!" Hee-Haw. Made us laugh every time we saw it.

It's not so funny being the victim of gossip, though. Can you relate?

God makes it very clear that He hates gossip. He lists it among murder and pride and lying right there in Proverbs. The dictionary defines gossip as "idle talk or rumor, especially about the personal or private affairs of others." OK, so what is "idle talk"? Since scripture warns us about such, we should know what it is. Gossip, or idle talk, consists of things said about other people that are not profitable to the subject, the hearer, or the speaker. They are untruths or things that stir up strife among others.

Gossip can be lies sprinkled with some truth or words that cause the hearer to think less of the person being "discussed." It can destroy relationships and murder reputations. Other times, the juicy morsels are all lies, and irreparable damage is done. But sometimes, gossip consists of things that are true but would have been better left unsaid. Words that are not profitable for the one being discussed. Secrets shared that should have never been disclosed.

Take a look at these verses with me:

- Proverbs 16:28 - *A troublemaker stirs up dissension, and a gossip separates close friends.*

- Proverbs 11:12-13 - *A man who lacks judgment derides his neighbor, but a man of understanding holds his tongue. A gossip betrays a confidence, but a trustworthy man keeps a secret.*

I don't know why we are tempted to do it. When we do, we have fallen prey to the deception that such "sharing" will be beneficial to US and that by tearing someone else down, we will look bigger. But that's the biggest lie of all. We not only do damage to others with our gossipy words, but we also destroy our own selves.

Maybe we will be motivated to curb our gossipy tongue when we remember the truth of Proverbs 18:21, *"Death and life are in the power of the tongue, and those who love it will eat its fruits."*

Will we enjoy the fruit of life-giving words, or we will reap the consequences of death-inducing words?

My Mama says it this way, "What goes around, comes around." Amen, Mama, amen.

Living Letters

Day 4

I was blessed to grow up in a home where criticism was not part of our vernacular. We simply did not criticize or complain, not even when it was "merited." How my parents achieved that, I do not know! I assure you. On my own I managed to master the art, even falling prey to the idea that criticism was "helpful" to others. How would they ever change their ways, I reasoned, unless I told them where they were wrong? This "skill" grows exponentially when practiced even a bit, I soon learned. The more I criticized, the more things I saw that "needed" criticizing. Once put into motion, criticism can quickly become a way of life and a lens through which all persons and activities are filtered. A lens that turns toxic towards those on the receiving end, but also on the viewer. A critical spirit is not only difficult to live with, but also to house inside one's own soul.

One day I stumbled on a verse. James 4:11, pretty simply says, *"Do not speak against another."*

We can try and "adjust" it to say something else but it translates very clearly–do not criticize. The verse doesn't have parentheses to include exceptions for poor service or irritating people or trampled rights. It just says do not.

And then there's that verse in the next chapter of James, verse nine, *"Do not complain, brethren, against one another."*

I am not saying there is never a time to report bad service or share an unfortunate experience, but I do suggest a heart check first and a prayer for wisdom. I also suggest a longing to err on the side of being TOO UNcritical and UNcomplaining.

God said not to complain or criticize. Remember what my Mama said, and Proverbs 18:21.

Day 5

We are going to take one more look at this idea of complaining and criticizing.

Do all things without grumbling or complaining. Philippians 2:14

Whoa. ALL things? Really?

Yep. That's what it says. ALL things. Hmm.

The audacity of the Apostle Paul to pen these words, ALL things indeed! Did he have to put up with the mate that you do, or the co-worker, or the toddler? Did 30% of his paycheck go to a government that wastes his money frivolously? Did his family dump all their work on him and then neglect to appreciate him properly? And what about his in-laws–did Paul even have in-laws? Did he plan all sorts of wonderful family activities, in an attempt to be a marvelous parent, and raise marvelous children with marvelous memories, and then have the weather ruin the whole day? And what about health–does he know what it's like to battle a terminal disease? Or live with debilitating pain day after day? Maybe if Paul had to put up with some of what you put up with, well, then maybe he wouldn't be so glib about instructing us to do this stuff without any sort of grumbling or complaining.

For sure.

Did you know that Paul wrote those words while chained to a Roman soldier? Did you know that he had been beaten and whipped and robbed? Not to mention rejected and ridiculed and repudiated. Yet he continued to teach and preach and serve and make tents without grumbling and complaining. And he tells us in this letter to the believers at Philippi that God expects us to do the same.

Oh.

Seems pretty impossible. I mean, really, everybody complains at least a little! Even if it's just about the weather! It would be odd not to, wouldn't it?

That seems to be precisely the point. Check out the next verse: *That you may be blameless and innocent, children of God without blemish in the midst of a crooked and twisted generation, among whom you shine as lights in the world,*

So maybe, just maybe, if we Christ-followers don't grumble and complain like everybody else does, we might stick out like lights in the darkness. And the world might take notice that we are different and wonder why.

And maybe, just maybe, we could then give an account for the hope that is within us, and gladly explain that we can do all the things we do cheerfully without complaint because we trust our loving and sovereign Heavenly Father who directs our lives and is always at work for our good.

ALL things. Oh.

Day 1

O Lord, who shall sojourn in your tent? Who shall dwell on your holy hill? He who walks blamelessly and does what is right and speaks truth in his heart; who does not slander with his tongue and does no evil to his neighbor, nor takes up a reproach against his friend. Psalm 15:1-3

Psalm 16:11 tells us that, *"In His presence is fullness of joy,"* so we can extrapolate that these verses tell us how to find joy, because they explain who can live in His presence. Notice that activities of the tongue are included...

1. Blameless living: Note that I didn't say perfect, but blameless. The word used here does not mean unblemished but rather without fault. Big difference. Unblemished would mean that we were without sin, but without fault means that God no longer finds us guilty. That is only possible if we are in Christ. Even if we were to somehow be able to do all the other things listed in this passage, if we are not blameless, then we cannot get into His presence. Therefore, no fullness of joy.

2. Does right: Pretty simple, does right. When I was a little girl, my Mama's parting words many days would be, "You do right, now." I knew exactly what she meant–do the right thing. I don't know if Mama realized that her counsel was more than just avoiding trouble, but it was also the path to joy. Do right.

3. Speaks truth in his heart: Speaking truth in our hearts is more than telling the truth; it's knowing what the truth it...and believing it. It's not being deceived and telling ourselves the truth. Since we behave what we believe, this results in speaking...and living...the truth. We need to ask the Lord frequently to show us any areas where we are not speaking the truth in our hearts so that He can remove the deceit...so that we can walk the path to joy.

4. Not slander other people: News flash–what we do to others affects our own measure of joy. Slandering others, saying things that reduce another's opinion of someone, is not the path to joy, even though we might be tempted to think so in the short term. My husband often tells our children that there are two ways a tree can feel tall–grow tall itself or cut down all the other tall trees in the forest so that it can feel tall in comparison. Point made.

5. Interesting how the psalmist separates speaking evil and doing evil: Making a double point, perhaps? One who wants to live in joy does not take revenge, do harm, or fail to pay the debt of love we owe to others. Tall order.

6. Does not take up reproach: The word means not to blame others. Sounds like forgiveness, doesn't it? Path to joy...forgiveness...connection....

The path to joy...Psalm 15:1-3

Day 2

When words are many, transgression is not lacking, but whoever restrains his lips is prudent.
Proverbs 10:19

I think I would be wise to let this passage speak for itself. Just sayin.

Day 3

Put to death therefore what is earthly in you: sexual immorality, impurity, passion, evil desire, and covetousness, which is idolatry. On account of these the wrath of God is coming. In these you too once walked, when you were living in them. But now you must put them all away: anger, wrath, malice, slander, and obscene talk from your mouth. Do not lie to one another, seeing that you have put off the old self with its practices and have put on the new self, which is being renewed in knowledge after the image of its creator. Here there is not Greek and Jew, circumcised and uncircumcised, barbarian, Scythian, slave, free; but Christ is all, and in all. Put on then, as God's chosen ones, holy and beloved, compassionate hearts, kindness, humility, meekness, and patience, bearing with one another and, if one has a complaint against another, forgiving each other; as the Lord has forgiven you, so you also must forgive. And above all these put on love, which binds everything together in perfect harmony. And let the peace of Christ rule in your hearts, to which indeed you were called in one body. And be thankful. Let the Word of Christ dwell in you richly, teaching and admonishing one another in all wisdom, singing psalms and hymns and spiritual songs, with thankfulness in your hearts to God. And whatever you do, in word or deed, do everything in the name of the Lord Jesus, giving thanks to God the Father through him. Colossians 3:5-17

List the actions or attitudes that we are to put away/put to death or stop:

1.

2.

3.

4.

5.

6.

7.

8.

9.

10.

11.

How many of these have to do with what we say, or what comes out of our mouth?

Instead of these things, what are we to put on?

Verse 16 gives us the key that enables us to put off the old and put on the new–what is it?

Day 4

He who goes about as a talebearer reveals secrets, but he who is trustworthy conceals a matter. Proverbs 11:13

Let's face it–it is a very real temptation to tell what we know, especially if it's true and no one listening has heard the news! It makes us feel significant to be "in the know," and to "have the inside scoop." And we want to share it so badly.

Sometimes we disguise it as a "prayer request" so that we look spiritual on top of significant.

But this verse exhorts us to know when to keep quiet–when someone's reputation is at stake, when nothing good is to be gained by sharing what we know, or when we are just trying to gain personal advantage by telling instead of concealing.

I am not talking about covering up darkness that God says to expose to the light, and I am not talking about protecting evil and risking further injury to innocent victims.

I am talking about sharing juicy tidbits of information because we want to look important.

We've all done it.

Lord, forgive us.

Lord, help us to conceal the matters that can be concealed and to protect the reputation of our brothers and sisters...help us to have Love that covers.

Day 5

For the righteous falls seven times and rises again, but the wicked stumble in times of calamity.
Proverbs 24:16

This series on "the tongue" might have been discouraging for you. Maybe you've realized lots of failures in this area and you don't feel much hope for improvement. Then read the above verse again.

Everyone loves to applaud winners, and rightly so! Winning takes talent, but especially hard work and perseverance. The winners that I most admire are the ones who have overcome obstacles, who didn't seem to have a chance of winning, and who had failed before–a lot.

What is true in sports arenas is even more so in life. How are folks able to not only "survive," but in most cases "thrive," in the midst of wayward children, financial downturns, marital crises, parental rejection, and even substance abuse? Especially if there's at least some blame to lay on themselves?

To me, that's the most painful part–feeling like I own the blame of a mess, even just part of it. There is something actually noble about bearing up well under problems that happen "to us" ...but when we know deep down inside that this "calamity" is (at least in part) "by us," well, it's hard to bear.

This verse tells us that the righteous man falls seven times, and I can certainly identify with that! Probably more the "seventy times seven," boy, can I relate to the falling! I have days, weeks, and months where I feel at best misunderstood, and at worst, like I have offended every person in my path. I don't know how you react when you fall but I often hear the whisper of temptation to give up or to just quit trying, because obviously, I can't get it right!

What does the righteous woman do, though? Yes, she falls, but she gets back up. Instead of staying in the stumble, she gets back up and tries again. It looks like this:

- Admit you fell: If calamity knocks you down, you can't get up unless you realize you fell in the first place.

- Accept the responsibility that belongs to you: While we're not responsible for everything that happens, we need to own our own falling without blaming others.

- Figure out what tripped you up: If #2 wasn't humbling enough, this should help! Don't wallow in the failure with a pity party and don't figure all problems since the dawn of time are attributable to you–ask for input and insight and stick to the truth.

- Purpose to try anew: "*Rise again*," and ask God what a new try looks like. Then do it.

This verse tells us that the righteous and the wicked both fall...but the only mention of getting up belongs to the righteous. I don't know what your "*calamity*" looks like today, but my prayer is that you'll rise again. Please don't quit. Take a breather for a minute if you need replenishing, but please don't quit. Don't give up on that child or that spouse or that friend...or yourself.

Day 1

Probably a bazillion times, we will tell someone "I'm praying for you." Probably less than a bazillion times do we actually do it. Now, I'm not being cynical or critical...just honest. We are well-intentioned and we really do care about the one we commit to pray for, but sometimes we just don't do it. Or if we do, it's one of those "arrow prayers" that we shoot up towards heaven, "please bless Bobby." We'd be hard-pressed to know if God ever answered many of those.

So let's find out about prayer. We will use Matthew 6:9-13 as our basis. This is most often referred to as "The Lord's Prayer."

Pray then like this:

Our Father in heaven, hallowed be your name. Your kingdom come, your will be done, on earth as it is in heaven. Give us this day our daily bread, and forgive us our debts, as we also have forgiven our debtors. And lead us not into temptation, but deliver us from evil.

Most Bible scholars agree that we should refer to this as "The Model Prayer" because Jesus is instructing us how to pray. They say that "The Lord's Prayer" is what we should call John 17, when Jesus prayed for us! Whatever we call it, it is a set of instructions that can guide us as we pray, instead of a routine prayer to only memorize and repeat.

These verses contain different index sentences that serve as topical areas for the believer to cover in prayer. We will break this model down into each different area over the next few days so as to learn how we are to pray. Following that, we will address some questions about prayer. Things like why do some prayers go unanswered? If God is omniscient, why should we pray? What makes God answer yes? How often should I pray? Is public prayer acceptable to God?

For now, just pray.

Day 2

Don't you read passages such as I John 5:14-15 (*And this is the confidence that we have toward him, that if we ask anything according to his will he hears us and we know that if he hears us in whatever we ask, we know that we have the requests that we have asked of him.*) and James 5:16 (*The prayer of a righteous person has great power as it is working.*) and wish you could pray with confidence that you would see results? Me too!

Well, we can. I believe we can experience the joy of seeing extraordinary things accomplished through prayer. I also believe that the longing for such is from the Lord. Just as the disciples asked Jesus in Luke 11:1, *"Lord, teach us to pray,"* we, too, can go to Him and be instructed. The prayer in Matthew 6 is the set of instructions He gave us. Elsewhere in scripture we have other guidance for our prayers but here we have a collection of sentences that provide an outline of topics for us. The rabbis of Jesus's day gave their followers a set of brief sentences or "index prayers" that suggested the subjects they should cover when they prayed. This is that same format, so we will use this guide to learn *"an effective prayer that will avail much"* (James 5:16 in King James English).

The very first phrase *"Our Father who art in heaven"* is where we begin. Jesus wants us to be assured that we are coming to the one who loves us, provides for us, knows us, delights in us... and beckons us to come. We are not approaching a distant sovereign whom we have to beg from, or convince against His will. No, we are invited to ask with the confidence of a child coming to his father, knowing that his father not only possesses the resources with which to grant his request but also deeply desires to share his abundance.

Maybe the word father doesn't hold good meaning for you. Maybe you have painful memories or an empty place in your heart that should be filled by a loving Daddy. That makes me so sad. I am so sorry if that is your story. Please hear me when I say that your Heavenly Father is not distant or negligent or abusive or cold. Don't let an earthly failure eclipse your view of Him. HE is the model all other fathers should follow, not a projection of someone who hurt you or failed you. You can come to your HEAVENLY FATHER with utmost confidence that He is drawing you to Himself, and that He delights in you and desires to have the most intimate relationship with you. And your Heavenly Father is pleased to give good gifts to His children.

First thing to know in our school of prayer–God is our Heavenly Father. And *"he who comes to God must believe that He is, and that He is a rewarder of those who seek Him."* (Hebrews 11:6)

Our Father who art in heaven. Amen.

Day 3

Our Father, which art in heaven, hallowed be Thy Name.

This always makes me think of the story told of the little fella writing a letter to God—he addressed it "Dear Howard." When asked how he knew God's name was Howard, he replied, "The Bible says so. 'Our Father, which art in heaven, Howard be thy name'." Don't you love that!

Maybe the little guy had the semantics wrong but I think he also had something right. God wants us to know Him by name. Howard or whatever!

So we are going to unpack His name today. But first, what does "hallowed" mean? Webster defines "hallowed" as holy, respected, revered. Vines expository dictionary explains another dimension to the Greek word, "the opposite of common."

Thus, our prayer begins with the assurance that we are approaching our loving, compassionate, omnipotent Father. Lest we dare to adopt a cavalier attitude, though, we are reminded that He is HOLY, hallowed, NOT COMMON. We tend toward erroneous extremes, I think. Either we wrongly perceive God as remote, detached, unapproachable, stern, and austere...or we interpret Him as our genie in the lamp, ready to grant our wishes, if we can just figure out the right formula.

He is neither. Our finite minds, flawed by sin and misinterpretations, have an impossible time understanding Him. So often, that leads us to avoid Him, to neglect prayer, and to trudge along in our own feeble strength—which takes us straight to failure and disappointment and anguish. Praise Him that *"He knows our frame; he remembers that we are dust"* (Psalm 103:14). He knows our propensity to doubt and fear and misunderstand and forget and especially to go our own stubborn way, so He goes to great lengths to help us believe, trust, understand, remember, and follow Him...He explains Himself with His names.

Throughout scripture, God refers to Himself with different titles so that we can get a glimpse of His character, His attributes, and His nature...so that we can get a better grasp of who He is and respond to Him in worship, proclaiming His "worth-ship." So that we will trust Him, come to Him, join Him in His plan, and make His name known to all the world. Learning who God is by name equips us to view every situation through His eyes.

Tomorrow we will look at some of God's names for Himself. Today, let's close by asking Him to open our eyes and see what nuggets of truth He has for us personally as we learn more about who He is through His names.

Day 4

The name of the Lord is a strong tower; the righteous runs into it and is safe. Proverbs 18:10

Here are some of the ways the Lord reveals Himself to us:

Elohim: God as creator - all things were made by Him, and for Him.
El Elyon: Sovereign, the most high - He is in complete control; His purposes will be accomplished.
El Roi: the God who sees...and cares...and can do something about what He sees!
El Shaddai: the God who *"pours forth,"* sheds blessings, is an all-sufficient refuge
Adonai: master, owner
Jehovah: self existent one - that is too high for me to comprehend!
Jehovah–Tsidkenu: The Lord, our righteousness - He is righteous in our place and He is sufficient.
Jehovah-Jireh: The Lord will provide. No matter what we need, He will provide.
Jehovah-Raah: The Lord, our shepherd - remember what all we learned studying Psalm 23?
Jehovah-Shalom: The Lord send peace - in the midst of confusion and chaos, He is our peace.
Jehovah-Nissi: The Lord our banner - in battle, our source of strength and confidence.
Jehovah-Rapha: The Lord who heals; healing of all kinds
Jehovah-Saboath: The Lord of hosts - over all principalities and powers, none are more powerful!
Jehovah-Shammah: The Lord is there - He exists in eternity past, eternity future, and now, at once
Jesus: the one who saves His people
Christ: the anointed one, chosen
Emmanuel: God with us, not distant and far away
Mighty God: as in ALL POWER
Prince of Peace: peace, not as the world gives
Everlasting Father: Father forever
Wonderful Counselor: compassionate, wise, comforting

As you read over these names, what attribute of God resonates with you right now? Go to Him in prayer in the confidence of that name. Are you battle-scarred? Jehovah-Nissi supplies strength. Are you afraid? Jehovah-Saboath is more powerful than anything that threatens you. Have you failed...again? Jehovah-Tsidkenu is your righteousness. Do you feel lonely? El Roi sees and He cares. Do you need direction? He is your Wonderful Counselor.

He is worthy of our worship. Truly, holy–hallowed–is His name. Let that be our first order of business as we come into His presence. Worship and acknowledgement of who He Is.

Day 5

The first index, or topic, we find in the Lord's prayer is that of worship. We acknowledge the holiness of God and His Worthiness. We come as His beloved children, but we come aware that, apart from the righteousness of Christ bestowed on us when we trust Him to save us, we could not enter into His presence.

That realization causes us to worship Him in wonder and love and reverence. Knowing His name, we attest to the attributes that reveal His glory, and we praise Him for His majesty, sovereignty, power, compassion, provision, and on and on. That's what it means to fear God. We are so aware of our UNworthiness to be in His presence—we realize that we deserve to be melted to nothingness in the fire of His holiness. And, yet, because of Jesus's righteousness and the mercy of God to accept His payment on our behalf, we can approach the throne of God...confidently, even with boldness. That's practically scandalous!

On to the next topic that Jesus instructed us to cover in prayer, *"Thy Kingdom Come."* Our worship gives birth to allegiance. We line up our desires to be in order with His, and we express that He is indeed the King of Kings and Lord of Lords and that we are citizens of His Kingdom. As such, we focus our hearts on the furtherance of His Kingdom here on earth and our priorities are consistent with His. We seek His Kingdom and His righteousness first.

This topic sentence includes our longing for heaven, when we will be with Him forever, our commitment to pursue Him above all else, and our desire to see others come to Him. As we respond to His glory in worship, we then acknowledge His rightful claim on our lives. Our hearts are ready to listen as He reveals any area where our allegiances are to this world rather than His kingdom, any place in our lives where something else is preeminent to His glory, anything less than denying self to daily take up our cross for His Kingdom, or any love that matters more than His.

Wow. No wonder He commanded that we pray without ceasing.

Worship and allegiance = the first steps of prayer.

Let's practice right now.

Day 1

Thy will be done.

That sounds an awful lot like *"Thy kingdom come."* Is there a difference?

There must be or Jesus wouldn't have included them both in His example for us to follow in prayer. Here's how it looks to me: as we bow before the throne of our Heavenly Father, we respond with worship. His character is revealed in part through His names and we praise Him, which flows into aligning ourselves with His kingdom purposes. Then, agreement with Him emanates into submission to His will...whatever it means for our lives.

Although Jesus gave us this as a pattern for prayer, it's not a magic formula. Breaking down this model into its ingredients like this might make us think that prayer is routine or scripted, and that every time we pray, we need to proceed in order through each step. (That's pretty much what happens when we just recite this prayer.) But that's not why Jesus gave it to us. Instead, this passage of scripture is an explanation of what prayer is. It helps us understand what the posture of our hearts is to be when we approach Him. Prayer is not about getting our will done in heaven but rather about getting God's will done on earth.

Prayer is not about begging God to do something for us. He is the giver of every good and perfect gift and He loves to bless us with those gifts, He encourages us (pretty much commands, actually) to come to Him and ask, and He wants us to be in an intimate relationship with Him and to delight in what He gives us. He wants us to be cognizant of our need for complete dependence on Him. So, do we regard prayer as a list of steps to check off...and when completed, we can expect our wishes to be granted? No, of course not. Prayer is communing with the Father, and getting close enough to discern His heart and HIS will. Which leads us to the next point that we will cover tomorrow.

Today we will close with worship and rest in the glorious truth that His will is good!

Day 2

And this is the confidence that we have toward him, that if we ask anything according to his will he hears us. And if we know that he hears us in whatever we ask, we know that we have the requests that we have asked of him. I John 5:14-15

When we say "Thy will be done," we are submitting our desires to the perfect plan of our Father because we trust Him. We are confident that Psalm 84:11 is true, *"For the Lord God is a sun and shield; the Lord bestows favor and honor. No good thing does He withhold from those who walk uprightly. O Lord of hosts, blessed is the one who trusts in you!"*

We can submit to Him because He is committed to our highest good. If we ask for something that isn't His will, we can rest in the assurance that His ways are higher, His plans are better, and He will accomplish them. Prayer is not simply believing that I can have what I want and expecting Him to give it to me. No, effective prayer is being in communion with the Father and discerning what His will is, desiring to see His will accomplished, and asking Him to do so.

That's what *"Thy will be done"* means.

Let me close with a personal story. When my Chip was a little boy, it came time for him to move out of his crib and into a "big boy" bed. This was, of course, very exciting and we made a big deal out of it, including new sheets and blankets and the whole deal. I found some nice flannel sheets that were an Indian pattern and thought those would be perfect. (OK–full disclosure–they were on sale and were the only full size ones in the store, but they really were cool. Promise.) Being the amateur psychologist that I am, I knew not to just present the sheets to Chip but rather to make sure that he saw them as a fulfillment of a wish. So I planted the idea of Indian sheets in his head. For days, I talked about how cool Indians were; we played cowboys and Indians and had a great time. I even went so far as to imply that only boys got to play cowboys and Indians so that he was set apart from his sisters. Then we began to daydream about Indian sheets. If only we could find some, that would make his big boy bed perfect. Yes, I am completely aware that this is unabashed manipulation, but work with me here–the sheets were cool. He needed some and I'd just as soon he be happy with them! Fast forward to Christmas morning. (Yeeeessssss, I did...but it wasn't his main gift, OK?)

Let me assure you, he loved them. And although he's long since outgrown Indian flannel sheets, the story still has an illustration. Now, know that God is not manipulative, but He does place desires in our hearts for the very answer He wants to give us. And, His choice of gifts isn't limited to sale items!

Day 3

The question of how to know God's will is one of the major concerns of a Christian. Particularly for 20-somethings who want to know what to study in college and whom to marry! All of us wrestle with wondering if this or that is what God wills for us. How can we know? Do we just tack "if it's your will" at the end of our prayers to be safe? If He is sovereign and accomplishing His purpose for the world, why even pray? If I just believe hard enough, can I have whatever I want? Is that what the passage in Matthew 21:2 means?

And whatever you ask in prayer, you will receive, if you have faith.

A misunderstanding or misapplication of this verse has led to much heartbreak, much self-condemnation, and even some abandonment of the faith. Surely we have all prayed for some particular something and then it didn't happen as we asked. If we don't know what this truth is, we are left with anger at God or at ourselves. Either He lied to us or our faith was inadequate.

Neither of these is correct.

When studying scripture, know that the best commentary on scripture is scripture itself. In other words, look at other passages on the topic to get the explanation. Consider the whole counsel of God, not an isolated verse.

So to gain understanding of this passage, we look at Hebrews 6:18, "*so that by two unchangeable things, in which it is impossible for God to lie, we who have fled for refuge might have strong encouragement to hold fast to the hope set before us,*" and Numbers 23:19, "*God is not a man, that he should lie, nor a son of man, that he should change his mind. Does he speak and then not act? Does he promise and not fulfill?*"

God does not lie. Period. Then, is my faith inadequate? If I had believed better, would my request have been granted? No, that's not what it means. And we can know this because of Matthew 17:20 which says, "*For truly, I say to you, if you have faith like a grain of mustard seed, you will say to this mountain, 'Move from here to there,' and it will move, and nothing will be impossible for you.*"

Ok, then, how do we get our prayers answered?

That is all for today, tomorrow we will look further. Ponder these truths for now and worship Him.

Day 4

And this is the confidence that we have toward him, that if we ask anything according to His will He hears us. And if we know that He hears us in whatever we ask, we know that we have the requests that we have asked of Him. John 14:14-15

HIS will. There it is again. HIS will. When we pray in accordance to His will, He grants what we ask. A couple of questions come to mind:

1. What's His will? The answer is in John 15:7, *"If you abide in me, and my words abide in you, ask whatever you wish, and it will be done for you.* God's will is His Word. When we pray His Word, we are asking according to His will. For example—when I pray for my husband, I ask God to cause him to *"walk in a manner worthy of His calling"* (Ephesians 4:1) or for my children to *"love God with their whole heart"* (Mark 12:30). In fact, I have a whole set of verses that I pray regularly for my family and myself. Even for specific things like breaking down strongholds of pride or despair or anger (2 Corinthians 10:3-5), praying God's Word is praying His will. We are assured that His Word is His will for us, so we can pray with confidence that He will grant what we ask.

2. What about things that are not precisely addressed in scripture, such as whom to marry, what to major in, where to live, etc.? Well, many of these concerns are addressed in principle and God calls us to search His Word and seek His direction. But sometimes, it's not. In those instances, I pour out my heart and tell God my desires. I ask for His guidance about what to ask and how to pray. And then I submit to His will. I like how Henry Blackaby puts it, "And, Lord, if you have something better in mind than what I'm asking, then cancel my request!" As I have practiced prayer longer, I have learned to "listen" with my heart and often the Holy Spirit directs me how to pray. Sometimes I don't hear correctly, to be sure, but what a delight when I do. It is so exciting to be led in prayer to ask God for something and then see Him give me what I asked for. Remember the story of Chip and the Indian sheets? God Himself puts His desires in our hearts, so that He alone can fulfill them. What a faith-strengthener!

And, remember, prayer is God's means for getting His will done on earth...for changing us and conforming us to His image. Learn to listen to Him and learn to want what He wants.

Sometimes we think God hasn't answered, but He does. He often says "yes" and we see the answer and we rejoice. Other times He says "no," and it's perfectly OK to be disappointed or sad for a time. Tell Him! Pour your heart out to the one who can do something about it, to the one who can bind up your broken heart. But sometimes, He just says, "wait." Those can be very difficult times. We can wait on Him a long long time and we can be tempted to think He has said no. Or nothing. But don't give up, please don't give up. He is good, He gives good gifts, and His plans (His will) for you are good.

Day 5

Give us this day, our daily bread. Matthew 6:11

Let's briefly recap the components of prayer: come into His presence with worship, and acknowledging His character and attributes; then align ourselves with His purposes, and subject ourselves to His sovereign rule; desire His will and submit our plans to His, above all.

Only then do we make our requests, our petitions, and we need to do it daily.

Remember the story of the Israelites in the wilderness? They were without food and desperate. God sent them bread from heaven, manna, every day. Every day, He provided what they needed and every day, they were to gather what He sent. What they gathered one day didn't last for the next–His provision was abundantly sufficient for each day, one day at a time. He didn't allow them to super-store once for all time. Instead, He allowed them a daily reminder of not only their dependence on Him but also of His faithfulness to supply.

That's the principle at work here. Every day, we ask God for what we need for that day–the strength, wisdom, and guidance for the needs of that particular day. We can't store up on Monday and have it last until Friday. We need a consistent "diet" of His provision in order to meet the demands for each day. And we need the continuous remembrance of His faithful presence and of His abundant generosity and grace.

Which leads us to the second point here, not just the "daily" aspect, but also the "bread." It is no coincidence that Jesus described Himself as the "Bread of Life." He is our sustainer, our strength, and our very life. HE is what we need when we lack wisdom or power or joy. He IS all that and more. All through the day I cry out to Him for the "bread" I need at that moment, for wisdom as I climb the stairs to address an issue with one of my children, for humility to ask forgiveness of my husband, for understanding when trying to understand a passage of scripture, for financial provision, and the wisdom to handle what He sends, for self-control when I really don't want to exercise but I do want to eat an entire bag of chocolate, for compassion for others, for meekness instead of anger, for kindness towards someone who has hurt me, for grace to extend forgiveness, and for faithfulness when I'd rather be self-indulgent. The list of my needs goes on and on, and on and on I ask for His bread…over and over and over. And He gives generously, without reproach. Every day, more than I ask.

He does give good gifts. But what He really wants us to have is Himself. He is all we need.

Day 1

Forgive us our debts as we also have forgiven our debtors. Matthew 6:12

This is an area we often overlook in prayer. If we aren't careful, we will see prayer as a one-way conversation, a chance to tell God what we need or want and just look forward to seeing His answers.

We would be grossly mistaken to view prayer that way, and we would also find our prayer life sadly ineffective.

This index, or topic sentence, involves two aspects. The first is confession, our confessing to God. We are to invite God to examine our hearts and show us areas that displease Him, not so that we can feel like a failure (although, we are!) but rather so we can be cleansed from our sin and turn from it. So that we can see we owe God a debt of righteousness that we cannot pay. It is our reminder of our need to have that debt forgiven–not just the one time need for forgiveness that results in salvation but also the daily need to have our relationship with God unhindered. There is something so powerful about confession. It's not just telling God what we have done wrong but it is actually agreeing with Him about it, and acknowledging that any sin is an impediment in our relationship with Him. Although our sin has been paid for (if we are in Christ), unconfessed sin is a barrier in our relationship with Him. Scripture exhorts us to be serious about our sin, even going so far as to let us know that If I regard wickedness in my heart, the Lord will not hear (Psalm 66:18). We need to regularly examine ourselves, asking the Lord to reveal our sin, and then admit that sin along with our need for forgiveness. I John 1:9 is such a comfort–when we confess whatever His Spirit reveals, He cleanses us from ALL unrighteousness, even the sin we don't know about! I think that if He were to reveal all our sin at one time, we would be so overcome with grief that we couldn't function.

Tomorrow we will look at the rest of this passage but for today ask the Lord to speak to your heart about anything that is between you and Him...then confess it and agree with Him.

Living Letters

Day 2

It is so beneficial to spend time letting God's Spirit reveal the areas that fall short of God's standards. We have the opportunity to address whatever is hindering our relationship with Him, to make things right with Him...and with others. God is really specific about having us make things right with other people before we can expect to come to Him in prayer.

So if you are offering your gift at the altar and there remember that your brother has something against you, leave your gift there before the altar and go. First be reconciled to your brother, and then come and offer your gift. Matthew 5:23-24

Confession of our own sin keeps us humble. When I make confession a priority, I am much less prone to judge others, and much more prone to extend mercy and compassion. I know how fallible I am so I don't condemn others for failing.

And confession should also make us compassionate.

Look at the entire sentence: *"Forgive us our debts as we forgive our debtors."* If you think you notice a connection between our being forgiven by God and our forgiving others, you are absolutely correct. Wow, this is not an oft-mentioned doctrine! But the Bible is crystal clear that if we don't forgive others, our own spiritual well-being is in serious danger. I have done much study on this issue and I believe that unforgiveness towards others is often the root of much depression, anxiety, rage, and other tormenting emotions. In fact, I believe this is what scripture is explaining in Matthew 18 when the parable concludes with the admonition, *"And his lord, moved with anger, handed him over to the torturers until he should repay all that was owed him. So shall my Heavenly Father also do to you, if each of you does not forgive his brother from your heart."*

As we pray, asking God to forgive our sin, we are also to be very sure that we forgive those that have wronged us. Mark 11:25 says, '*Whenever you stand praying, forgive, if you have anything against anyone, so that your Father who is in heaven will also forgive you your transgressions.* Notice the all-inclusive phrase, *"anything against anyone."* Wow. Pretty much covers it.

Tomorrow we will look a bit more at what forgiveness is...and what it's not, and how to do it! For today, let's just go to the Lord and ask His forgiveness for whatever His Spirit reveals. Amen.

Day 3

We've already seen why we should forgive, but it's always good to remind ourselves. When we forgive, we are acknowledging the forgiveness that God has extended to us. If we refuse to forgive others, then we put our own relationship with God in danger (Matthew 18:21-35). No, I'm not saying we lose our salvation, but I am saying (because the Bible says so) that our prayers will be hindered and we subject ourselves to all kinds of emotional torment.

OK. Now we're convinced, we want to forgive others. But what is it, exactly? And how can we do it? What does it look like?

Forgiveness is literally the erasing of a debt. When someone has sinned against you, they have not paid you what you are owed. We use that analogy all the time—"I owe you an apology" or "I'll make him pay for that." Just like we owe God righteousness, we owe all mankind love, and the same is owed to us (Romans 13:8). Unfortunately, just like we cannot pay God what we owe Him, we also do not always pay the debt of love we owe to others. We owe others and they owe us, and God requires that we forgive others what they owe us.

Ouch, that's hard to do. How in the world can we do that? We hurt, and we fear getting hurt some more. Does God really expect me to forgive? To just say "it's OK"? Really?

The answers are: yes, no, yes. Yes, He expects me to forgive. No, it's not OK. And yes, really.

Here's the deal. Forgiveness does NOT mean that what someone did to you is OK. Most often, it's not. Sometimes it's a really big deal, life-altering kinds of things. Sometimes it's not, but oftentimes it is. And it is NOT OK, nor does God say that it's OK. To say that would contribute further to our hurt, trivialize it, and not result in healing. Instead, forgiveness means acknowledging that there is indeed a debt owed (and it helps me to tell God exactly what I think I am owed) and choosing to not make the debtor pay. It means no longer holding them responsible for what they owe us, and not trying to extract some form of payment from them. It's letting God be their bill collector and our debt repay-er.

This is the way to not only an effective prayer life, but also to a life free from bitterness and anxiety. Our attempts to make the other person pay what they owe rarely result in getting the debt paid. Rather, new debts result! But if we tell God they don't owe us anymore, we are free from the chains of unforgiveness that bind us to the debtor, free from the torment that ensues when we refuse to release someone from what they owe, and we are out of God's way so that He can also work in the life of our debtor.

So that's what forgiveness is. How do we do it? We will look at some things that might be helpful tomorrow. Today let's just commit to the Lord that we want to be women who forgive others faithfully.

Day 4

Forgive us our debts as we have forgiven our debtors. Matthew 6:12

How can we forgive, practically?

Here are a few things that have been really helpful for me. First, I pray about the person who owes me. The Psalmist pours out his complaint in this way (see Psalm 17, 21, 22, 26, 28, 29)... you get the idea. It is perfectly Scriptural to tattle on those who hurt you! I tell God what they did and how it hurts and how much I think they owe me. Not that He doesn't already know, mind you, but because it helps me to get it out of my heart, instead of leaving it in there where it can fester. Only after that am I able to pray for them. To begin with, it might be through clenched teeth but, as I continue in obedience, I am eventually able to pray with a heart of compassion for them, praying that God would bless them the same ways that I want Him to bless me. I pray this over and over and over until my wounded heart stops bleeding and is able to beat in normal rhythm and I begin to heal. If my feelings try to override my choice to forgive, I start the process all over again. And I choose to subject my thoughts about the offender to the obedience of Christ. For instance, if I am tempted to think mean thoughts about them, I re-direct my thoughts to ones that please Christ instead. Repeating this over and over and over literally creates a new pathway of thinking in my brain and eventually new feelings follow. (This is actually scientifically verifiable!) Perhaps this is part of what Jesus was conveying to us when He said to forgive others not 7x7 but rather 70x7.

One last thought on forgiveness: that debt we are owed still needs to be repaid. We've made the choice to forgive, to not demand payment from the offender, but the debt remains. How do we get it paid?

We pay it ourselves.

Scandalous! Pay it ourselves?

Yep, by God's grace we pay it ourselves, but not in a conventional way. God's economy is unique. The way to get what we are owed is to pay it ourselves by investing in the life of the offender. Sometimes it is just through praying for them, but often it is through God-initiated, God-directed installment payments. It may be writing a note of congratulations when some blessing has come to them or speaking kindly to them in the grocery store. And only in God's economy can payment be made by NOT doing something, not telling the story of the offense (even if you're just sticking to the truth!), not pointing out their deficiencies to another person, not avoiding them like the plague, or not trying to rally others against them.

It means following God's directions to do good to the enemy and being an avenue of blessing.

But wait, you say! They will just hurt me again!

Maybe. Possibly. But we are never more like Christ than when we forgive. And if we choose to walk in the path of forgiveness and blessing, He will see to it that we are repaid far more than what we are owed. He promises.

Day 5

The last couple of days have been intense so today will be rather brief.

The final topic that Jesus instructed us in prayer says, *"And do not lead us into temptation but deliver us from evil."* That sounds confusing, doesn't it? Because elsewhere in scripture, we are told that God doesn't tempt anyone (James 1:13). Not just confusing, that sounds contradictory! Is it?

No, because scripture doesn't contradict itself. Remember, the best commentary on scripture is scripture, so let's unpack it in order to understand what we are to pray.

A helpful amplification of the verse in translation might be something like this, "Lord, I am prone to sin and I know it. But I don't want to! So please don't answer any of my prayers in a way that would result in increased temptation to sin. And, if you see fit to bring trials or temptations my way, I ask you for the grace that I need not to sin in them."

This phrase is an acknowledgement of our fallibility, our tendency to sin when temptations and trials come, and of Satan's desire to *"sift us like wheat"* (Luke 22:31). It's like an admission of our need to pray so that we don't fall, such as Jesus exhorting the disciples in the hours before His death to watch and pray (Matthew 26:41). What an appropriate reminder to end our prayer time, a reminder of our need to depend on Him continuously and our inability to live life victoriously in our own strength.

The final phrase, *"For Thine is the kingdom and the power and the glory, forever Amen,"* is like an exclamation point of worship on our prayers. Let's end there today, Hallelujah to His Name!

Day 1

Today we are going to revisit the verse at the beginning of the model prayer, *"Our Father who art in heaven."*

Our Father.

We have a close family friend who has two daughters. Those girls are all grown up now, but when they were little, their Daddy did the sweetest thing with them.

He gave them a very generous weekly allowance. Truth be told, they were probably the envy of all their friends. He provided well for them, taking care of each and every need but the allowance was the sweetest of all. The girls didn't have to earn their allotment in any way but their Daddy did have one stipulation. He would only dispense it to them on Sunday nights and they had to remember to ask him in order to get it. If they forgot, he never scolded them or deprived them of other things but the allowance, well, they had to ask for it. In fact, they had to climb up in his chair, snuggle close, spend some time talking, and just love on their Daddy. Then they could ask. And he most gladly complied, delighted to be with them and provide what they asked for. Seems like I remember that he often gave them more than they expected, just 'cause he was so kind and generous and, 'cause he could. All they had to do was ask.

Reminds me of my Heavenly Father, my Abba. Now I know I'm getting awfully close to some dangerous UNtruth like "name it and claim it" but I think there's a real parallel here. Maybe God's point in having us pray is so we can snuggle up close to Him.

Maybe we miss out on a lot He'd love to do for us because we never get around to asking. Maybe we all ought to climb up in His lap right now, snuggle close, and love on our Daddy. He loves to give good gifts to His children.

Day 2

Martha therefore said to Jesus, "Lord, if You had been here, my brother would not have died. Even now I know that whatever you ask of God, God will give You." John 11:21-22

Have you ever felt like God didn't answer your prayers? Well, I have! Those feelings are not accurate, though because God answers all prayers of His children. (Not so for those that don't belong to Him, but you can bet the bank that He will answer ours.)

He does always answer...but the answer isn't always "yes." Sometimes He says "yes," sometimes He says "no," and sometimes He says..."wait." But He always answers.

Let's talk for a minute about how we handle those "no" and "wait" answers. Both of those can be difficult.

When God says "wait" or "not now," it can feel like He is saying nothing. That makes us wonder if He's not listening or doesn't care or "maybe this prayer stuff just doesn't work for me." I understand. In those times of not seeing God's answers, I find it so very helpful to focus on His attributes, like when we are told in Philippians to set our minds on what is TRUE (not what might be true or could be true or what feels true). What IS true, and the truth is that God is always good, always faithful, always loving, always sovereign, and always at work on our behalf in a thousand ways that we cannot see. His Word is true-er than our circumstances. Always. He calls us to walk by faith, not by sight, which means trusting in who He is, not what I can see, or especially not what I think I see! When I am tempted to be discouraged or frustrated at the apparent lack of His answer, I remind myself to persevere. His Word is very clear that we are to be persistent in our prayers to keep on asking, knowing that in due time, He will answer. There are times we need to strengthen those spiritual muscles, break out in a little prayerful sweat, and purpose not to give up. In those times, I believe He sends His angels to encourage us, to minister to us, and to infuse hope and endurance. Just like Mary and Martha experienced when their brother Lazarus had died. It surely felt and seemed and looked like God had ignored them, but then Jesus showed up...on time, even though it looked like He was four days late. I haven't had the experience of seeing one who was dead walk out of the tomb but I can personally attest to the TRUTH that God answers prayer. And He rewards our persistence.

If you are in a "wait" time right now, don't give up. Keep praying. You very well might be just about to see God do something beyond your wildest expectations. He's like that!

Living Letters

Day 3

And He went a little beyond them and fell on His face and prayed saying, "My Father, if it is possible, let this cup pass from Me, yet not as I will but as Thou will." Matthew 26:39

What about the times God says "no"? Even as I type this, tears are welling up, recalling times He has said "no" to me or to people I love. And the cry of "why" either screamed through every fiber of my being...or got stuck in my throat in an attempt to deny the pain. I wish I had a three-point message that would answer our questions and resolve the anguish, but I don't. And I don't think there is one, in spite of what some people say. I don't know the "why" but I do know the who, and He is with us. He is supporting, sustaining, and comforting.

I know that one day, the answers to the "whys" will be there. Some things are explained in this life, but a whole lot will be revealed in eternity. Until then, may we draw strength from the truth of who He is. He is love, wisdom, power, understanding, compassion and holy.

In times of "no," I always think about a time when my husband made a decision for our family to move from North Carolina to Georgia. Our children could not understand why we would leave a place where we were so happy, where their friends were, where their entire lives were anchored. As parents, we were unable to explain to our sobbing seven year old that this was a good thing, that God had directed us to leave, and that this move would also provide happiness and new friends and all that she thought she was leaving. Then, in a moment only orchestrated by God, our 10 year old said through her quiet tears, "Mary, Mary. Don't you know Daddy loves us? And he would never do anything that wasn't best for all of us."

God spoke to me in that moment. In the whisper of my daughter, He strongly explained that I would face times when I was sobbing in His arms about decisions He had made on my behalf. And in those times, He wanted me to know that He loves me, and He will never do anything that wasn't best for all of us.

If He is telling you "no" right now, I fervently pray that you will feel the assurance of His love. And in the goodness of His plan.

Keep praying.

Day 4

If you then, who are evil, know how to give good gifts to your children, how much more will your Father who is in heaven give good things to those who ask Him! Matthew 7:11

Today's thought on prayer is brief, but significant. Sometimes we act as though we are bothering God and we practically apologize for coming to Him. We approach prayer as though we need to beg Him to grant our request.

That's baloney and I want to help you change that stinkin' thinkin'. God is the one that thought up the whole idea of prayer anyway! It's His chosen means of communicating with us, of forging an intimate bond, of sharing His goodness, and of letting us participate in what He's doing.

His plans for you and me are good, and better than we could dream up ourselves. And He possesses all power and controls all things so He can engineer anything He wants in order to accomplish His plan.

Do you need to make a decision? Ask Him for wisdom. Do you have a strained relationship? Ask Him to show you how to repair it. Is someone you love living dangerously? Ask Him to show Himself strong on their behalf.

Don't be deceived. Come to Him, knowing the truth.

Let us then with confidence draw near to the throne of grace, that we may receive mercy and find grace to help in time of need. Hebrews 4:16

Also read:

Hebrews 10:19

Ephesians 3:12

PRAY!

Day 5

The prayer of a righteous person has great power as it is working. James 5:16b

We've looked at the prayer Jesus gave us as our model and unpacked the topics to cover in our communication with the Father. Worship, allegiance to God's Kingdom, submission to His perfect will, petition for what we need (on a daily basis!), confession/forgiveness, and supplication for help in trials. Great stuff. I hope it's helped our prayer lives, remembering that prayer is not to inform God of what we need (He already knows–see Matthew 6:32) but rather to strengthen our relationship with our Heavenly Father, increasing our intimacy with Him so that we are transformed into the image of His Son.

Let's touch on prayer once more by digging into that verse in James. The familiar King James translation of this verse says, *"The fervent prayer of a righteous man availeth much."* We want to "avail much" through our prayer life–so what are some other things we need to know?

Scripture tells us at least four things that reveal what it means to be fervent and righteous:

1. Right reason: James 4:2,3 *"You do not have because you do not ask; you ask and do not receive because you ask wrongly, so you can spend it on your passions."* Pretty straightforward. No need for me to expound.

2. Right request: John 14:14 *"If you ask me anything in my name, I will do it,"* and I John 5:14 *"This is the confidence we have in approaching God: that if we ask anything according to his will, he hears us."* A righteous person will ask God for things that are consistent with His Word, i.e., according to His will. That's why they get answers and *"availeth much."*

3. Right relationships: with God, as in sins confessed, John 9:31 *"We know that God does not listen to sinners, but if anyone is a worshiper of God and does his will, God listens to him"* and Psalm 66:18 *"If I had cherished iniquity in my heart, the Lord would not have listened;"* and with others, Matthew 6:14-15 *"For if you forgive others their trespasses, your Heavenly Father will also forgive you, but if you do not forgive others their trespasses, neither will your Father forgive your trespasses"* and Matthew 5:23-24 *"So if you are offering your gift at the altar and there remember that your brother has something against you, leave your gift there before the altar and go. First be reconciled to your brother, and then come and offer your gift."*

4. Right requirement: *"fervent prayer"* is one of faith and persistence. James 1:6-8 tells us the key ingredient is faith, *"But let him ask in faith, with no doubting, for the one who doubts is like a wave of the sea that is driven and tossed by the wind. For that person must not suppose that he will receive anything from the Lord; he is a double-minded man, unstable in all his ways."* And we are told of the importance of persistence in Matthew 7:7-11, lest we think a casual thought tossed heavenward would yield great fruit.

Prayer = God's chosen method of getting His will done on earth and conforming His saints to the image of His Son. Amen. Pray on, Sisters, pray on!

Day 1

For we do not have a high priest who is unable to sympathize with our weaknesses, but one who in every respect has been tempted as we are, yet without sin. Let us then with confidence draw near to the throne of grace, that we may receive mercy and find grace to help in time of need. Hebrews 4:15-16

So many times I have heard, "God's trying to teach me something." So many times I have said it.

I have realized it's wrong. Here's why:

First of all, God doesn't need to "try" anything. He "does" stuff, He doesn't "try" it.

But that's not my main problem with the phrase. It's really an issue with the concept that God is "teaching us a lesson." Think about how else we use that phrase, "I decided to teach him a lesson" or "I taught her a lesson she'll never forget." Not a positive tone.

When we use that phrase, most likely we are going through a difficulty and we try and explain it by "God's trying to teach me something." The assumption is that we are somehow deficient and God is getting us up to par by sending us through pain and suffering. Maybe we don't intend to portray Him that way, but this phrase makes Him sound like a stern schoolmaster, leaning up against the wall, paddle in hand, watching a subordinate struggle.

God's not like that. At all.

When His children are hurting–in small ways or in big ones–He isn't distant or passive. He isn't waiting on us to figure out the lesson so that He can move us on. He's in the thing with us, holding us, and not teaching us some lesson but rather revealing His love and grace and power and truth to us.

Yes, He often allows, even orchestrates, circumstances for His children that we probably wouldn't have chosen for ourselves. But He's not "trying to teach us a lesson." He's offering us...Himself.

Next time we're struggling or enduring pain or in the midst of a problem, let's abandon the idea that this adversity is "God teaching us a lesson." Instead, let's remember that He wants this to be an opportunity for us to see Him for who He is, full of grace and truth, extending mercy and love and power to help us in our need.

Day 2

And we prayed to our God and set a guard as a protection against them day and night.
Nehemiah 4:9

A little background: God's people are rebuilding the walls of Jerusalem, which had been devastated by enemies and looters. They returned from long years of exile and were set on restoring their city to beauty and safety. Although commissioned by Almighty God, the work was not without setbacks and discouragement. The opposition came initially in the form of jeers and verbal abuse and eventually led to threat of invasion. Thus, verse 9. (Ultimately, the source of discouragement came also from within their ranks, not from the outside. Wow!)

Let's take note of these things. First, God's people were doing what He had told them to do, but that didn't mean smooth sailing. Note to self: difficulty and discouragement are not necessarily the signs that God intends me to go in another direction. Often, just the opposite is true! When I find it tough to complete the task I believe God has given me, that might just mean God wants me to flex a little spiritual muscle and resolutely stand. Just sayin.

So the opposition is going to come. It might be intimidation or ridicule or antagonism, or it might be distraction or resistance or negativism. Don't be surprised, but don't give up. This verse tells us exactly what to do. *And we prayed to our God and set a guard as a protection against them day and night.*

Two things are the example. I think, though, that we as believers tend towards one or the other in exclusion, and then we think God failed us when we are without success. But scripture is very clear here. First, pray. Pray because God is the only one who has the power we need. The only one who has the wisdom we need. The only one who has the love and grace and strength we need. The only one who can affect the situation...because He engineered it for His purposes and our benefit to begin with! And prayer is His chosen means of getting his will done. It's how He changes us, it's how He keeps us connected to Him, and it's how He gets the glory and honor of which He is worthy.

Tomorrow we will look at what else we are to do. For today, let's pray about whatever opposition we are facing right now.

Day 3

So in the lowest parts of the space behind the wall, in open places, I stationed the people by their clans, with their swords, their spears, and their bows. And I looked and arose and said to the nobles and to the officials and to the rest of the people, "Do not be afraid of them. Remember the Lord, who is great and awesome, and fight for your brothers, your sons, your daughters, your wives, and your homes." When our enemies heard that it was known to us and that God had frustrated their plan, we all returned to the wall, each to his work. From that day on, half of my servants worked on construction, and half held the spears, shields, bows, and coats of mail. Nehemiah 4:13-16

We saw yesterday that, when God's people are doing what He has called them to do, opposition is going to come. We need not be surprised nor alarmed when that happens. We need to pray.

Notice, though, that His people didn't just pray. Prayer was not all God called them to do. Sounds practically blasphemous, doesn't it? Well, it's not. They set up a guard to watch and protect against the enemy. Now don't hear what I'm not saying. In no way am I advocating some kind of works-based theology. Our life of salvation (justification, sanctification, and glorification) is completely a product of God's grace. But as His grace works through us, He calls us to do some things. In this case, the people prayed and worked and stood guard, ready to terminate invaders.

The next time you face a little opposition (like maybe before you have your second cup of coffee this morning?), remember Nehemiah and his people. They prayed. And they also worked.

Oh, and the wall? Well, read on through chapter 6 of Nehemiah and see what happened.

So the wall was finished on the twenty-fifth day of the month Elul, in fifty-two days. And when all our enemies heard of it, all the nations around us were afraid and fell greatly in their own esteem, for they perceived that this work had been accomplished with the help of our God. Nehemiah 6:15-16

God will finish what He starts. We get the privilege of participating!

Day 4

But the Lord answered and said to her, "Martha, Martha, you are worried and bothered about so many things; but only one thing is necessary, for Mary has chosen the good part, which shall not be taken away from her." Luke 10:41-42

This passage is rich with not only spiritual but also practical meaning and application. You might be familiar with the story: Jesus has come to visit His dear friends, Mary, Martha, and Lazarus. Martha can hardly enjoy the visit because she is so busy trying to get dinner on the table, and she's irritated with her sister who, instead of helping Martha accomplish her agenda, is just sitting with Jesus. She even (self-righteously?) implores Jesus to make Martha come help her. Verses 41 and 42 record His gentle answer...simplicity. Not being "worried and bothered about so many things." First, let's apply that spiritually, because in reality, all other application flows from that. If we are "too busy" to have adequate, consistent times where we worship the Lord, meditate on His Word, and listen to His voice, then we can be completely sure that we are doing a whole lot of things that He doesn't intend for us to do. Mark this down—we will always have enough time to do what He calls us to do. If we can't "get it all done," then some of "it" doesn't need to be there. I used to hear myself answer "BUSY" when people asked how I was doing. His still small voice corrected me, speaking softly that I was being prideful and boastful. So I stopped.

I have consistently found that if I make it my priority to listen to Him, then I greatly reduce my stress and prevent getting into a frazzled state. It's helpful to take a look at what causes our frazzled state to begin with. Here are some thoughts (most of which are up close and personal, if you know what I mean):

- Trying to make things "perfect."

- Trying to impress others.

- Doing more than is truly necessary.

- Placing importance on the wrong things.

Excellence and planning are good things, to be sure...but so is simplicity. Knowing what matters and what doesn't, and staying in constant touch with Him so I know the difference, keeps me from being pulled away into things that don't matter.

Amen

Day 5

Then Jehoshaphat stood in the assembly of Judah and Jerusalem, in the house of the Lord before the new court, and he said, "O Lord, the God of our fathers, are You not God in the heavens? And are You not ruler over all the kingdoms of the nations? Power and might are in Your hand so that no one can stand against You. Did You not, O our God, drive out the inhabitants of this land before Your people Israel and give it to the descendants of Abraham Your friend forever? They have lived in it, and have built You a sanctuary there for Your name, saying, 'Should evil come upon us, the sword, or judgment, or pestilence, or famine, we will stand before this house and before You (for Your name is in this house) and cry to You in our distress, and You will hear and deliver us.' Now behold, the sons of Ammon and Moab and Mount Seir, whom You did not let Israel invade when they came out of the land of Egypt (they turned aside from them and did not destroy them), see how they are rewarding us by coming to drive us out from Your possession which You have given us as an inheritance. O our God, will You not judge them? For we are powerless before this great multitude who are coming against us; nor do we know what to do, but our eyes are on You." All Judah was standing before the Lord, with their infants, their wives and their children. 2 Chronicles 20:5-13

To better grasp the significance of these verses, we need a little background. Jehoshaphat, King of Judah, was reigning well. God was allowing him and his nation to live in peace and prosperity. It certainly looked like they had God's favor and I'll bet King J was quick to praise his God, don't you think?

This is where the story picks up. Suddenly things turn south, King J got word that a couple of neighboring nations decided to make war against the nation of Judah and verse 3 tells us that he was afraid. I would be, too! That same verse tells us his response. It would be completely understandable and reasonable and wise if Jehoshaphat had gone out to examine his army and beefed them up a bit, maybe purchased a few more weapons and stocked up on supplies. Being prepared is approved by God, after all. But that's not what verse 3 tells us he did. Yes, he was afraid and he "turned his attention to seek the Lord and proclaimed a fast throughout all Judah." Hmmmm. Pause for self-examination. Is that what I do when I'm afraid?

Then, he gathered the people together and led them in prayer. Talk about a model to follow! First, he acknowledged who God is and His power and might. That's a great place to begin indeed! Then he remembers what God had done in the past for His people. Finally he asked for help, admitting *"nor do we know what to do, but our eyes are on Thee."* And I absolutely love verse 13, *"And all Judah was standing before the Lord, with their infants, their wives, and their children."* Everyone got to see how King J handled fear–what a great life lesson!

Pray that we would turn to prayer when the enemy attacks and that all around us would see our response.

Day 1

Then in the midst of the assembly the Spirit of the Lord came upon Jahaziel the son of Zechariah, the son of Benaiah, the son of Jeiel, the son of Mattaniah, the Levite of the sons of Asaph; and he said, "Listen, all Judah and the inhabitants of Jerusalem and King Jehoshaphat: thus says the Lord to you, 'Do not fear or be dismayed because of this great multitude, for the battle is not yours but God's. Tomorrow go down against them. Behold, they will come up by the ascent of Ziz, and you will find them at the end of the valley in front of the wilderness of Jeruel. You need not fight in this battle; station yourselves, stand and see the salvation of the Lord on your behalf, O Judah and Jerusalem.' Do not fear or be dismayed; tomorrow go out to face them, for the Lord is with you." And Jehoshaphat bowed his head with his face to the ground and all Judah and the inhabitants of Jerusalem fell down before the lord, worshipping the Lord. And the Levites, from the sons of the Kohathites and of the sons of the Korahites, stood up to praise the Lord God of Israel with a very loud voice. 2 Chronicles 20:14-19

In response to Jehoshaphat's prayer, God tells His people not to fear for the battle is not yours but God's. Powerful words. Mighty words. He tells us the same—the battle is not ours but His.

And, how does the King respond? In song!

Do you get the picture? King J was praising God and that led to a group-sing! Seriously. The Korahites were the group of Levites in charge of singing, for real. And they broke out in song at this point, but it doesn't end there. The next day, the people of Judah went out to face the invaders, and guess who King J sent out first? Yep, those who praised Him in verse 21. That's like putting First Baptist's praise band on the front lines!

And what did God do?

When they began singing and praising, the Lord set ambushes against the sons of Ammon, Moab, and Mount Seir, who had come against Judah; so they were routed. For the sons of Ammon and Moab rose up against the inhabitants of Mount Seir, destroying them completely; and when they had finished with the inhabitants of Seir, they helped to destroy one another. When Judah came to the lookout of the wilderness, they looked toward the multitude, and behold, they were corpses lying on the ground, and no one had escaped. When Jehoshaphat and his people came to take their spoil, they found much among them, including goods, garments and valuable things which they took for themselves, more than they could carry. And they were three days taking the spoil because there was so much. 2 Chronicles 20:22-25

And the dread of God was on all the kingdoms of the lands when they heard that the Lord had fought against the enemies of Israel. So the kingdom of Jehoshaphat was at peace, for his God gave him rest on all sides. 2 Chronicles 20:29-30

Great story. Greater application. Praise is the fire that lights the wick of God's power...triumphing over my enemies, spreading His glory, and securing my peace. Amen!

Day 2

Thus Samuel took a stone and set it between Mizpah and Shen, and named it 'Ebenezer', saying, "Thus far the Lord has helped us." I Samuel 7:23

I love hymns. The tunes are beautiful (especially the re-mixes that are vogue now), but mostly I love the truths that are imparted through the rhyming lines with deep insight, doctrine of the faith, and meaningful encouragement. Frankly, few songs of today can do the same. Love those hymns. One of my most favs is *Come, Thou Fount of Every Blessing* sung by David Crowder band. I think I favor it because it's one of the few hymns I can still bang out on the piano! But this time I began to pay close attention to the words and "Ebenezer" caught my ear.

In verse two, the song says, "Here I raise my Ebenezer, hither by Thy help I'm come." It goes on to relay the treasured principle that God pursued us, chose us, initiated the relationship, and He sustains it. Glory! Well, what in the world is an Ebenezer? Makes me think of someone hoisting that cranky old miser, Scrooge, from Dickens' *A Christmas Carol* high in the air! Somehow I don't think that's what songwriter Robert Robinson meant when he penned those words in the late 1700's, but I didn't know, so I looked it up. And I thought you'd be interested, too.

In this passage in Samuel, the Israelites had just defeated the Philistines and recovered the Ark of the Covenant after being defeated twice previously, in the same place. The prophet Samuel erected a monument to celebrate the victory and commemorate that God Himself had given it to them. He named the place Ebenezer, which literally means "stone of help," signifying God's provision to secure the victory for them. Thus Samuel took a stone and set it between Mizpah and Shen, and named it Ebenezer, saying, *"Thus far the Lord has helped us."*

"Here I raise my Ebenezer, hither by Thy help I'm come. And I hope by Thy good pleasure safely to arrive at home. Jesus sought me when a stranger, wandering from the fold of God. He to rescue me from danger, interposed His precious blood."

These lyrics remind us that it is God's powerful and divine love that not only secures all kinds of life victories for us but also draws us to Him, keeps us in Him, and will bring us home. The hymn depicts an act of worship that acknowledges what the Apostle John says in his Gospel, chapter 6, verse 44, *"No one can come to Me, unless the Father who sent Me draws him; and I will raise him up on the last day."*

The Israelites put up a memorial to remind themselves that God's help acquired the victory for them. That was their Ebenezer. The songwriter penned a hymn to prompt his heart to the remembrance that it was God's initiation and intervention that begins, sustains, and completes our relationship with Him. What victory is eluding you? Are you experiencing defeat... repeatedly? Then turn to God for help. And when He gives it, what stone of remembrance is erected to remind you that without His help, we have no victory, no salvation, nothing? But with His help, His grace, and His provision, we are reconciled to Him, restored to wholeness, and reassured of triumph. No matter how many previous defeats we suffered.

Raise your Ebenezer. Remember His help.

Day 3

The effectual fervent prayer of a righteous man availeth much. James 5:16

The King James Version is so rich. It's an oft-quoted verse that rolls off our tongue but do we really grasp what I it means? Let's unpack it...

"Effectual"–this means "effective." Well, duh, of course we want effective prayers! The question is–how to do that? How can we pray effectively? How do we pray so that He will answer with "yes"? How do we pray "according to His will"?

We pray His Word! His Word is His will! So when we pray His Word, we can know He says yes! How do we do that? We will see in just a second. Let's unpack the rest of the verse first...

"Prayer of a righteous man (woman)"–you might think, there's the catch, I'm not righteous enough! Thankfully, the effectiveness and the much availing of our prayers does not depend on our righteousness! If we are in Christ, then His righteousness is counted as ours. Hallelujah! Our fellowship with the Father can be affected by our sin (Psalm 66:18) but our right standing before Him–and His hearing of our prayers–is not based on our ability to be righteous.

"Availeth much" means it brings about great and mighty work. The work of our powerful and loving Heavenly Father working good in the lives of people, granting good gifts, changing the hearts of those in authority, bringing light into darkness, guidance and direction for us to follow, and provision for our lack. Yes, that is the "much" we desire!

All this is the work of God. What is our part?

"Fervent." Showing great intensity and perseverance. That is our part, persistent praying, faithful faith, and deep desire. Although even this is only possible because God grants us His grace, this is where we have a part in seeing our prayers answered. God is looking for women who are willing to pray (Ezekiel 22:30) so that He might answer. He wants women who will not give up but will persevere in praying.

Will you be one?

Here are some effectual prayers we righteous women can pray fervently...and watch Him avail much!

- For joy (Philippians 3:1)

- For no bitterness (Hebrews 12:15)

- For Godly friends (Proverbs 13:20)

- For diligence (Romans 12:11)

- To not be critical (Romans 14:13)

- To have a servant's heart (Philippians 2:3)

Day 4

If I regard iniquity in my heart, the Lord will not hear me. Psalm 66:18

Let's dig deeper into the verse we looked at yesterday in conjunction with praying effectively and seeing God avail much.

We already established that God's answers to our prayers are not based on our own goodness or righteousness but rather that Christ's righteousness is counted as ours, and that all God's promises are found in Him. (*For as many as are the promises of God, in Him they are yes; therefore also through Him is our Amen to the glory of God through us.* 2 Corinthians 1:20)

So does our sin have no impact on our prayer life? Can we dismiss our attitudes and behaviors as irrelevant? The answer is a resounding no! (Romans 6:1)

The psalmist does not mean that we are to be sinless, but rather that we are to be blameless. *"Regarding iniquity in my heart"* does not mean that I look into my heart and see defilement but rather this is telling us that an unwillingness to forsake sin is what blocks our communication with the Father. The cherishing of sin, a love of evil, or a secret purpose to sin is certain to prevent the hearing of our prayers. In order to be acceptable, to be effective, to see the Lord avail much on our behalf, we must regularly and consistently ask Him to show us anything that stands as a block between us and Him.

It might be wrong motives (James 4:3), or a breach in a relationship (Matthew 5:23,24), or hidden sins (Psalm 51:6-10), or a prideful attitude (Psalm 139:23,24). Spend some time today reading each of these passages and ask the Lord to shine His light into your heart...and get ready for Him to "availeth much" in your prayer life!

Living Letters

Day 5

And I sought for a man among them who should build up the wall and stand in the breach before me for the land, that I should not destroy it, but I found none. Ezekiel 22:30

The interconnectedness of God's sovereignty and man's accountability are complex and too deep for us to fully comprehend, at least this side of heaven. It's tempting to lean way too far to one side or the other. Either thinking that, apart from our hard work (even in prayer), all manner of folks will go to hell, and God's whole plan will fall apart. OR we rest so solidly on our "blessed assurance" that we figure God's got it all worked out and there is no need for us to pray.

Both are wrong...and dangerous.

Elsewhere we will focus on the sovereignty of God but for today, let's see what this passage has to say to us.

Here, God reveals to us that He is looking for men (and women) to pray so that He can respond with healing and power and salvation. But clearly at the point in history of this passage, there were none to be found. Consequently, God's indignation is poured out upon the land (see verse 31).

What does this mean for you and me?

Are there times God wants to spare us or our family or even our country from destruction but there was no one crying out to Him for mercy, for wisdom, for protection?

Will you be a woman who stands in the gap?

Day 1

And He made from one man every nation of mankind to live on all the face of the earth, having determined allotted periods and the boundaries of their dwelling place, that they should seek God, and perhaps feel their way toward Him and find Him. Acts 17:26-27

It seems to be human nature to wonder if one's life would be different (aka better...) if one's life circumstances were different (aka better...). We sometimes think, "if only I had been born in a different place," or to different parents or in another time or socioeconomic situation, "life might be better." Maybe, instead of thinking "if only," we feel guilty that we don't have adverse beginnings to overcome and feel compelled to succeed lavishly so as to "earn" the good life spot we've been given.

How can we not only accept our lot in life, but actually be joyfully content? And help others to do the same?

By grasping these verses.

God, in His loving sovereignty, orchestrated all the details of your birth and mine to put us in exactly the right spot so that we would seek Him. Whatever circumstances best cultivated the soil of our hearts to receive the Good News of our need for Him and His gift of grace are the ones He designed for us. "*Having determined allotted periods and the boundaries of their dwelling place,*" when and where and to whom. Not an accident. Not an oversight or a tragedy. But rather purposed with love..."*that they should seek God, and perhaps feel their way toward Him...and find Him.*"

Close out today by thanking God for that one thing about yourself that has always bothered you: your parents, your financial situation, your talents (or lack thereof!). Whatever. He is speaking to you even now, that you might seek Him....

Day 2

But God has chosen the foolish things of the world to shame the wise, and God has chosen the weak things of the world to shame the things which are strong and the base things of the world and the despised, God has chosen, the things that are not, that He might nullify the things that are, that no man should boast before God. 1 Corinthians 1:27-29

I was thinking about Mary today. Thinking about how God choose a young girl (she was most likely 14 or 15 years old!), from a not-famous-or-wealthy-or-influential family, about to marry a young boy under less than ideal circumstances, from an insignificant little town, traipsing to an obscure little village, and nine months' pregnant. (Moms, pause for just a moment and ponder riding on the back of a donkey on dirt and gravel roads for 69 miles, hours away from delivery. Uh, right. Lots of loving communication for "couple time," I am sure.) Then birthing a baby, apparently without a midwife (certainly without an ob/gyn staff that she had months to become attached to and trust with her very life) in a stable, with animals around. So much for freaking out over dropping a pacifier on the floor and handing it to baby without first sterilizing it. Then He announced the world's greatest news to a bunch of shepherds–dirty, smelly, uneducated shepherds that came to look at Mary's newborn. Most of us shudder (or maybe scream at poor Joseph, surely this is all his fault?).

God could have done it differently. He could have sent His Son as an adult, surrounded by angels, and with an entourage fit for the King that He is. Or He could have chosen pristine birthing conditions in the center of the Roman Empire with all the medical specialists of the day. At least He could have chosen some more impressive characters to bring forth His Son and to welcome Him to the world. Some folks that others would have looked up to, paid attention to, helped with a room or at least a casserole!

But He didn't. God's choices. Nearly all of the time, He rests His plans in the hands of the insignificant ordinaries, or the obviously wrong option. On purpose!

Maybe you need to be reminded about God's choices. As in, if you don't feel gifted, remember Moses. As in, if you have a not-so-perfect past, remember Rahab (we're talking prostitute, people!). As in, if you have messed up since He called you–think about Abraham (uh, turned his wife over to another man because he was afraid...twice!). Or Noah's drinking binge on the heels of being saved from worldwide destruction (actually, after 40 days cooped up on the boat with those animals, that's kind of understandable....). If you're just an ordinary nobody, think Gideon. If you have had every advantage and you still blew it, think David and Solomon and Paul. If you feel defeated because you've proven yourself a failure or a coward or hopeless...think Peter.

God's choices. He seems to always be about the unlikely and the ones that nobody believed in or counted on or even noticed.

And, just in case you are one of the other folks...if you are important or significant or gifted or have never messed up royally...well, thankfully, for YOU, God is not a respecter of persons. He will still take you, too, and turn you into part of His plan. But, just to warn you, you probably have some humbling to do. Cuz, really, none of us are significant or gifted or important.

Day 3

All discipline for the moment seems not to be joyful, but sorrowful; yet to those who have been trained by it, afterwards it yields the peaceful fruit of righteousness. Hebrews 12:11

This verse may be very familiar to you. Let's ask the Lord to show us fresh truth in it today. Here are some thoughts to ponder...

- All discipline seems hard (sorrowful). Physical, emotional, mental, spiritual–all of it. So I shouldn't be surprised when it is difficult to work out or learn a new skill or change a wrong attitude or grow in grace. Nor should I whine about it. Fact of life–it's hard. For everybody. Get over it.

- Seems...yet, discipline seems sorrowful but it is bearable because of the hope of its fruit. Peaceful fruit of righteousness. That's what we are after. Discipline is the transport to get there.

- To those who have been trained by it, news flash–not everyone who receives discipline automatically gets to enjoy the peaceful fruit of righteousness! No, that is only for those who have been trained by it. So that means that I can thwart or nullify the work of discipline in my life. If I don't cooperate with God's activity of discipline in my life, I will not only have to endure the unpleasant disciplinary work but neither will I enjoy the fruit He desires to produce by it! For sure God is always at work in my life but just as surely, I have a choice about how I respond to what He plans to accomplish.

How do I get trained by it, instead of short-circuiting His intention for me? We will dig that out tomorrow. For today, ask Him to plant His truth in our souls.

Day 4

All discipline for the moment seems not to be joyful, but sorrowful; yet to those who have been trained by it, afterwards it yields the peaceful fruit of righteousness. Hebrews 12:11

If we want to run a marathon, we have to be trained for it (at least we do if we intend to finish the race!). If we want to improve our musical ability or our computer skills or our parenting, we need training. The Christian life, too, requires training in order to enjoy success. Scripture tells us that we need discipline, and God lovingly supplies it throughout our life. But we saw yesterday that, while He provides the training opportunities, we have the option of being trained by them in order to enjoy the peaceful fruit He intends for us to have.

How can we participate in His training sessions in such a way as to be successfully trained? Here are some thoughts:

- Self-examination: Is there sin in my life that God wants to address? Sometimes discipline is a result of sin. Other times it is a catalyst to reveal sin that I was unaware of, but it is always a call to examine myself and see what God wants to remove from me (Psalm 26:2; 139:23,24).

- Development of endurance: Struggling is not always bad. Not at all. We get stronger as a result of wrestling and enduring and not quitting. Numerous passages in scripture exhort us to hang in there and not give up. Persevere. We don't know what is ahead of us and today's discipline may very well be the opportunity to generate some muscle strength that will be needed in the demands of tomorrow, so don't give up (James 5:11).

- Embrace it: What? Embrace the suffering? I already admitted discipline was sorrowful–why in the world would I embrace it? Endure, maybe, but embrace? Why... and how?

Tomorrow we shall see what God says. Today, ask Him to illuminate your soul and reveal any ways you are not rightly responding to discipline.

Day 5

All discipline for the moment seems not to be joyful, but sorrowful; yet to those who have been trained by it, afterwards it yields the peaceful fruit of righteousness. Hebrews 12:11

Discipline is hard, not fun, because it is shaping us into a form that is not natural. That is painful. If we want to enjoy the blessings of the new and better shape, we must embrace the discipline… including the suffering. Why? How?

- Why: Because *"God deals with you as sons; for what son is there whom his father does not discipline? But if you are without discipline, of which all have become partakers, then you are illegitimate children and not sons"* (Hebrews 12:7). In other words, I realize that discipline is proof that I belong to God, that He loves me as His child, and His purpose is for my good (Genesis 50:20). If I cling to the absolute truth that He is always sovereign and always loving, then I can accept that whatever happens in my life is allowed by Him…for my good and His glory.

- How: By clinging to that truth. Repeating it over and over to my weary and broken soul. He is good and He loves me and He is accomplishing His purpose in my life. 2 Thessalonians 1:3 indicates that discipline enlarges our faith and grows our love. Wow. And choosing not to feel sorry for myself, *"knowing that the same experiences of suffering are being accomplished by your brethren who are in the world"* (1 Peter 5:9). Other people have endured and accomplished–I can, too. And by relying on the comfort God provides to me…and others who are also afflicted (2 Corinthians 1:3-5). And by getting my eyes off myself and ministering to somebody else.

Neglecting these things can cause me to forfeit the fruit God desires to bring about through the discipline. But being trained successfully by the discipline God permits in my life allows me to *"be considered worthy of the kingdom of God"* (2 Thessalonians 1:5) and gives me the opportunity to experience the truth of James 1:12, *"Blessed is a man who perseveres under trial; for once he has been approved, he will receive the crown of life which the Lord has promised to those who love Him."*

Amen.

Day 1

Have you ever noticed that some people have a depth that sets them apart from other folks? For some, it is manifested in a quiet compassion that not only feels the pain of others, but also moves to meet their needs. For others, it's insight that surpasses prevailing wisdom. Or it might be a heart that seems to always notice the needs of every situation and matches with a willingness to serve. But it is always with an attitude that never seeks to be applauded or even noticed. Confident humility.

I've studied these folks and found a common denominator. Each one has known difficulty, brokenness, disappointment, heartache, pain, and even defeat, but then survival. Sustaining endurance.

That's where the depth of character came from. Isaiah 45:3 says, "*And I will give you the treasures of darkness, and hidden wealth of secret places, in order that you may know that I am The Lord, the God of Israel.*" Treasures aren't found lying around on top of the ground. They are located deep down, in dark places. To get to them, one has to go to the depths, to the darkness, and through the hard spots.

Treasures only come from the darkness, it is wealth that is hidden but shared with those that go into the deep places. Places immersed in trials or heartaches or pain.

We don't usually choose to go into life's hard places, but maybe if we remember they are the only places that these treasures can be found, we won't run away from them when God takes us there.

Treasures in the darkness mean getting to know that He is the Lord. Treasure indeed.

Day 2

Therefore, since we are surrounded by such a great cloud of witnesses, let us throw off everything that hinders and the sin that so easily entangles. And let us run with perseverance the race marked out for us, fixing our eyes on Jesus, the pioneer and perfecter of faith. For the joy set before him he endured the cross, scorning its shame, and sat down at the right hand of the throne of God. Hebrews 12:1-2

My Betsy is a swimmer. She was blessed with the long torso and lean body type that proves an advantage for competitive swimming. She also has the tenacity and work ethic that have resulted in some summertime blue ribbons. She's a natural in the water. There's this one habit, though, that her coach has worked hard with her to break. When Betsy is speeding through the water, she has a hard time not glancing over to the lanes on either side just to check on the competition. More than once, this has cost precious milliseconds that made the difference between first and second. That wasted motion means time lost for the lead. Betsy has been swimming for a while, but even so, she has to fight hard that natural tendency to look at the other lanes. She measures her progress, not by the finish line, but by the other swimmers. On the side of the pool, her coach shakes his head wondering how he can keep her from worrying about somebody else's race.

I don't swim competitively but, like my Betsy, I wrestle with looking in the other lanes of those in the race around me. I've walked with Jesus a long time but I can still get distracted by some of those in the other lanes. It's so tempting to see others in the lanes around us and think they are winning. Cuz they look like they're "ahead." So we pull harder, try to swim faster, all the while losing time because we are measuring our race by somebody else's...instead of focusing on the finish line. Do you know what I mean? We get distracted by all sorts of "wonder if's." Should I go to that church where so and so goes? Or get the same kind of Bible? Or take that Bible study? We look at the lane on the other side of the pool and assume that we should homeschool or adopt or be involved in a particular ministry just because someone else is and they sure look like they are winning. It's not that we want to beat somebody else–we just want to be sure we're doing the right thing to win the race. And we can focus all too quickly on someone else's race and assume we are losing because we aren't running the same one.

But notice that the verse says, *"the race marked out for us."* This means we have an individual, particular race that we are to run. It's ours, not somebody else's. While we are all called to the same commands to love and serve and show mercy and obey God, our races are not all marked out the same. We are called to finish this race–not to swim in somebody else's lane. Time spent wondering or worrying about the other lanes distracts me from my own race, makes me lose not only focus and time, but also joy and contentment. Of course we should clap and cheer for all those swimming beside us but they should not be a gauge of how well we are doing in our own lane.

The solution? Right there in that passage, fixing my eyes on Jesus. He called me to the race that He marked out for me. He equips me to run that particular race. And He promises joy in the running if I keep looking at Him. Gonna work on focusing on the finish line and less on the lanes of friends.

Day 3

We will, in all things, grow up into Him who is the Head, that is, Christ. From Him, the whole body, joined and held together by every supporting ligament, grows and builds itself up in love, as each part does its work. Ephesians 4:15-16

The physical body is made up of a bazillion cells (can you tell this is in my own words?). Each cell is distinct, yet connected. Every cell in my body contains my own unique DNA, which links each one to another, making them all belong together. Yet they are separate from one another, individual. Some work together and function as a group, different from other cell groups, yet all are orchestrated to operate in harmony with one another. Every single cell in my body responds to orders from my brain...and every single cell recognizes an inherent bond with every other cell in my body, responding to their needs. When cells, at least most of them, work as they are designed to do, I am healthy. If enough rogue cells have their distorted way, my whole body can suffer.

Indeed, this is the picture of the body of Christ. We are all separate individuals, yet, because we are imprinted with the DNA of Jesus, we not only respond to His commands but also to the needs of others. In fact, many of His commands involve meeting the needs of others! Think of the numerous "*one another*" exhortations in scripture, "*wash one another's feet,*" "*love one another,*" "*serve one another,*" "*teach and admonish one another,*" "*pray for one another,*" "*confess your sins to one another,*" "*comfort one another,*" "*bear one another's burdens,*" and "*forgive one another.*" When we all "*do to one another as we would have them do unto us,*" the body of Christ functions in beautiful, beneficial, healthy harmony.

And the world takes note.

Day 4

For even the Son of Man did not come to be served but to serve. Mark 10:45

Good service...we all want to get it. Actually, we all expect it. How good are we at giving it? Christ set the example for us. He, for whom and by whom all things are created, sets His priority on serving. What can we learn from that?

- There is much joy in serving: Especially when it's inconvenient. When I meet a need for someone else, I am rewarded with a deep satisfaction, a treasured happiness that can only come when I strive to please someone else instead of myself. From simple things to complex acts–doesn't matter. Joy!

- Begin at home: Frankly, it's harder to serve here than at church or in the community. Even though these are the folks we love the best and presumably want to serve the most! Go figure. But service should be at home first and best above all other places. I think we women have an advantage over fellas when it comes to serving. We seem to have serving programmed into our DNA, but trust me it still is a choice. A daily choice. Now I firmly believe that children should do chores (yes, little urchins of mine–lots of them!), but Mom should be the greatest servant of all. "Great" in terms of not only quantity of service but especially quality: cheerful service, glad spirit, willing heart, doing things noticed and unnoticed, and without complaining. Wives don't let your husband out-serve you. Allow me a brief moment on the soapbox here...the Church has done a great job instructing husbands in being servant-leaders, and so they should. But I fear that we have all too happily seated ourselves in our easy chairs while our husbands perform their "rightful" service. Treat your hubby like a king.

- Serve at home and then serve at church: Most folks I know are doing a great job at this. It hardly needs a mention. In fact, I worry more about folks that are doing too much rather than not serving at all! But just in case you are merely warming a pew, I suggest that you find a place to serve–a regular commitment, a place where it matters if you don't show up, and then serve your heart out!

- Look for the serendipitous chances to serve: Picking up paper towels off the floor in public bathrooms is a favorite of mine. (Yes, Mom, I wash my hands after!)

- Serve others in their times of need: Now, I gotta tell you–I think the community I am part of does a great job at this. Taking meals, helping out with others' kids, acting as personal moving service, providing Christmas for needy families, praying for each other faithfully, and on and on and on.

I have heard folks excuse their lack of serving with "It's not my gift." Well, my goodness, how convenient. But how wrong. All those spiritual gifts that we seem to want to pick and choose, well, scripture actually commands us to exercise each one of them. Yep. Check it out. We will have one or two that dominates our motivation but we are all exhorted to give, show mercy, teach, prophesy, have wisdom and faith...and to serve, especially to serve. Christ is our example.

Don't expect to be applauded or even noticed for your service. In fact, hold out hope that you won't be because your Father who sees in secret will reward you.

Day 5

Ever since I was a teenager, I've read books and heard talks that sought to inspire the recipients to reach for the stars, dream the big dreams, and do the impossible. Those messages are appealing and inspirational indeed, and I am all for doing things excellently, not shabbily. But today, I'd like to examine these messages through the microscope of scripture and see if perhaps we need to exercise caution in our reaching and dreaming and doing...

First, I concur that we should heed Colossian 3:23, *"Whatever you do, do your work heartily, as for the Lord rather than for men."* Christians should be known for being the best workers, for having the most cheerful attitudes, and of providing the greatest service to the organization. The problem I have with some of these books and talks, though, is that the last phrase of this verse is often unheeded. They don't encourage us to do great work for the Lord's reputation, but rather to enhance our own...how to "get ahead," how to "succeed," how to "have a great career/marriage/kids," etc. Including "how to have a big church," as opposed to how to advance HIS fame.

Next, on the "dream big" thing, check out this verse and see if you think it is consistent with that mindset...

And to make it your ambition to lead a quiet life and attend to your own business and work with your hands, just as we commanded you, so that you will behave properly toward outsiders and not be in any need. I Thessalonians 4:11-12

I know I am in unusual territory. I know it doesn't sound right for me to suggest to teens and young adults, "Don't aspire to be great. Just aspire to lead a quiet life and work hard and treat people right." I know that doesn't make for great conference speeches or book titles or conversation fodder. But isn't that exactly what this passage teaches?

Work hard, yes, but not to advance your own interests. Be ambitious, yes, but let your ambitions be to lead a life that is not "grand" or "admirable," but rather one that treats others right. Sometimes grand things do indeed come but they should come from God's hand, not from our pursuit, and for His fame, not our pleasure.

The world will probably not take note of our accomplishments if we obey these verses. Most likely, we won't be applauded or acclaimed or emulated very much, at least not here. But check out what God says in Malachi 3:16, *"Then those who feared the LORD spoke to one another, and the LORD gave attention and heard it, and a book of remembrance was written before Him for those who fear the LORD and who esteem His name."*

A book of remembrance written for the Lord Himself is better than any earthly listing in Who's Who.

Day 1

Read Colossians 1:17 and meditate on it for a moment.

I was playing with my grandson, Jonathan, on the floor one day and we were having the best time! (Primarily because he is so handsome and extremely smart and winsome and obedient and...well, you get the idea). One of our toys was one of those wooden peg and hammer things. You know what I mean–the colored pegs fit into nice snug holes and you can hammer them in, and out, and in, and out...again and again. It's a lot of fun.

Except that we have misplaced one of the pegs. That empty hole doesn't bother Jonathan too much but it drives me crazy. I keep looking under furniture, on the porch, in the toy box, trying frantically to locate that missing peg. No such luck.

As I crawled around on the floor, I pondered my peculiar obsession against missing pieces. I don't like incomplete puzzles or unattractively mismatched china or broken door handles or light bulbs that need replacing or holes in my screen door or books with the covers torn off or toys without all their proper attachments. Shabby chic, I like. Missing pieces–not so much.

This quirk of my personality is probably a physical manifestation of my emotional state. I prefer Hallmark movies to horror flicks, fairy tales to reality shows, and I surely do wish that "happily ever after" applied to here and now. My heart is broken continually over mommies that get cancer...and mommies who leave their children willingly. Over daddies who valiantly serve their country across the ocean from their families...and daddies who selfishly abandon their families in hopes of something better. Over children lost to seasons of life...or devastating decisions...or the grave. Over babies who need a home...and scared would-be moms who are not given hope and encouragement and support. Over marriages that break, and especially over the partner left crying with the glue in her hand, hoping for one last chance to try and fix it. Over families and friends hurt by sin, and over the sinner that needs fixing in all of us.

I want so badly for life to go well all the time for all of us. I don't like it when it doesn't. I don't like it when things don't fit right. I want all the puzzle pieces to be there and make the picture complete.

I have yet to find that missing peg, but as I searched through the dust bunnies under the sofa, the Holy Spirit reminded me that, in the midst of lost puzzles pieces, and AWOL people, and broken hearts, Colossians 1:17 tells is that, *"In HIM all things hold together."* And when life's more like a horror film than a Hallmark movie, He will hold onto me. And you. And He will hold us together. Amen

Day 2

You shall not worship them or serve them [idols]; for I, the Lord your God, am a jealous God, visiting the iniquity of the fathers on the children, on the third and the fourth generations of those who hate Me, but showing lovingkindness to thousands, to those who love Me and keep My commandments. Exodus 20:5-6

I don't have any parenting advice but I do have some encouragement to share from the one from whom every family in heaven and on earth derives its name. Just take a look at what our Heavenly Father promises to do for us in Exodus 20...

In verse 5 He warns His people not to worship or serve anyone or anything but Him. To say that the consequences of such sin are undesirable is a major understatement. Our disobedience predisposes subsequent generations to fall prey to the same thing. That's what is meant by, *"visiting the iniquity of the fathers on the children and on the third and fourth generation."* The verse does not mean that God punishes the children for the sins of the parents! The Hebrew word for "visiting" is "paqad" and it means, "to review, inspect, number, take a census." In other words, God's not going to zap your kids on account of your critical spirit, addictive behavior, immorality, selfish ambition, greed, or obsessive fears–but if you were to take a spiritual/emotional family history, those same sins would show up through the line, time after time. God is stating what will result, not what He causes.

Here's the good news in Exodus 20:6–*"but showing lovingkindness, to thousands, to those who love Me and keep My commandments."* The word for "showing" is "Asah." While verse 5's "visiting" is a passive observing, "asah" is active–it means to create, to construct, to labor, to accomplish. WOW! Do you see what God is saying? He will take our obedience and love, frail as they may be, and He will build into our posterity fortresses of grace and blessing and love and benevolence and favor and honor–His lovingkindness. It's too good to be true! Except that it is true. So very like Him. Above and beyond what we can ask or imagine. He will take my heart to serve Him and my obedience and then, He will build into my children and my grandchildren and my great grandchildren BLESSING. Favor that they did not earn. Just cuz I believe and obey...and cuz He's good and generous.

Every parent I know tries to do the best job possible. Every parent wants their child to be better off than they were. And they will do everything they know of to make that come true. Well, now you know how to be sure it happens- cooperate with God. Don't worry about what the parenting books tell you to do–just obey God, serve Him with your whole heart.... and it'll show up in your children.

Now, I know. You're thinking of some great parents whose kids messed up royally. Yeah, me too, as in all of us. We have the perfect Heavenly Father...and we still rebel. To be sure, all of us, including our children, have the freedom to choose our own way. Sometimes we all do. But here's what I have to say about that–first, the story isn't over yet. God's not done. And second, I trust His construction. If He says He is building blessing and grace and honor and favor into their lives because I believe and obey Him, then that's all I need. I plan to continue to do my part–to love and serve Him. And I'll trust Him to do His work.

Day 3

Do not neglect to do good and to share what you have, for such sacrifices are pleasing to God. Hebrews 13:15

Today's verse is short...but long on application. Pause before continuing to read and ask the Lord to personalize this for you.

Such a simple precept: doing good, sharing what we have. But sometimes we neglect it, don't we? The word for today is to consider what you have in terms of time, skills, material goods, and money. Just think about it for a moment. Take inventory, so to speak. Don't let yourself be deceived into thinking you don't have much–if you are reading this, then you obviously have enough time and skill and material goods to share. (You're welcome!) Maybe you have enough time to make a phone call of encouragement. Maybe you have enough skill to bake a cake or sew some window treatments or mow a lawn for someone. Maybe you have enough material goods that you can donate some furniture to a homeless shelter or some skills to a ministry or money to a mission trip.

Maybe you have enough of all three. Let's ask God what we can share? How? And with whom? Begin with surplus...then move to sacrifice. This pleases Him.

What is He speaking to your heart about right now?

I'll just say that I think I have enough surplus of material goods that it'll take a while to get to the "sacrifice" level. How about you?

Day 4

The eye is the lamp of the body. So, if your eye is healthy, your whole body will be full of light, but if your eye is bad, your whole body will be full of darkness. If then the light in you is darkness, how great is the darkness! Matthew 6:22-23

I wear contact lenses and whenever I get a new pair, I am once again reminded of what a difference clear vision makes. Being able to read without squinting. Seeing things at a distance without blur. Wow. I find myself functioning with more confidence and less self-consciousness. Walking and driving (especially at night) and just life in general becomes easier. I laughed out loud when my mind recalled the first time I got glasses. I was ten years old and apparently had not realized what I had been missing. As we drove home from that ophthalmologist's office in LaGrange, I provided a running commentary for my mom on all the sights. As in, the fact that trees have leaves...I was amazed then, and still am now, at the difference it makes when one can see clearly.

Our physical experiences often have spiritual parallels and this is certainly true for our ability to see. Just like my walking physically is affected by my inability to see clearly, so it is with my spiritual life. When my spiritual vision is clouded—by sin or a lack of truth—my "walk" is clumsy and faltering and ineffective. I am more conscious of myself, and less conscious of others. I don't have the proper view of my circumstances, of other people, or of myself.

New contact lenses give me great vision. Clearer. More light. But it's not without adjustment. My brain has to adjust to one lens that sees close up and one that sees far away. I'm working on it :)

In the same way, I'm asking God to give me healthy spiritual eyes. Eyes that see life from His perspective. Light to see His truth in the darkness. Clear vision that will help me walk with confidence and focus on others instead of myself. And it takes practice and work to get it right, but eventually, it becomes easier...second nature.

When my eyes are full of His light, I walk well. When they aren't, I stumble. And great is the fall. My prayer today—Lord, fill me with your light. Help me set my eyes on things above. Amen.

Read these other passages and write out the insight from the Lord today:

1. Luke 11:34-36

2. Matthew 6:24

3. Deuteronomy 15:9, and Proverbs 28:22

Day 5

But He said to me, "My grace is sufficient for you, for my power is made perfect in weakness." Therefore I will boast all the more gladly of my weaknesses, so that the power of Christ may rest upon me. 2 Corinthians 12:9

Sometimes God says "no." It is true that lots of times He says "yes," and sometimes what seems to be a "no" is really a "not now–just wait." But sometimes He says "no." And that's hard.

There are different ways to respond to His "no" -

• The refusal

• The tantrum

• The withdrawal

First, there's the refusal. When God doesn't give us what we ask for, we can refuse to acknowledge His answer and insist on getting our way. Sometimes He intervenes and saves us from our stubborn heart but many times He lets us go ahead and have our way. Then we find out we didn't really want what we thought we did. Things don't turn out so well.

Then there's the tantrum. We cry and pout and tell God that we can't believe He's treating us like this. We deserve so much better than what He's giving us. Often, we pile up evidence of our worthiness by noting all the things we've done for Him. We shake our puny fists in the face of His majestic throne and demand that He do better by us. The thought of it makes me shudder. It's a wonder He doesn't remove our existence with His breath.

And last is the withdrawal. This is not an angry response. It's more aloof. There's acceptance but it's more like resignation. Sort of...well, ok God, if this is what You're gonna do, OK. Then pulling away. No angry stomps. No clenched fists, but it leaves you with a heavy heart that can quickly harden if the burden isn't lifted.

How does God desire that I respond to His "no"? And how do I train my heart to do so? He wants me to trust Him. I do not believe that He expects me to clap and cheer when I don't receive the answer I have asked for. I believe He welcomes my honesty and that includes admitting when I am disappointed or hurt or sad. So when I am grieved over His answer, He wants me to pour my heart out to Him. He lets me sit in His lap and tell Him just how upset I am. I believe He would rather soothe my sobs than have me resist His embrace in stony silence because He cares for me. My feelings matter to Him. And the bad feelings need to be depleted before the right ones can fill me up.

Sometimes His reasons become apparent after I embrace His answer. But there are some reasons I've yet to be shown. So I must choose to wait...and trust. In the waiting, I will cling to what I do know. I know that He is always good, always loving, and always at work on my behalf. His Word tells me so. And His Word is more true than my circumstances. Acceptance because of trust is what He desires. Knowing His heart for me is how I get my heart to that place, and I can only do that because of His grace.

Living Letters

Day 1

Look after each other so that none of you fails to receive the grace of God. Watch out that no poisonous root of bitterness grows up to trouble you, corrupting many. Hebrews 12:15

At the end of our driveway grew some crepe myrtles. Beautiful bushes with deep pink blooms through the summer and brilliant color all fall. Gorgeous, really, but they grew too large for that spot and, well, it was time for a change. So we (I use the royal "we," it was totally my husband!) cut them down and dug up the roots. Then on to the new landscape plan. Except that those gorgeous crepe myrtles didn't want to leave us, and after we thought we had removed them, they grew back. We dug up some more and, just to be on the safe side, got a professional tree cutter to dig them out for good.

Or so we thought.

The following spring, those stubborn crepe myrtles reappeared. Ruining my planting plans at the end of the driveway. Not gorgeous. Tacky.

Try as we might, we couldn't seem to rid ourselves of those plants. They had obviously established for themselves a vast root system. We could chop off what we could see, and even dig out until we thought we had it all, but those persistent roots kept producing fruit. Fruit that we no longer wanted.

There is another obstinate root that all too often grows in the lives of God's people. It is willful and ornery, and unlike those crepe myrtles, these roots produce no beauty. Anywhere.

Bitterness.

Do you know anyone who's bitter? Have you ever felt those pangs yourself? Bitterness is fairly easy to detect–in someone else, at least! They carry an air of defensiveness and a desire to "tell their story" over and over, at least their side of it. They have a one-sided perspective, an attitude that seems to think they deserve better, and an unwillingness to let goodness inside that hard shell in spite of a desperate desire to embrace it.

We tend to keep our distance from bitter people, just like we would spit out banana peels or coffee grounds to rid ourselves of that taste. However, just like the initial taste of bitter chocolate or coffee, it can become not only tolerable but also eventually delicious after repeated exposure. So it is with bitterness that we allow to remain in our own lives. Keeping it close makes it livable...then comfortable...then preferable. But to those around us, that cloak of bitterness creates a hard shell of distrust and insensitivity to others, while being overly sensitive about our own feelings. It creates a tension in relationships and a spirit of ingratitude and rejection.

Truly, that poisonous root grows up and brings trouble to its host and to all those around.

Close out today by asking the Lord to reveal any root of bitterness in your life. Tomorrow we will begin to dig it out.

Day 2

Look after each other so that none of you fails to receive the grace of God. Watch out that no poisonous root of bitterness grows up to trouble you, corrupting many. Hebrews 12:15

The process of digging up those crepe myrtles was a lot of physical labor; digging up the bitterness in our hearts will likewise require some work. But it will be worth the effort! Go to His Word to find out...

This verse in Hebrews teaches that bitterness takes root because we fail to receive the grace of God. What does that mean? Grace is God's favor that He bestows on us, the power to desire and to obey His will. He makes it available to us if we humble ourselves before Him, because He gives a greater grace. Therefore it says in James 4:6, "*GOD IS OPPOSED TO THE PROUD, BUT GIVES GRACE TO THE HUMBLE.*"

Since this passage is written to God's people, it is not referring to the time He grants us grace at the moment of salvation. (Ephesians 2:8 says, "*For by grace you have been saved through faith. And this is not your own doing; it is the gift of God.*") The passage in Hebrews and the passage in James are a reminder that, just as it is His grace that saves us, so it is His grace that enables us to live a life that pleases Him. ("*And God is able to make all grace abound to you, so that having all sufficiency in all things at all times, you may abound in every good work.*" 2 Corinthians 9:8)

God presents us opportunities to need His grace for those good works, about a zillion times a day. Good works in the form of serving others without being appreciated...or even noticed. Good works in the form of being content with what we have...instead of comparing our lives to someone else's. Good works in the form of not returning evil for evil...and giving a blessing instead. Good works as in accepting personal responsibility for sin...instead of blaming your own failure on someone else's. And especially the good work of forgiving others the debt they owe you...just as God in Christ has forgiven you.

So, how do we fail to receive the grace of God for these good works?

See James 4:6 again, and I Peter 5:5.

Yep, you guessed it. Pride. The attitude that thinks we deserve better than what we got.

Pride is what blocks our reception of grace. Pride prevents our ability to receive what we need to live a life of joy and peace and freedom and obedience. Pride clings to a belief that we deserve better than we got. Instead of hope, though, it's more an attitude of entitlement. One that expects...or rather demands...that life produces better circumstances or gifts or people for us.

But pride never delivers what it demands.

Pride spawns instead...a root of bitterness.

Living Letters

Day 3

Look after each other so that none of you fails to receive the grace of God. Watch out that no poisonous root of bitterness grows up to trouble you, corrupting many. Hebrews 12:15

So, then, how do we get rid of this poisonous root?

We get rid of this poisonous root with basic steps. They sound simple, but I'll warn you, they are hard. Digging out those roots is hard work...and painful.

1. Accept personal responsibility for the roots: Quit the blame game. Humble yourself. No matter what happens to us, we are in charge of our response. Own it. Confess the sin to God...and anyone you've poisoned (even if they are the offender!).

2. Forgive anyone you perceive as an offender: This includes anyone who didn't measure up to your expectations. This doesn't mean you say, "it's ok, no big deal." Sometimes it's a mighty big deal indeed! Forgiveness does NOT mean to dismiss the offense. It means instead that you don't make the other person pay what they owe you. This is hard to do, and it takes a lot of work. Here's some stuff that helps:

   a. Ask God for help. Tell Him what the other person did and why it hurts. Then ask for His help in forgiving them.

   b. Pray for the other person (no, not, "God, get them and get them good!"). Pray for God's blessing in the life of your offender.

   c. "Invest" in them by showing them love. God will give you the ideas if you ask Him.

3. Trust God when He says He is at work on your behalf, bringing good to those who love and obey Him: See Him as the giver of good gifts. Instead of blaming Him–and others–for what you perceive as "shortfalls." And, ask Him if your expectations need adjustment...Open your eyes to the good gifts and thank Him. Then, thank Him even for the offenses. (I Thessalonians 5:8 - when it says *"everything,"* it means EVERY thing!) Know that His ways are above our ways. He is the ultimate alchemist...turning what others meant for evil, into our good.

Pulling out the root of bitterness is hard work, long hard work, sometimes. It's repeated efforts. But, just like those crepe myrtles needed to go before the plan of beauty I had in mind for my driveway could be developed, so it is with bitterness. Removal of bitterness makes room for beauty.

The very process of "bitterness removal" can accomplish what God had in mind in the first place...

Let us then with confidence draw near to the throne of grace, that we may receive mercy and find grace to help in time of need. Hebrews 4:16

Day 4

Therefore, do not throw away your confidence, which has a great reward. For you have need of endurance, so that when you have done the will of God, you may receive what was promised. Hebrews 10:35-36

We all want to be confident, don't we? We want that feeling of security, of certitude, of poise. You know what I mean, don't you? The way we carry ourselves when we know our outfit is hip and our new haircut is stylin'. That state of mind we are in when we know we're prepared for that presentation and we stand up tall and convey a sense of calmness to the crowd. That tenacity of spirit when we stand at the free throw line and the fate of the game is in our hands. (Wait, I have no idea what that feels like. I love basketball but I was so terrible at it that my position was tailback...as in "get your tail back on the bench"! I still love to watch it, though, and I imagine what the clutch players must feel like in these situations...)

Confidence. We want it. We are drawn to people with it. We need to know how to get it.

There is a pervading philosophy about confidence that sounds good but is really counterproductive. It's toxic, actually. It tells us that in order to have confidence, we have to get good enough not to fail. So we focus on getting good at something but all the while, we are afraid to fail. So afraid, in fact, that we spend more energy on insulating our environment against that possibility. You know what I mean—we tell kids that they are all winners, everybody gets a trophy, and they can be whatever they want. We try to create an attitude of success by avoiding failure. We don't dare fail or let our kids fail so we wind up just playing it safe and not trying to do anything hard. Just don't fail, we tell ourselves.

But that doesn't produce confidence, does it? It seems as though it would make us feel safe and secure but instead it makes us feel weak. Fearful. Insignificant.

Playing it safe is throwing away our confidence.

Is there any area of your life where you need more confidence? Are you willing to write it down, to admit it to God, to ask Him about it?

Tomorrow we will look at the last part of this passage and see what we need to do.

Living Letters

Day 5

Therefore, do not throw away your confidence, which has a great reward. For you have need of endurance, so that when you have done the will of God, you may receive what was promised. Hebrews 10:35-36

Let's begin today with prayer. (Actually, that's how we need to begin every day, isn't it?) I hope you wrote something down yesterday that you need to gain confidence in. I hope you're open to finding out what God wants you to do about it.

Do you know what it is?

Endurance. In order to gain confidence, we need endurance. Success is not a result of not failing; rather it is a by-product of failing and refusing to quit! Confidence comes when we have tried and failed and not given up, but kept on trying until we got it right.

Proverbs 24:16 say, *"For the righteous falls seven times and rises again, but the wicked stumble in times of calamity."*

How can the righteous man fall seven times? Because he kept getting back up! Then he finally got it right! The wicked falls down when things are difficult...and stays there.

That is where confidence is birthed–in the getting up, the enduring, and the struggle. Safety is not what produces success.

It is painful to fail, even more so to watch our children fail. But we must not fear the failure. That is the breeding ground for confidence. What we should fear is the insulation from failure.

I don't know where you are lacking confidence today. Maybe it's parenting (as in potty training, maybe?). Perhaps it's an area at your church where you would love to serve but you feel so unqualified, so you just stay where you are in the shadows. It might be in some other area where you have become so discouraged that you don't even have hope of change.

You need confidence.

And the way to get that is endurance.

Will you ask the Lord to help you persevere? One tiny step at a time, one tiny step UP at a time.

Remember my failure at basketball? Well, when that didn't work out too well, I redirected my efforts towards cheerleading. And I've continued that art to this day. Maybe not the cartwheels and pompoms but I still love standing on the sidelines, loudly encouraging my friends in the game. Don't be afraid to fail, my friend. God wants to develop confidence in you, Let Him help you endure.

You go, girl!

Day 1

I will instruct you and teach you in the way you should go; I will counsel you with my eye upon you. Psalm 32:8

I've always been told that I have my Daddy's eyes. Clear blue. Squinting nearly closed when I laugh. Piercing when I am focused. Revealing my heart...always.

My Daddy's physical eyes are closed now but as long as he lived, he was always looking out for me. "Be careful," he called, when I headed out to the store. "Do you need some help unloading?" upon my return. And, every day, several times a day, "Are all the babies OK?"

My father's eyes were protective, helpful, and compassionate.

My Father's eyes.

What does it mean that His eye is upon me?

I think first that it means He protects me. Just like my earthly Daddy is always interested in my protection. And like when I tell Chip to keep an eye out for his baby sister. I want him to take care of her, and make sure she's safe and secure, especially in unfamiliar surroundings.

Unlike earthly protection, though, my Heavenly Father is omnipotent and omniscient. He is capable beyond any earthly power and He knows my needs for security and defense far more than I know myself. He is my shield and protector and no one and no circumstance can touch me without the express consent of His sovereign loving eye. Ever.

My Father's eye upon me also means that He is there to help me. Yes, to instruct and to guide but also to help me go in the way I should. Help to do the right things. Help to carry the loads He assigns. Help to turn away from the ways I should NOT go. In the same way that my Daddy was continually looking for ways to help me...and yet with divine power, knowledge, love.

So we can confidently say, *"The Lord is my helper; I will not fear; what can man do to me?"* (Hebrews 13:6). Because He has His eye upon me, His omniscient, omnipotent, loving eye, I do not worry about my life. Not my people, nor my to do list, nor my needs. He is my helper.

2 Chronicles 16:9 puts it this way, *"For the eyes of the Lord run to and fro throughout the whole earth, to show Himself strong on behalf of those whose heart is perfect toward Him."*

He is always looking for ways to show Himself strong on my behalf! Unfathomable!

Let's end today by praising Him for having His eye upon us, protecting us, and helping us. Tomorrow we will look at how His eye is compassionate.

Living Letters

Day 2

I will instruct you and teach you in the way you should go; I will counsel you with my eye upon you. Psalm 32:8

Our Heavenly Father has His eye upon us, protecting us, helping us. Always. That is so encouraging, so reassuring! And yet there is more.

My favorite thoughts about what it means for my Father's eye to be upon me is the same favorite I had about my Daddy. Compassion. My Daddy...and my Heavenly Abba...care what happens to me. And the matters of my heart matter to them both.

Zechariah 2:8 puts it this way, *"For he who touches you touches the apple of his eye."*

The apple of His eye connotes tenderness, affection, and being cherished.

Now neither my earthly Father nor my heavenly one have favorites...but amazingly they are able to make each child feel as though they are. Cherished. Treasured. Held dear.

And, just like my reaction when something pokes the center of my own eye, if something...or someone...does me harm, my Father rapidly and powerfully responds to remove the offender, to soothe the hurt, and to prevent recurrence. I'm the apple of His eye.

One last thing...

In the context of this verse, I wonder if there is another layer of meaning. Something additional the psalmist wants to convey. He speaks of the Lord teaching us, instructing us, and guiding us in the way to go.

Maybe, just maybe, He is telling us that we will know what to do, where to go, how to be, by watching our Father's eyes. Just like a quarterback can telegraph a pass by looking at his intended receiver, maybe we can discern what God wants us to do by looking at what His eyes are focused on.

What situation needs our attention? What wrong needs to be made right? What person needs our concern?

Watch His eyes. Where is He focused...where is His gaze fixed...where is He directing you?

Then go towards what He has set them on.

Day 3

Make glad the soul of Your servant, For to You, O Lord, I lift up my soul. Psalm 86:4

I believe God made us to long for joy, to crave satisfaction and happiness.

The problem is not that we want to be happy–it's that we seek that happiness in the wrong places!

Yes, God wants us to be happy, but He wants us to know that only He can provide it.

What does it mean to *"lift up one's soul"*? It means to be dependent on, to look expectantly toward. It's so easy...so human, *"to "lift up our soul"* to all sorts of things. A spouse, a child, a friend, a job, our appearance (God help us!), recognition, approval of others, being needed/ appreciated by others, financial security, prestige, and we can even become dependent on being good to make us feel joy!

But we all know what happens. Those things we expect to bring us joy, to complete us, to appease the insatiable appetite for significance and value, well, they disappoint. Our mate seems disinterested and we panic. Our child's behavior falls short and our parenting comes into question. A friendship suffers a permanent fracture and the pain of rejection unravels us. Job loss. Being overlooked, undervalued, and unappreciated. Beauty and financial stability are so incredibly relative that as soon as either of those imposters appears to be stable, one glance in either direction catapults you into insecurity.

Ok, so how do we *"lift up our soul to the Lord"*? If we agree that He is the only reliable source to satisfy and bring joy, then what do we do, practically speaking, to lift our soul to Him?

1. Truth: First of all, I tell myself the truth. If I'm lacking in the gladness area, I admit it. Then I ask God to shine HIS truth into my heart. Have I been lifting up my soul to something else instead of Him? I run through the usual suspects of family, friendships, performance, need for acceptance, financial issues, etc. I know the truth that none of these can deliver what I need with any measure of sustainability but am I living in ignorance of that truth? Am I expecting more of these gifts than they are capable of providing?

2. Trust: After poking around a bit to find where I've lifted up my soul, I purpose to change direction and place my expectations in the only constant of the universe–God Himself. I speak His truth over and over to my needy heart, reminding myself that He alone is worthy of my trust, my dependence, and my expectations. I refresh my soul with the truth that He loves me, that He is always faithful, and always at work on my behalf in a thousand ways I cannot see. And that I will walk by faith and not by sight because His Word is true-er than my circumstances. Just like the psalmist expects–trusts–that God is the place to lift up one's soul because He is the one who can gladden it, so do I. I trust.

There is one more "T" to help us get to a happy heart. We will examine it tomorrow.

Living Letters

Day 4

Make glad the soul of Your servant, For to You, O Lord, I lift up my soul. Psalm 86:4

Yes, we long to be happy, to be glad.

And God wants us to have joy, satisfaction, and happiness. Why, then, are so many Christians unhappy?

Because we look for it in places that cannot provide it...we *"lift up our soul"* to the wrong things.

Yesterday we saw two things that help us lift up our soul to the only one who can make us glad, two steps to take towards happiness.

Today is #3.

3. Thankfulness: The third "T" is like the last leg on a stool–my quest for gladness won't stand up very well on just two legs. This last step puts the first two into action. It's the proof of the pudding, so to speak. I get the truth. I trust the truth of who God is. And then I thank Him, in totality. Thankfulness for the gifts He gives that I enjoy, as well as the ones I'd probably rather refuse...except that I trust Him. I trust that even the gifts I think I'd rather not have are still gifts from Him. And I trust Him that it's just their packaging that makes me think I should shun them. All the things that He allows into my life are for the purpose of His accomplishing His good, in me, for me, and through me. So I thank Him. For all the gifts. And as I begin to thank Him, as I lift up my soul in worship of Him, and as I acknowledge His worth, my eyes begin to open to more and more good things to praise Him for. So many blessings flood into my heart that He has given. Thankfulness has cleared my vision. My soul is lifted up to Him in expectation, and like a baby bird waiting for its mother to bring food, I am replenished. Because of gratitude. Thankfulness.

Today, list things that you can thank Him for. Good things that He has blessed you with. Write them here and praise Him aloud.

Day 5

Make glad the soul of Your servant, For to You, O Lord, I lift up my soul. Psalm 86:4

Being made glad is a result of where we lift up our soul. And learning to do that involves:

1. Truth

2. Trust

3. Thankfulness

Yesterday we focused on blessings He has graced our lives with. We praised Him for the good things and saw that there are many indeed!

But thankfulness for only the things we consider "good" is incomplete. He tells us to thank Him for all things (I Thessalonians 5:8).

That is hard and seems counterintuitive. But we lift up our soul in truth and in trust...so we will thank Him for the things we wish we could change, the things that seem to be the source of our pain, and the things that, if only could be removed, would make us glad.

What are those things in your life?

Thank Him today.

Day 1 - The Book of James

James, a bond-servant of God and of the Lord Jesus Christ, to the twelve tribes who are dispersed abroad, greetings. James 1:1

For the next several weeks, let's look at one of my most favorite books, the book of James.

James, the author of this book, is the (half) brother of Jesus. He didn't become a Christ-follower until later in his life, possibly after the resurrection of Jesus. But he went on to become the leader of the New Testament church, known for his prayer life. Can you imagine growing up with Jesus as your older brother? Talk about pressure of having a perfect older sib! James describes himself as a bond-servant. What is that? Does that conflict with Jesus saying, *"I no longer call you servants but rather friends"*? Of course scripture does not conflict with itself so we need to find out what a bond-servant is to understand why James uses that term. The Old Testament explains it to us in Exodus 21:1-6. The Law given to Moses established that slaves were to be set free after six years. If, however, after serving for six years, the slave freely decided that he would rather remain in the service of his master, then he would receive a piercing of his ear which distinguished him as being bonded to his master for life. Obviously, that would have to be a remarkable master to entice him to serve rather than to be free! In his epistle, James is making that claim. That serving Jesus is so far preferable to being without Him that he chooses to bond himself to his master for life. What a tribute to Christ and what a testimony to the world.

"To the twelve tribes" is a reference to the nation of Israel, and specifically to those who have been spiritually adopted into the family of Abraham. James's epistle is written to believers; it is not an appeal to the unconverted Jew.

"Who are dispersed abroad" is sometimes translated using the word *"scattered"* instead of *"dispersed."* When I think of the word *"scattered,"* it brings up images of the floor of my closet or the Legos in the playroom or some other disorder. *"Dispersed"* is a much better term! The Greek word is "diasporo" which means, "to sow as seed." It is an agricultural term that conveys the idea of deliberate placing a seed in a chosen place so as to produce optimal results. What a choice of words for God's people! At the time of James's writing, they were being persecuted for following Christ. Attempting to find safety, the believers often moved from one area to another. James is encouraging them that their locations are not by chance but rather intentional placement by God to further the progress of the Gospel, as well as to achieve His transformation of them into the likeness of Christ.

"Greetings" or the Greek word "chairo" is more than a simple salutation. It conveys a desire for blessing on the recipient and carries the meaning of joy...but not any ole joy. Rather a joy as a result of God's grace. What a great segue for the next section of the letter! Does my life testify to the world that my Master is so incredibly awesome that He is worth giving up my life for? Do I acknowledge that every single place He plants me–regardless of whether I would have chosen it myself–is a deliberate placement on His part? A place where He intends to grow me into His likeness and show the world the fruit of His labor? And, can I embrace the life-giving truth that real joy is a result NOT of my circumstances, my desires being met, or people behaving like I want them to...but rather, only because of His grace?

Day 2

Today, let's look at the verse again and see what's NOT there...

James, a bond-servant of God and of the Lord Jesus Christ, to the twelve tribes who are dispersed abroad, greetings. James 1:1

Most all Bible scholars agree that the author of this book is James, the half-brother of Jesus. He grew up with Jesus and yet wasn't convinced that He was the promised Messiah until after Christ had risen from the dead (John 7:5, 1 Corinthians 15:7). After his conversion, though, he became a wholehearted follower of the one he used to share an earthly home with. James went on to become the head of the church in Jerusalem and was the "go to guy" when early believers had questions, concerns, or disputes (Acts 15). Reliable historians refer to James as "Old Camel Knees" because he was so faithful in prayer that his knees developed callouses from kneeling so often and so long.

Yet, in the only epistle history records him to write, we don't see any mention of his kinship to THE MESSIAH or any attempt to leverage his position in the church.

No effort to boost his ego or establish his prestige among the readers.

No pursuit of earthly laudation or the praise of men.

No focus on his own accomplishments or burdens or interests.

In a word, what is absent from this verse, and indeed the entire letter, is due to the presence of...humility. What is it? What benefit does it bring? How do we get it if we want it?

First, what is it? It's the antithesis of pride. So a definition of pride is in order. Pride is not only self-aggrandizement but it's also equally the evil twin of self-deprecation. Pride, we must understand, is not only thinking too much of oneself, it's also thinking of oneself too much. That shows up in boasting of achievements as well as hosting a pity party. The key component is focus on self.

Humility, then, is a proper view of self. We see ourselves in desperate need of a Savior, unable to save oneself through anything we could possibly do or be, and a pathetic "zero" without Him. Simultaneously, humility enables us to see ourselves as precious, valuable, and significant to the Savior. So much so that He designed us to be in relationship with Him, He pursues us incessantly, and He transforms us to reflect His glory.

And humility sees others (and their needs, accomplishments, and burdens) as more important than our own. Humility doesn't get caught up in one's own highs or one's own lows but instead focuses on ministering to others. Humility is so focused on others that there is no room to think about impressing them with whom we know or what we've done.

What is the benefit of humility?

Tomorrow.

Living Letters

Day 3

James, a bond-servant of God and of the Lord Jesus Christ, to the twelve tribes who are dispersed abroad, greetings. James 1:1

What benefit does humility bring? James himself tells us in chapter 4, verse 6, *"But he gives more grace."* Therefore it says, *"God opposes the proud, but gives grace to the humble."* God's support, instead of His opposition, is the benefit of humility. It's God's support in the form of guidance when I don't know what to do, wisdom to solve problems, strength when I'm weary, His favor over the plans of my life, and His encouragement when I want to give up... instead of His insurmountable opposition.

Yes, the benefit of humility is more desired than anything else. Indeed, we want it. So, how do we get it? James tells us that, too just a few verses down. James 4:10 says, *"Humble yourselves in the presence of the Lord and He will exalt you."*

Humble yourself. Be aware of your need for His grace and your inability to help yourself. Acknowledge the propensity of self-focus and intention your gaze to Him instead. When we see Him for who He is, we can't help but see ourselves in proper perspective.

Instant humility.

And in walks grace.

And we are all in need of grace.

So are our relationships.

I can't think of a single relationship or a single situation that wouldn't be helped immensely by the presence of (and hurt perhaps irreparably by the lack of) humility.

The H factor.

James had it.

I want it, too.

Day 4

Count it all joy, my brothers, when you meet trials of various kinds, for you know that the testing of your faith produces steadfastness. And let steadfastness have its full effect, that you may be perfect and complete, lacking in nothing. If any of you lacks wisdom, let him ask God, who gives generously to all without reproach, and it will be given him. But let him ask in faith, with no doubting, for the one who doubts is like a wave of the sea that is driven and tossed by the wind. For that person must not suppose that he will receive anything from the Lord; he is a double-minded man, unstable in all his ways. James 1:2-8

It's no secret to any of us that this life is full of trials. Seems like we're either in one, coming out of one, or about to head into one. *"Of various kinds"*—all sorts of things that cause pain, angst, or grief. Trials. I don't like them and you probably don't either. I'd rather have comfort and ease and pleasure, thank you, just the same.

Interesting that James tells us that our perspective on these trials should instead be...JOY. Joy. Joy?

Really?

Why?

And, how?

First, the why. That's found in the second phrase, *"because the testing of our faith produces steadfastness and the full effect of steadfastness at work brings about a life lacking in nothing."* Lacking in nothing? WOW! Read that again—lacking in nothing. Sign me up!

Oh, wait. The path to that life is the road marked *"trials."*

And James says our countenance on that path should be *"joy."* The word *"chara"* literally means little lambs jumping and skipping without a care in the world.

Gulp, in the midst of trials. Trials bring suffering and pain and discomfort. But James says our attitude about them should be joy...because of what they can bring about in our lives.

We will look at "how" tomorrow.

Day 5

Count it all joy, my brothers, when you meet trials of various kinds, for you know that the testing of your faith produces steadfastness. And let steadfastness have its full effect, that you may be perfect and complete, lacking in nothing. If any of you lacks wisdom, let him ask God, who gives generously to all without reproach, and it will be given him. But let him ask in faith, with no doubting, for the one who doubts is like a wave of the sea that is driven and tossed by the wind. For that person must not suppose that he will receive anything from the Lord; he is a double-minded man, unstable in all his ways. James 1:2-8

How in the world can we have the perspective of joy towards our trials?

Well, James tells us to *"count it"*–another translation says, *"consider it."* There's the key. *"Consider."* Choose the thoughts. Think carefully about, especially in order to make a decision. Contemplate.

Deliberate with intentional thoughts.

Thoughts that require divine intervention because they are not our natural default. That's why James exhorts us to ask God for wisdom.

Wisdom that enables us to trust that whatever God has allowed into our lives is there so that He can prove our faith to be genuine, so that He can let steadfastness operate in us...and result in lives that lack nothing. Wisdom that clings to the character of God–always faithful, always loving, always good–and trusts that His purpose for us is good.

"Doubting" isn't emotional wavering. The Greek word used here is "judging...coming to a wrong conclusion about." James is encouraging us here to cling to the truth about God. In the midst of a trial, it's easy to instead believe that God's not always good. That He doesn't love us. That He should've done some things differently.

Wisdom–"Sophia"–is the ability to see life from God's perspective and to trust who He is... always good, always at work on our behalf, and always loving towards those who follow Him.

Trials. Testing. Like gold going through a fire to "proof" it. And once it comes out, it is more valuable than before.

That's the reason for our joy.

Genuine faith more precious than gold.

Day 1

Let the lowly brother boast in his exaltation, and the rich in his humiliation, because like a flower of the grass he will pass away. For the sun rises with its scorching heat and withers the grass; its flower falls, and its beauty perishes. So also will the rich man fade away in the midst of his pursuits. James 1:9-11

At first glance, it seems a bit odd that James inserts this comment about the rich man and the poor man right after he implores us to ask God for wisdom when we are handling trials. He's told us that our thoughts ("consider") towards trials are to be those of joy...because we can trust that God is doing a great work to develop endurance in us and that endurance will make us whole, lacking nothing. Indeed, that is reason for joy. Even in the midst of trials.

And we don't default to that position naturally—we need God's wisdom for that. We have to ask Him for that perspective, for that ability to see trials like He sees them, for the grace to trust His purpose.

But why then the comment extolling the poor man and pretty much feeling sorry for the rich man? And why in this context? Maybe lots of reasons but I think this is at least one of them...

Because when times are tough, our human tendency is to think that something we can see, like money, would ease the pain, solve the problem, or make the trial go away.

Think about it for a minute. Focus on a tough time you've had recently or are in right now.

Did it cross your mind that an additional influx of cash would make you feel better?

Chances are, somewhere in the midst of that problem, you at least entertained the thought that money might be a help.

But James turns that thought upside down to tell us that God's economy is different. Unlike Elizabeth Taylor who said, "Money is the best deodorant," God tells us that money is not able to make a bad situation into good. Instead, it has the potential to make it worse. If we don't have "enough" money to get us out of a tight spot, then we are more likely to realize the truth that our only hope is God. That's what James calls "*exaltation*"...a high position.

On the other hand, if we have "enough" money, James exhorts us to focus instead on the truth that in reality, we are spiritually impoverished, "*humiliation*" and in desperate need of a Savior.

Trials. They stink.

Maybe so. But we gotta be careful not to trust that money is gonna make 'em smell better.

It won't.

Only realizing our helplessness and clinging to God will help.

Day 2

Let no one say when he is tempted, "I am being tempted by God," for God cannot be tempted with evil, and he himself tempts no one. But each person is tempted when he is lured and enticed by his own desire. Then desire when it has conceived gives birth to sin, and sin when it is fully-grown brings forth death. Do not be deceived, my beloved brothers. In the midst of trials, there always comes a temptation. James 1:13-16

Already we examined God's purpose in trials: to proof our faith, and to make it more precious and valuable. Going through this process (if we cooperate with Him!) results in a life "*perfect and complete, lacking in nothing*" (James 1:4).

And that is what we long for–to lack nothing, to be whole, complete.

However, the enemy is opposed to God's purposes. When he sees a trial coming our way, rest assured that he has a counterplan for us.

That's where the temptation comes from.

So when we're considering trials a reason to find joy, knowing that God is at work in our lives, producing a precious faith, completing us and supplying all we need so that we lack for nothing, well, it's at that point that the enemy of our souls opens his arsenal of weapons.

He wants us to fail the test. He doesn't want us whole and complete and drawing near to our Father.

So he tries to get us to fall...

What does a fall look like?

We shall see tomorrow. For today, let's ponder the truth that the enemy's plan for our trials is directly opposed to God's.

Whose side are you gonna be on?

Day 3

Let no one say when he is tempted, "I am being tempted by God," for God cannot be tempted with evil, and he himself tempts no one. But each person is tempted when he is lured and enticed by his own desire. Then desire when it has conceived gives birth to sin, and sin when it is fully-grown brings forth death. Do not be deceived, my beloved brothers In the midst of trials, there always comes a temptation. James 1:13-16

So we know the enemy of our souls wants to see us fall. What does a fall look like?

It can look like any number of things. Depends on what appeals to the one in the trial.

It might be to get angry and declare, "it's not fair." If we don't process this appropriately, a full-fledged pity party can ensue and bitterness is likely to set in, along with resentment towards those around us, including God. "How could He do this to me?" Questions like that are understandable...but not helpful.

Or the enticement to follow a path of destructive behavior might be his choice of armament against us. Opportunities for wickedness and folly present themselves, usually disguised as much more benign than they really are.

Or the appeal might even be to abandon faith altogether. After all, what's it gotten you so far, the enemy whispers.

And if one takes the bait, if one fails and falls, then the normal tendency is to blame the one who is sovereign over all. Surely this failure is somehow His fault.

James stops us short in this line of thinking. No, he says. That is deceptive thinking. Don't be deceived, he warns.

Yes, the trial is from God. But the temptation is not; it's from our own inner desires. Our "lusts"– the desire to please ourselves–is present within us. And if we don't know/believe/act on the truth, we will believe that something other than God's plan will get us out of that trial, fill up the hole that's screaming to be filled up, or satisfy the longings of our soul. It is oh so very easy to be deceived into thinking that something...or someone...will slake our thirst, appease our appetite, mollify our yearning...and we bite the lure the enemy dangles in front of us. We bite. Sin.

But the decoy that entices us fails to deliver what seemed to be promised.

Instead, the process of death is set in motion. Maybe not instantly, but eventually it sets in. If we don't let go of the lure and run towards truth, death is inevitable in the form of the end of a dream or a relationship or even a life. It's death of trust and faith and blessing.

In a trial, God's purpose is to produce a faith more precious than gold. The enemy, however, is bent on destruction. Yours. And mine. We don't have to fall, though. Next time we'll look at how to beat him at his own game.

Day 4

Do not be deceived, my beloved brothers. Every good gift and every perfect gift is from above, coming down from the Father of lights with whom there is no variation or shadow due to change. Of his own will he brought us forth by the word of truth, that we should be a kind of first fruits of his creatures. James 1:16-18

The preceding verses in this chapter address the fact that the enemy of our souls presents temptations in the midst of our trials. He sends the temptation in an attempt to thwart God's purpose in the trial. God's purpose is to make us perfect...Satan's is to make us fall.

The root of most every temptation can be found in these verses, in the temptation to doubt the goodness of God.

And to be truthful, we are very easy to deceive!

When we are suffering in a trial, the enemy wants us to doubt God's goodness, His capability to help, His faithfulness, and to believe that something (or someone) else is the answer to the bleak feeling in our soul.

So James reminds us of the truth, the truth about God's character.

1. His goodness to us: He only gives good gifts. Sometimes we are confused by the package they come in, but we need to know that everything He gives us is good. And if there is a gift we are seeking but He is withholding, well, then, it isn't what it seems because no good thing does He withhold from those who walk uprightly (Psalm 84:11).

2. His power for us: When James describes God as the Father of Lights, it is helpful to know that not only does the word "lights" convey energy, warmth, and light, this word specifically means THE SOURCE of light. It describes one that is never kindled, never quenched, and that gives light. Surely this source is able to keep His promises to us!

3. His consistency with us: No variation or shifting shadow...no matter what our circumstances, God's Word is always true. He is not a respecter of persons and He never changes. He is always good. Always powerful. Always loving.

4. His love towards us: He chose us. Not because He had to but because He delighted to. Of His will, He chose us. He doesn't love us because He made us...He made us because He loves us.

During a trial, it's hard to hold onto the truth because we get distracted by our pain. And that makes it easy to fall for the temptation to doubt God's character.

Don't let that happen to you. Everything God does is good. He loves you. He is able to keep His promises. Always.

Day 5

Let's hit the pause button for a moment today and digest what we have covered so far in James.

Read James 1:1-18 again.

James, a bond-servant of God and of the Lord Jesus Christ, To the twelve tribes who are dispersed abroad: Greetings. Consider it all joy, my brethren, when you encounter various trials, knowing that the testing of your faith produces endurance. And let endurance have its perfect result, so that you may be perfect and complete, lacking in nothing. But if any of you lacks wisdom, let him ask of God, who gives to all generously and without reproach, and it will be given to him. But he must ask in faith without any doubting, for the one who doubts is like the surf of the sea, driven and tossed by the wind. For that man ought not to expect that he will receive anything from the Lord, being a double-minded man, unstable in all his ways. But the brother of humble circumstances is to glory in his high position; and the rich man is to glory in his humiliation, because like flowering grass he will pass away. For the sun rises with a scorching wind and withers the grass; and its flower falls off and the beauty of its appearance is destroyed; so too the rich man in the midst of his pursuits will fade away. Blessed is a man who perseveres under trial; for once he has been approved, he will receive the crown of life, which the Lord has promised to those who love Him. Let no one say when he is tempted, "I am being tempted by God"; for God cannot be tempted by evil, and He Himself does not tempt anyone. But each one is tempted when he is carried away and enticed by his own lust. Then when lust has conceived, it gives birth to sin; and when sin is accomplished, it brings forth death. Do not be deceived, my beloved brethren. Every good thing given and every perfect gift is from above, coming down from the Father of lights, with whom there is no variation or shifting shadow. In the exercise of His will He brought us forth by the word of truth, so that we would be a kind of first fruits among His creatures.

Make a list of at least five things you have learned these past two weeks from James.

    1.

    2.

    3.

    4.

    5.

Now write how you have applied them in your life.

Day 1

Know this, my beloved brothers: let every person be quick to hear, slow to speak, slow to anger; for the anger of man does not produce the righteousness of God. James 1:19-20

The context for this passage is the topic of trials. Pretty safe to say, then, that it applies to each of us every day. We're either in the midst of a trial, just coming out of a trial, or headed into one soon! So, it's pertinent.

What counsel does brother James have for us?

1. Be quick to hear: There's a difference between "listening" and "hearing." We can "listen" for the sound of the whistle but until it reaches our ears and conveys the message to our brains, we haven't "heard" it. The same is true for the sounds around us. James is telling us to "hear" what is said in such a way that we comprehend the message. Sound advice.

    Quick to hear whom?

    God, first of all. In the midst of life, He is speaking to us. In our pleasure, He whispers, "be grateful and know that all good gifts come from Me." In our concern, He urges us to trust Him. In our pain, as CS Lewis puts it, God "shouts in our pains: it is his megaphone to rouse a deaf world."

    We must be attentive to what He is saying. Quick to hear.

    Also, we must hear those around us. May we not presume we know what they are saying before we hear their words! Proverbs 18:13 declares if one gives an answer before he hears, it is his folly and shame.

    Many many times conflict could be avoided if we would be quick to hear what another is saying rather than assuming we know already.

2. Be slow to speak: The Greek word for "slow" here implies control. Not slow as in lackadaisical or negligent but rather managed, regulated, and disciplined. Wow. What a difference that kind of speech can make! Just think about what Proverbs 10:19 says, *"When words are many, transgression is not lacking, but whoever restrains his lips is prudent."*

James has one more admonition in this passage. We will look at it tomorrow.

Day 2

Know this, my beloved brothers: let every person be quick to hear, slow to speak, slow to anger; for the anger of man does not produce the righteousness of God. James 1:19-20

The counsel from James is clear. Direct. He says:

1. Be quick to hear.

2. Be slow to speak.

And then he says...

3. Be slow to anger.

Proverbs 16:32 tells us why it's profitable to be slow to anger:

Whoever is slow to anger is better than the mighty, and he who rules his spirit than he who takes a city.

This verse tells us that in self-control there is power, but what else do we need to know about anger?

Mainly, that anger is not a sin. It's an emotion. It's like an indicator light on the dashboard of my car–when it starts flashing, it's a sign to check under the hood.

It's the same with anger. When that emotion surfaces, we need to check our hearts and see what's going on in there.

Anger isn't the sin; it's the response of our souls when what we want to be is not achieved. Aristotle defined anger as "desire with grief." We want something (might be comfort or pleasure or significance). And something, or someone, blocks the reaching of that goal.

Result = anger.

No, anger isn't the sin...but what we do with it can be.

So James urges us to be slow in what makes us angry, and be controlled in how we handle it. When that light is flashing, check under the hood. What is at the root of this emotion? Is it a right desire? Or is it a selfish one? After that introspection, then we can ask God what we should do about it.

Oh, and then we should be quick to hear!

In the remaining verse, James reminds us that anger won't fix the problem we're trying to solve. Because underneath every desire, every longing, every wish is really a soul that needs the righteousness of God. And nothing else will satisfy.

Living Letters

Day 3

Therefore put away all filthiness and rampant wickedness and receive with meekness the implanted word, which is able to save your souls. But be doers of the word, and not hearers only, deceiving yourselves. James 1:21-22

We spend an awful lot of time trying to fix ourselves, and an awful lot of energy and money, too. And I don't mean physically (although that's true as well!) but I mean emotionally, relationally, and psychologically. Even though we are slow to admit it, I think deep down we know that much of what's wrong in our lives has to do with the fact that we are broken people. People that "need fixing."

Trouble is, we don't know how to do it.

I think this verse tells us.

When James uses the phrase "save your souls," I don't believe he is referring to the establishment of a relationship with Christ. Rather, I think he is explaining the "working out" of our salvation, the sanctification process whereby Christ-followers are transformed (slowly as it may be!) into the image of Christ.

It's about "fixing ourselves." Making whole and healthy the parts of us that are broken.

Our self-image. Our relationships. Our speech. Our attitudes. Our priorities. Our treatment of others. Our use of resources. Our own selves.

Here's what James says:

- Putting aside all filthiness and all that remains of wickedness: get rid of the wrong stuff. Take personal responsibility (as in, it's not your parents' fault or your mate's fault or your boss's fault or your circumstances' fault) and get rid of the things in your life that don't line up with holiness.

- In humility: have a correct assessment of yourself. Not only take personal responsibility but also see yourself in desperate need of God's grace. That becomes the point at which He showers His favor upon you, when you realize and acknowledge your need for it.

- Receive the Word implanted: the Word was implanted in you when you trusted Christ for salvation. Now you need to embrace it. "Receive" means to embrace and accept like an organ transplant. Let it become part of you. Meditate on the Word. Memorize it. And then...

- Mind it: prove yourselves doers of the Word and not merely hearers who delude themselves. As you study the Word and learn what God tells you to do, then, well, just do it. Nike time. Just do it.

Obey what He shows you. That's what transforms you, changes you, fixes you, and saves your soul. It's Nike time, y'all, just do it.

Day 4

Do you ever slap yourself on the forehead and say, "I knew better than that!"? I surely do! I cannot count the times that I hear a sermon or read a passage of scripture or just plain remember a truth and think, "I used to do that right but somewhere along the line, I've stopped." Or I find myself repeating the same commissions or omissions over and over again.

How does that happen to us?

Well, basically, we're human! And humans forget. Like James tells us, *"For if anyone is a hearer of the Word and not a doer, he is like a man who looks intently at his natural face in a mirror. For he looks at himself and goes away and at once forgets what he was like. But the one who looks into the perfect law, the law of liberty, and perseveres, being no hearer who forgets but a doer who acts, he will be blessed in his doing."* (James 1:23-25)

Just as I look in the mirror everyday to check my hair and makeup before I leave the house. More than once, if I have time! And then, based on what I see, I adjust. And tweak. And look again. Because I can't remember what I look like from one glance to the next!

It's the same with our spiritual life. God's Word is the mirror that we look into in order to know what we look like spiritually. And, based on what He shows us, we adjust and tweak and look again. And what helps us remember what we saw is to obey what He shows us to do. Being a doer, not just a hearer, or a looker!

I love what the word "intently" means in Greek, it means to stoop down and focus. Isn't that powerful? We don't need to merely read God's Word, we need to humble ourselves and examine how to apply what it means to live it out. It means being willing to let the word show us where we need to adjust, and then to obey it. That's what helps us remember.

This mirror of God's Word that we are to look into isn't just another law to follow, thankfully not. Rather it is the perfect law...the law of liberty.

What does that mean, a law...of liberty? Seems contradictory. Except that it's not.

The perfect law is the Gospel of Christ. He fulfilled every point of God's law, which we can't do, and, in so doing, He set us free from our inability to keep it. God counts His perfection as ours...and then He abides within those who believe in Him and transforms us into people who look like Him. Not immediately, to be sure. But, little by little as we obey Him, being an effectual doer and not just a hearer of His Word, we grow in our likeness to Him. Blessed in what we do.

Living Letters

Day 5

If anyone thinks he is religious and does not bridle his tongue but deceives his heart, this person's religion is worthless. Religion that is pure and undefiled before God, the Father, is this: to visit orphans and widows in their affliction, and to keep oneself unstained from the world.
James 1:26-27

First, let's check our context. In the preceding verses (21-25), James exhorts believers to obey God's Word, clinging to it, embracing it, and receiving it in the same way one would receive an organ transplant! (Although he didn't use that exact phrase...the idea is the same. Make His Word a part of your life by meditating on it, memorizing it, and most of all, minding it!) James warns us that it is highly possible to merely listen to God's Word and never get around to obeying it. That, he says, is worthless. That kind of faith will do nothing to change anyone, and will not transform anyone into the image of Christ Jesus.

However, faith that is characterized by obeying the truth of His Word translates into big results. Verse 25 says that one who is an *"effectual doer"* is *"blessed in what he does."* And verses 26 and 27 reveal to us some of the blessings that come: one who obeys God's Word is changed in the way she speaks, what she does, and what she loves.

1. The way she speaks: "bridle the tongue." She is able to direct the tongue in the way it should...and should not...go. Speaking words of comfort and encouragement and instruction that need to be spoken. And NOT speaking words of anger or bitterness or divisiveness. Controlling the tongue. The power of life and death are in it, so controlling it by giving life instead of death is a result of embracing God's Word.

2. What she does: caring for those that cannot repay you, those whom the world deems unvaluable, instead of serving/giving/doing in order to be appreciated or recognized or somehow rewarded. It is a trademark result of being transformed into the image of Christ.

3. What she loves: to *"keep oneself unstained by the world"* cannot happen if we love the world. If we place value on material things or the approval of men or having a position of power/influence, our life gets stained. The values of the heart show up in how we live, in our priorities, in our longings, and in our responses. Do we crave attention for our physical appearance? Then that stain shows up in excessive resources being spent to obtain beauty...as well as in fear of losing the same. Do we long for recognition in the eyes of others? Then we become stained by activities that deceive us to believe they offer that approval, things like debt to acquire "status symbols" or gossip to appear "in the know" or a frantic pace of life based on FOMO (Fear of Missing Out), and especially pride at having to always appear to be right.

Receiving the word implanted...changes the way we speak, what we do, and what we love. Amen.

James surely packs a lot of punch into just a few words, doesn't he?

Day 1

My brothers, show no partiality as you hold the faith in our Lord Jesus Christ, the Lord of glory. For if a man wearing a gold ring and fine clothing comes into your assembly, and a poor man in shabby clothing also comes in, and if you pay attention to the one who wears the fine clothing and say, "You sit here in a good place," while you say to the poor man, "You stand over there," or, "Sit down at my feet," have you not then made distinctions among yourselves and become judges with evil thoughts? Listen, my beloved brothers, has not God chosen those who are poor in the world to be rich in faith and heirs of the kingdom, which he has promised to those who love him? But you have dishonored the poor man. Are not the rich the ones who oppress you, and the ones who drag you into court? Are they not the ones who blaspheme the honorable name by which you were called? If you really fulfill the royal law according to the scripture, "You shall love your neighbor as yourself," you are doing well. But if you show partiality, you are committing sin and are convicted by the law as transgressors. For whoever keeps the whole law but fails in one point has become accountable for all of it. For he who said, "Do not commit adultery," also said, "Do not murder." If you do not commit adultery but do murder, you have become a transgressor of the law. So speak and so act as those who are to be judged under the law of liberty. For judgment is without mercy to one who has shown no mercy. Mercy triumphs over judgment. James 2:1-13

In this passage, James addresses a timeless issue of the human condition...an attitude of favoritism. As old as history itself, James faced the same matter that churches and you and I and everybody else have to guard against today. Favoring one group over another. Preferential treatment for the "such and such's" or "so and so's." James calls it judgment, and he warns us not to do it.

So let's unpack this passage...

First what we see is the predicament.

In verses 1-3, James explains the predicament as preferential treatment based on superficial values. Here, it's rich over poor but it could be lots of other things. Position. Skin color. Gender. Belief system. Anytime we base a person's value on something other than what God values, we find ourselves in this same predicament...an attitude of favoritism.

Let's close out today asking God to speak to our hearts and show us if we have this predicament in our own lives. Tomorrow we will see the next steps.

Day 2

My brothers, show no partiality as you hold the faith in our Lord Jesus Christ, the Lord of glory. For if a man wearing a gold ring and fine clothing comes into your assembly, and a poor man in shabby clothing also comes in, and if you pay attention to the one who wears the fine clothing and say, "You sit here in a good place," while you say to the poor man, "You stand over there," or, "Sit down at my feet," have you not then made distinctions among yourselves and become judges with evil thoughts? Listen, my beloved brothers, has not God chosen those who are poor in the world to be rich in faith and heirs of the kingdom, which he has promised to those who love him? But you have dishonored the poor man. Are not the rich the ones who oppress you, and the ones who drag you into court? Are they not the ones who blaspheme the honorable name by which you were called? If you really fulfill the royal law according to the scripture, "You shall love your neighbor as yourself," you are doing well. But if you show partiality, you are committing sin and are convicted by the law as transgressors. For whoever keeps the whole law but fails in one point has become accountable for all of it. For he who said, "Do not commit adultery," also said, "Do not murder." If you do not commit adultery but do murder, you have become a transgressor of the law. So speak and so act as those who are to be judged under the law of liberty. For judgment is without mercy to one who has shown no mercy. Mercy triumphs over judgment. James 2:1-13

Yesterday, we say the predicament of favoritism. Today, we see what is behind it...

In verses 4-7, James explains that the problem that causes this predicament is because our value system is different from God's. The Greek word for "judge" is "krino." It means to separate into categories, to make distinctions among, and to cause a division between the parts. It's like deciding what something is and slapping a label on it so as to know what to do with it then. Only the "something" is a "someone" and the "it" is a "who." And when we do it, it's because we have an agenda...James is a bit more harsh with his words, he says we have evil motives.

We are inclined to treat people in ways that we believe will benefit ourselves.

So we assess someone else's value, and then determine if their label could offer an advantage to our own position. If so, we are tempted to adjust our behavior in a way that leverages the other person's assets.

And James just shakes his head at us, warning us that we are deceived. He knows the principle from Proverbs 29:5 applies, "*A man who flatters his neighbor is spreading a net for his steps.*" By trying to gain favor from people we think can give us an advantage, we are actually setting a trap for ourselves.

The only one qualified to determine a person's value is God, the only righteous judge.

And the basis of His acceptance is...mercy.

Not some superficial issue like skin color or position or net worth. Mercy. Tomorrow we will see what to do about this problem that puts us in this predicament.

Day 3

My brothers, show no partiality as you hold the faith in our Lord Jesus Christ, the Lord of glory. For if a man wearing a gold ring and fine clothing comes into your assembly, and a poor man in shabby clothing also comes in, and if you pay attention to the one who wears the fine clothing and say, "You sit here in a good place," while you say to the poor man, "You stand over there," or, "Sit down at my feet," have you not then made distinctions among yourselves and become judges with evil thoughts? Listen, my beloved brothers, has not God chosen those who are poor in the world to be rich in faith and heirs of the kingdom, which he has promised to those who love him? But you have dishonored the poor man. Are not the rich the ones who oppress you, and the ones who drag you into court? Are they not the ones who blaspheme the honorable name by which you were called? If you really fulfill the royal law according to the scripture, "You shall love your neighbor as yourself," you are doing well. But if you show partiality, you are committing sin and are convicted by the law as transgressors. For whoever keeps the whole law but fails in one point has become accountable for all of it. For he who said, "Do not commit adultery," also said, "Do not murder." If you do not commit adultery but do murder, you have become a transgressor of the law. So speak and so act as those who are to be judged under the law of liberty. For judgment is without mercy to one who has shown no mercy. Mercy triumphs over judgment. James 2:1-13

So what's the prescription for the problem that causes this predicament of preferential treatment?

James writes out the divine remedy in verses 8-11: the royal law.

Loving one's neighbor as one's own self. Instead of favoritism, which is loving one's neighbor in order to help one's own self.

Failure to keep the royal law is a serious matter and James reminds us of that. In Matthew 22:34-40, Jesus explains that all of God's Holy Word can be boiled down to just a couple of principles:

But when the Pharisees heard that he had silenced the Sadducees, they gathered together. And one of them, a lawyer, asked him a question to test him. "Teacher, which is the great commandment in the Law?" And he said to him, "You shall love the Lord your God with all your heart and with all your soul and with all your mind. This is the great and first commandment. And a second is like it: You shall love your neighbor as yourself. On these two commandments depend all the law and the prophets.

Love God...and love others, as much as we love ourselves.

That's the prescription that will heal the problem. And that will get rid of the predicament.

One more thought. Depending on how well we live out the royal law, James has a prognosis for our lives in verses 12, 13. These are definitely worth repeating as we close out today, "So speak and so act as those who are to be judged under the law of liberty. For judgment is without mercy to one who has shown no mercy. Mercy triumphs over judgment."

Day 4

What good is it, my brothers, if someone says he has faith but does not have works? Can that faith save him? If a brother or sister is poorly clothed and lacking in daily food, and one of you says to them, "Go in peace, be warmed and filled," without giving them the things needed for the body, what good is that? So also faith by itself, if it does not have works, is dead. But someone will say, "You have faith and I have works." Show me your faith apart from your works, and I will show you my faith by my works. You believe that God is one; you do well. Even the demons believe—and shudder! Do you want to be shown, you foolish person, that faith apart from works is useless? Was not Abraham our father justified by works when he offered up his son Isaac on the altar? You see that faith was active along with his works, and faith was completed by his works; and the scripture was fulfilled that says, "Abraham believed God, and it was counted to him as righteousness"—and he was called a friend of God. You see that a person is justified by works and not by faith alone. And in the same way was not also Rahab the prostitute justified by works when she received the messengers and sent them out by another way? For as the body apart from the spirit is dead, so also faith apart from works is dead. James 2:14-26

Faith. Works. How do these two go together?

This passage can lead to some confusion so let's be clear right from the start...we cannot be made right with God by doing good works. Scripture is crystal clear on that truth (see Ephesians 2:8-10, Isaiah 64:6). So what is James telling us here?

Simple. Not that our works justify us before God, but rather that our works are the evidence that we have faith in God. Like the green leaves on a tree in the spring aren't what makes the plant alive but it is proof that it is indeed alive.

And "alive" faith produces works–results–that change life for not only those who possess it but also those connected to that possessor.

Results like Mercy Health Center, providing free healthcare to the poor in our area. Results like Kupendwa, saving lives of women and their babies in Uganda. Results like Sparrows Nest and Downtown Academy and Samaritans Purse...to name a few.

Results like an encouraging word for the dental office receptionist, like extending a helping hand to an acquaintance that needs a job, like fostering kids in crises, like paying a power bill for a single mom, or like restoring a fractured relationship.

If we have faith, it will show up in how we live. And God will be made visible to those around us.

That's faith that works.

Day 5

Not many of you should become teachers, my brothers, for you know that we who teach will be judged with greater strictness. For we all stumble in many ways. And if anyone does not stumble in what he says, he is a perfect man, able also to bridle his whole body. If we put bits into the mouths of horses so that they obey us, we guide their whole bodies as well. Look at the ships also: though they are so large and are driven by strong winds, they are guided by a very small rudder wherever the will of the pilot directs. So also the tongue is a small member, yet it boasts of great things. How great a forest is set ablaze by such a small fire! And the tongue is a fire, a world of unrighteousness. The tongue is set among our members, staining the whole body, setting on fire the entire course of life, and set on fire by hell. For every kind of beast and bird, of reptile and sea creature, can be tamed and has been tamed by mankind, but no human being can tame the tongue. It is a restless evil, full of deadly poison. With it we bless our Lord and Father, and with it we curse people who are made in the likeness of God. From the same mouth come blessing and cursing. My brothers, these things ought not to be so. Does a spring pour forth from the same opening both fresh and salt water? Can a fig tree, my brothers, bear olives, or a grapevine produce figs? Neither can a salt pond yield fresh water.
James 3:1-12

James's letter is characterized by his direct approach and these verses are not an exception in any way. He moves from proclaiming to us in chapter two (by the way, remember that when these letters were written to first century believers, they weren't sectioned off in chapter and verse—we've just done that to help us break it down into more manageable pieces) that the evidence of the veracity of our faith is seen in our lives in chapter three...that the work of faith will have results.

And the first result he points to has to do with what we say.

What a concept. There's an undeniable connection between our faith and our tongue.

Here is a brief sketch of what James says in verses 1-12...

He gives a precaution about using our tongue to teach (v. 1). I don't think James is against teaching, not at all. Rather, I think he is urging believers to not take the teaching of God's truth lightly. It can be a thrilling task to be one who teaches the Bible to others, and it can easily cause one to stumble into pride and self-righteousness and vulnerability. So James is warning us to be cautious. To be mindful that teaching is a serious responsibility and God will hold those who teach to a higher standard than non-teachers. Matthew 12:37 says, "By your words you shall be justified and by your words you shall be condemned." Before you teach it, be sure you live it." Be careful about wanting an audience. Don't be selfishly ambitious in wanting to teach. See Matthew 12:36 for motivation!

I will share the rest of the sketch over the next few days.

Day 1

Not many of you should become teachers, my brothers, for you know that we who teach will be judged with greater strictness. For we all stumble in many ways. And if anyone does not stumble in what he says, he is a perfect man, able also to bridle his whole body. If we put bits into the mouths of horses so that they obey us, we guide their whole bodies as well. Look at the ships also: though they are so large and are driven by strong winds, they are guided by a very small rudder wherever the will of the pilot directs. So also the tongue is a small member, yet it boasts of great things. How great a forest is set ablaze by such a small fire! And the tongue is a fire, a world of unrighteousness. The tongue is set among our members, staining the whole body, setting on fire the entire course of life, and set on fire by hell. For every kind of beast and bird, of reptile and sea creature, can be tamed and has been tamed by mankind, but no human being can tame the tongue. It is a restless evil, full of deadly poison. With it we bless our Lord and Father, and with it we curse people who are made in the likeness of God. From the same mouth come blessing and cursing. My brothers, these things ought not to be so. Does a spring pour forth from the same opening both fresh and salt water? Can a fig tree, my brothers, bear olives, or a grapevine produce figs? Neither can a salt pond yield fresh water.
James 3:1-12

Last lesson we saw the precaution to be careful about wanting to teach. Take it seriously because we will be judged by the impact of our words, especially in teaching.

Next, James says that...

The proof of our faith is in our tongue. Verse 2 is pretty straightforward; the condition of our tongue is evidence of the maturity of our faith. Our words are the manifestation of who we are and our words reveal our heart. Luke 6:45 says, *"Out of the abundance of the heart, the mouth speaks."* What fills our heart spills out our mouth.

We are tempted to think that someone else is responsible for what comes out of our mouth (as in "You made me so mad!") but James says otherwise. Our tongue gives evidence of the maturity of our faith. If yucky stuff comes out of our mouth, then it is an indication that there is yucky stuff in our heart.

Does that convict you as it does me?

Day 2

Not many of you should become teachers, my brothers, for you know that we who teach will be judged with greater strictness. For we all stumble in many ways. And if anyone does not stumble in what he says, he is a perfect man, able also to bridle his whole body. If we put bits into the mouths of horses so that they obey us, we guide their whole bodies as well. Look at the ships also: though they are so large and are driven by strong winds, they are guided by a very small rudder wherever the will of the pilot directs. So also the tongue is a small member, yet it boasts of great things. How great a forest is set ablaze by such a small fire! And the tongue is a fire, a world of unrighteousness. The tongue is set among our members, staining the whole body, setting on fire the entire course of life, and set on fire by hell. For every kind of beast and bird, of reptile and sea creature, can be tamed and has been tamed by mankind, but no human being can tame the tongue. It is a restless evil, full of deadly poison. With it we bless our Lord and Father, and with it we curse people who are made in the likeness of God. From the same mouth come blessing and cursing. My brothers, these things ought not to be so. Does a spring pour forth from the same opening both fresh and salt water? Can a fig tree, my brothers, bear olives, or a grapevine produce figs? Neither can a salt pond yield fresh water.
James 3:1-12

We've already seen: 1) a precaution about teaching, and 2) that the proof of our faith is in our tongue.

And now we see...

The power of the tongue to direct the course of life, ours and that of others (vs. 3,4) because WORDS, not TRUTH, can destroy a career, ruin a ministry, and end a friendship. WORDS are small things that affect in big ways, like a bridle for a horse and a rudder for a ship. Proverbs puts it this way, *"The power of life and death are in the tongue,"* (Proverbs 18:21). Power. Words have the incredible power to give life or to bring about death...he power to give life, energy, and motivation, or the death of hopes, dreams, and confidence. Words can literally set the course of lives and James urges us to be careful. We might consider a word "little" or meaningless but the picture James paints shows us that little things have big impact. A tiny rudder changes the direction that a huge ship sails. A "little" word can change the direction of a life. For good or bad.

We also see the potential for evil in the tongue (vs. 5-12). Notice there are only negative descriptions: fire, poison, unable to be tamed. It's as though James is doing all he can to paint a frightening picture. Like In driver's education when they show the film of the awful carnage of car wrecks to convey the realm of possibility when you get behind the wheel of a car. James is making sure we get the picture–like a fire can be intentionally or unintentionally set, so our tongue can cause serious damage. Whether we mean for it to or not, the effect is still a burning ruin. And in verse 6 we see that our words not only have the potential for evil to others but also in our own lives, *"set on fire the course of our life and is set on fire by hell."* Not only do we speak from the overflow of our hearts but our hearts also become like the words we speak. And James doesn't stop there. In verses 7-8, the lack of encouragement continues. Not only is the tongue full of deadly poison, it is *"restless,"* the original Greek word here means "liable to break out." What a description! Just when we think we've got it under control, the tongue "breaks out" and casualty results. Just like that film in driver's education was the last thing they showed in class. He leaves us with a feeling of desperation, so that perhaps we will acknowledge the potential for evil in our tongue and desperately desire the only one who can transform it. The one who can produce good fruit in us and the one who can make sweet water flow from our mouth.

Day 3

Who is wise and understanding among you? By his good conduct let him show his works in the meekness of wisdom. But if you have bitter jealousy and selfish ambition in your hearts, do not boast and be false to the truth. This is not the wisdom that comes down from above, but is earthly, unspiritual, demonic. For where jealousy and selfish ambition exist, there will be disorder and every vile practice. But the wisdom from above is first pure, then peaceable, gentle, open to reason, full of mercy and good fruits, impartial and sincere. And a harvest of righteousness is sown in peace by those who make peace. James 3:13-18

The preceding verses were all about the tongue, how it holds such potential for evil, is liable to just break out with poison, and the impact it has on the hearer AND the speaker. In the passage for today, James exhorts us to apply the truth he's just imparted.

The first verse, in essence, asks who is willing to now live with regard to this truth, this truth of managing the tongue, in light of its potential for evil. The "wise" here is a different word than what usually occurs in the original Greek text. The expected word for "wise" is "Sophia" but here, the word "Sophos" is used. It translates as "a watchman," one who watches and is thereby able to regulate his course. The word for "works" is understood as results. And "meekness" is not weakness, but rather it is power under control. Think in terms of a mighty stallion, bridled and controlled so that his strength is used advantageously, not destructively. So James is telling us here that our tongues need watching over. And if we do it right, the results will be good conduct and power used to give life instead of bringing death.

In the next verses (14-16), scripture reminds us about what governs our tongue...our hearts. And if the heart is wrong, don't arrogantly ignore the truth that our tongue will display what's inside. As we learned earlier, what fills our hearts will spill out of our mouths.

These verses are radical. They run so counter to what the world offers us, to the "wisdom" that isn't wise at all. The world advises us to maneuver ourselves up over others, tearing them down as necessary. And a heart focused on its own selfish agenda will inevitably be jealous of those that seem "ahead" in some way. This "wisdom" isn't wise at all. It's not only toxic it's actually demonic. And it won't give us what we're after, a life full of joy and peace and satisfaction. Instead, this kind of "wisdom" results in chaos and unrest and evil. In spite of what it seems to promise.

This passage closes with a litmus test for our decisions. If we wonder what to do, whether it's a ruptured relationship or tension at work or a career choice, we can evaluate it in terms of verses 17-18. A wise decision is one that first has a pure motive (not a selfish one!), a desire to reconcile and restore, is gentle as opposed to harsh or pushy, is reasonable (do we women sometimes expect more than is reasonable?), shows mercy in how it treats others (not how they deserve but how they need), and is just (impartial) and sincere...without hypocrisy.

And this wisdom is like a seed, a fruitful seed that grows and blooms into a whole harvest of righteousness by those willing to make peace with themselves and with others.

Day 4

We ended yesterday with this verse:

And the seed whose fruit is righteousness is sown in peace by those who make peace. James 3:18

Pretty clear. If we want righteousness in our lives, and in the lives of those around us, we must be peacemakers.

Sounds good! But what's a peacemaker?

The need for a peacemaker certainly implies that there is a lack of peace...in other words, a conflict of some degree. We might label it tension, frustration, annoyance, or even war. It's the opposite of mutual harmony, serenity, and freedom from angst or disturbance.

So a peacemaker is one who can act as the catalyst to bring peace to a situation and to relationships, one who brings reconciliation, restoration. And this seed of peacemaking results in the fruit of righteousness. To all involved.

How can we be peacemakers?

First, know that the absence of visible conflict does not necessarily equal peace because, instead of "making" peace, we can merely be "faking" peace. Sweeping issues under the rug, pretending that all is well, all the while being bruised and battered by the inevitable bumps that accumulate under the rug is peace-faking. It is an escape response to the need for peace, either by denial or by flight (running away from the conflict such as withdrawing from a relationship, quitting a job or church, or ending a relationship). Peace-faking is terribly unsuccessful because it results in no resolution of the problems. Although this response might bring some temporary relief from the angst and tension, it will eventually make the situation worse.

Peace-takers are the opposite end of the spectrum from peace-faking. This response might be disguised to look like an attempt at reconciliation but is actually an attack. Peace-takers are interested in getting their own way rather than in preserving a relationship. They use control (bullying, intimidation, verbal attacks) or manipulation (gossip, slander, pouting, withholding approval or affection) to overcome the "opponent" in a conflict. This always makes the situation worse.

But a peacemaker is one whose example is Christ, whose inspiration is grace, and whose goals are genuine harmony, understanding, and restoration. Tomorrow we will look at some things a peacemaker does. Today, ask the Holy Spirit to speak to you about where you are regarding peace...

Day 5

And the seed whose fruit is righteousness is sown in peace by those who make peace. James 3:18

What does a peacemaker do?

- Overlook an offense: Proverbs 19:11 says, "*A man's wisdom gives him patience; it is to his glory to overlook an offense.*" Notice the verse doesn't say, "to pretend it didn't happen." To overlook it means to look past it, to see the bigger picture. To value the relationship so much (and to want to imitate Christ so much!) that we absorb the cost of the offense. Forgive. Move past it. Don't let it fester and develop into bitterness and pent-up anger. Overlook an offense. Much peace could be achieved if we would just be willing to overlook offenses.

- Seek reconciliation: Matthew 5:23-24 exhorts us, "*If your brother has something against you...go and be reconciled.*" If we have been the offender, this certainly applies. But we also need to consider it when we think we are in the right, but perceive our brother thinks otherwise. Tall orders, to be sure. This requires divine humility, the removal of the log in our eye so that we can see how our brother might be viewing things (Matthew 7:5). Again, valuing the relationship above our "personal rights." Just like Jesus, who, "*though he was in the form of God, did not count equality with God a thing to be grasped, but emptied himself, by taking the form of a servant, being born in the likeness of men. And being found in human form, he humbled himself by becoming obedient to the point of death, even death on a cross.*" (Philippians 2:6-8)

- Pursue restoration: Often, we are interested in resolving a conflict for selfish reasons. We want to enjoy the peace instead of endure the tension. But a peacemaker is focused on the restoration of the other person, even at personal cost. With Matthew 7:5 in mind (and applied!), a peacemaker pursues the good of the offender, "*Brothers, if someone is caught in a sin, you who are spiritual should restore him gently.*" (Galatians 6:1) Restoration. Not for the sake of pointing out how somehow has wronged us but rather with the goal of restoring their fellowship with the Father.

Peacemaking. It's costly. It requires humility and sacrifice and maturity...it's like Jesus. It bears a harvest of righteousness in our lives and in the lives of others.

Blessed are the peacemakers, for they will be called children of God. Matthew 5:9

Day 1

What causes quarrels and what causes fights among you? Is it not this, that your passions are at war within you? You desire and do not have, so you murder. You covet and cannot obtain, so you fight and quarrel. You do not have, because you do not ask. You ask and do not receive, because you ask wrongly, to spend it on your passions. You adulterous people! Do you not know that friendship with the world is enmity with God? Therefore whoever wishes to be a friend of the world makes himself an enemy of God. Or do you suppose it is to no purpose that the scripture says, "He yearns jealously over the spirit that he has made to dwell in us"? But he gives more grace. Therefore it says, "God opposes the proud, but gives grace to the humble." Submit yourselves therefore to God. Resist the devil, and he will flee from you. Draw near to God, and he will draw near to you. Cleanse your hands, you sinners, and purify your hearts, you double-minded. Be wretched and mourn and weep. Let your laughter be turned to mourning and your joy to gloom. Humble yourselves before the Lord, and he will exalt you.
James 4:1-10

The fights among us...are due to the battles within us...and the conflict on the outside...is because of the war on the inside.

What does this mean and how can it make a difference in our relationships?

In verses 1 and 2, we find the reason for the conflicts in our relationships. This translation uses the word "*passions*" but others use the word "pleasures" or "desires." What they all point to is that we experience conflict because, simply put, there is something we want and if we perceive someone is blocking the fulfillment of that desire, we fight to get it.

These passions, pleasures, or desires are not necessarily for bad things! We might long for a well-behaved child, or a loving husband, or a good night's sleep. And if those desires (which we all too often label as "needs") are unmet, then we fight, quarrel, or get angry (which, by the way, Jesus explains in Matthew leads to murder). Underneath our desires are foundational longings for security, acceptance, significance, and love. What we might label as "wanting to be pretty" could actually be a deep God-given need for acceptance and esteem. And it probably is.

It's not wrong to want to look pretty (or to be treated respectfully or to be appreciated or to feel safe), but when we assume we can find a consistent source of attainment apart from Christ, well, that's when we run into trouble. No other person can meet those needs deeply enough to satisfy us fully.

No matter how much we might fight to get them to, God stands ready and overwhelmingly able to meet our deepest needs.

We will unpack this more next time.

Day 2

What causes quarrels and what causes fights among you? Is it not this, that your passions are at war within you? You desire and do not have, so you murder. You covet and cannot obtain, so you fight and quarrel. You do not have, because you do not ask. You ask and do not receive, because you ask wrongly, to spend it on your passions. You adulterous people! Do you not know that friendship with the world is enmity with God? Therefore whoever wishes to be a friend of the world makes himself an enemy of God. Or do you suppose it is to no purpose that the scripture says, "He yearns jealously over the spirit that he has made to dwell in us"? But he gives more grace. Therefore it says, "God opposes the proud, but gives grace to the humble." Submit yourselves therefore to God. Resist the devil, and he will flee from you. Draw near to God, and he will draw near to you. Cleanse your hands, you sinners, and purify your hearts, you double-minded. Be wretched and mourn and weep. Let your laughter be turned to mourning and your joy to gloom. Humble yourselves before the Lord, and he will exalt you.
James 4:1-10

So we saw last time that the fusses and fights in our lives are because we don't get what we long for. We try to get our desires met from sources that are not able to do so–in spite of our best efforts to extract it from them!

Only our Heavenly Father can meet the desires of our heart and He longs to do so.

So why are we in conflict? We are in conflict because we either fail to ask Him or we ask for the wrong thing.

Now, granted, often He manifests Himself through the kindnesses of others. But we gotta realize that other people are just the delivery boy. God Himself is the source for what we need, and in verses 3-5, we see that He makes that very point by allowing us to experience conflict.

When we think someone or something other than God can fill our need for security, significance, or acceptance, in essence, we are seeking to worship it. And God loves us too much to allow that! He doesn't need to be "made Lord"–He IS LORD! And all those lesser things that try to set themselves up on the throne of our heart are waging a useless war. HE IS LORD. He will let the battle rage but He will not step down from His throne.

In the next few verses of this passage He explains how to resolve the conflict and how to find genuine fulfillment of those longings deep within. We will look at that tomorrow. For today, ask Him to reveal the unmet desires that are at the root of conflicts in your life.

Day 3

What causes quarrels and what causes fights among you? Is it not this, that your passions are at war within you? You desire and do not have, so you murder. You covet and cannot obtain, so you fight and quarrel. You do not have, because you do not ask. You ask and do not receive, because you ask wrongly, to spend it on your passions. You adulterous people! Do you not know that friendship with the world is enmity with God? Therefore whoever wishes to be a friend of the world makes himself an enemy of God. Or do you suppose it is to no purpose that the scripture says, "He yearns jealously over the spirit that he has made to dwell in us"? But he gives more grace. Therefore it says, "God opposes the proud, but gives grace to the humble." Submit yourselves therefore to God. Resist the devil, and he will flee from you. Draw near to God, and he will draw near to you. Cleanse your hands, you sinners, and purify your hearts, you double-minded. Be wretched and mourn and weep. Let your laughter be turned to mourning and your joy to gloom. Humble yourselves before the Lord, and he will exalt you.
James 4:1-10

When you are quarreling with someone, stop for a moment and ask the Lord what is the root of this fight? What is the desire you are trying to get met through the wrong source?

Then seek to resolve it as James instructs in verses 6-10.

Verses 6 -10 tell us to *"realize who He is... And who we are not."*

Humble yourself before God by submitting to His ways, which includes humbling yourself before others and confessing your sin. When we humble ourselves, He floods our hearts with grace and with the desire and the power to obey Him.

This grace is what we need to trust His goodness, to submit to His authority, and to withstand the one who tempts us to believe that anything else but Christ can satisfy. This grace is what we need to draw near to Him in worship, where we will see who He is, and who we are not. This grace shows us our sin and breaks our hearts over our unholiness, and empowers us to be made pure, to be cleansed.

This grace is only found in the presence of the Lord. It thwarts the power of the enemy and makes him flee. This is where our deepest needs are met...where our souls are exalted, in the presence of the Lord.

And the conflict will cease, within...and without.

Day 4

Brothers and sisters, do not slander one another. Anyone who speaks against a brother or sister or judges them speaks against the law and judges it. When you judge the law, you are not keeping it, but sitting in judgment on it. There is only one Lawgiver and Judge, the one who is able to save and destroy. But you—who are you to judge your neighbor? Now listen, you who say, "Today or tomorrow we will go to this or that city, spend a year there, carry on business and make money." Why, you do not even know what will happen tomorrow. What is your life? You are a mist that appears for a little while and then vanishes. Instead, you ought to say, "If it is the Lord's will, we will live and do this or that." As it is, you boast in your arrogant schemes. All such boasting is evil. If anyone, then, knows the good they ought to do and doesn't do it, it is sin for them. James 4:11-17

We need to remember that this book was written as a letter, so it flowed from one subject into another. This passage followed verse 10, which exhorts believers to humble themselves. Then the next thoughts from brother James are demonstrating the behavior we exhibit when we DO NOT humble ourselves...

The lack of humility, that would be, duh, PRIDE, shows itself in these three areas:

- Critical of people: (versus 11-12) When we don't embrace our place in relation to God's rightful place, we tend to put ourselves on the bench as judge. We evaluate people's actions, ascribe motives to them, decide the appropriate punishment, and then, often we execute it ourselves. Like a bailiff that usurps the role of the jury, the judge, and the jailer, all in one. As though we don't trust THE lawgiver, THE judge, to address the problems in someone else's life, we assume responsibility of doing so. Not that it's wrong to call sin "sin"–not at all. The problem comes when we assume the role of determining motive and punishment. That's pride.

Two more exhibitions of pride tomorrow...

Day 5

Brothers and sisters, do not slander one another. Anyone who speaks against a brother or sister or judges them speaks against the law and judges it. When you judge the law, you are not keeping it, but sitting in judgment on it. There is only one Lawgiver and Judge, the one who is able to save and destroy. But you—who are you to judge your neighbor? Now listen, you who say, "Today or tomorrow we will go to this or that city, spend a year there, carry on business and make money." Why, you do not even know what will happen tomorrow. What is your life? You are a mist that appears for a little while and then vanishes. Instead, you ought to say, "If it is the Lord's will, we will live and do this or that." As it is, you boast in your arrogant schemes. All such boasting is evil. If anyone, then, knows the good they ought to do and doesn't do it, it is sin for them. James 4:11-17

When our lives are not characterized by humility, we will see it evidenced by:

- Criticism of people

- Arrogance in plans: (verses 13-16) Now I'm a planner. I like to know my schedule and make plans accordingly. I don't like to rush at the last minute to do things that could've been taken care of in advance. Is this passage condemning such contemplations? No. Plenty of other verses commend and exhort planning. Proverbs 6:6-8 and Proverbs 10:5 to name a few. Rather, it's calling us to examine not only the making of our plans but especially the "why." Notice the motive in verse 13, *"to make money."* Other translations say, *"to make a profit."* The lack of humility is demonstrated when our goal is to advance our own agenda rather than submitting to God's plans for our time.

- Setting of priorities: (verses 17) When my life is characterized by pride (self-focus) instead of humility (God-centered), I am prone to ignore the promptings or conviction of the Holy Spirit. And then I don't do what I know to be right and/or I do what I know to be wrong. That is sin, of omission or commission. It's sin. And it's rooted in pride.

SO, how can we walk in humility instead of pride? If these verses reveal pride in us regarding our attitude towards people, our pursuit of personal agenda, our insistence on our own way–what can we do instead?

Go back to verse 10. Get in the presence of the Lord. Soak up who HE is and inevitably we see who we are NOT. Confess the sin His Spirit reveals. Ask for His transforming power. And ask Him to point out every manifestation of pride every time it occurs. Then repent. Change directions. Give grace to people instead of condemnation. Ask the Lord for His directions instead of your own. Respond in obedience to what He shows you is right.

Day 1

Come now, you rich, weep and howl for the miseries that are coming upon you. Your riches have rotted and your garments are moth-eaten. Your gold and silver have corroded, and their corrosion will be evidence against you and will eat your flesh like fire. You have laid up treasure in the last days. Behold, the wages of the laborers who mowed your fields, which you kept back by fraud, are crying out against you, and the cries of the harvesters have reached the ears of the Lord of hosts. You have lived on the earth in luxury and in self-indulgence. You have fattened your hearts in a day of slaughter. You have condemned and murdered the righteous person. He does not resist you. James 5:1-6

Without equivocation, James proclaims that judgment will be severe to those who misuse the wealth God has entrusted to them. What a departure from the worldview that what we have, believing that we deserve it and therefore we deserve to employ it to please ourselves.

James says NO.

He issues strong caution against:

- Placing trust in material wealth: No matter how secure that gold and silver and luxurious trapping seems, it cannot sustain your trust. It will fail you. You can't buy enough security or save enough security or display enough security to protect you because, ultimately, God controls it all. He's just entrusting it all around to see how it's handled. And however you handle whatever He allots you will be the evidence of your relationship to Him on the Day of Judgment. The consequences of trusting in wealth will be devastating. Horrific. Damning, and unavoidable at that point. The time to choose where to place trust is now. He alone can save.

- Mistreating people for the sake of your gain: This passage takes a severe view of oppression. As well it should! In James's time, many Christians relied solely on their wages as day laborers. (The same situation is also true in many places today.) They were so poor that their survival depended on this daily pay. Were it withheld from them, either from fraud or lack of opportunity, their very existence was threatened. James proclaims that God hears the cries of those oppressed and He will avenge them.

- Excess/personal indulgence: Here, James lashes out in righteous indignation at the excessive lifestyles of the rich. He points out the personal accountability of one living luxuriously while one nearby dies from lack.

The warning of these verses is abundantly clear. Judgment will come based on our use of the resources God has entrusted. He will not overlook greed and injustice and oppression. He will avenge the poor and weak and needy.

Day 2

Come now, you rich, weep and howl for the miseries that are coming upon you. Your riches have rotted and your garments are moth-eaten. Your gold and silver have corroded, and their corrosion will be evidence against you and will eat your flesh like fire. You have laid up treasure in the last days. Behold, the wages of the laborers who mowed your fields, which you kept back by fraud, are crying out against you, and the cries of the harvesters have reached the ears of the Lord of hosts. You have lived on the earth in luxury and in self-indulgence. You have fattened your hearts in a day of slaughter. You have condemned and murdered the righteous person. He does not resist you. James 5:1-6

We're in the home stretch of our trek through James, into the last chapter. I hope you've fallen in love with this letter as I have. More importantly, I hope it's taken up residence in your heart and that you've embraced its truth.

Let's take a deeper look at the passage from yesterday. Although its warning is clear (God will judge us based on how we use the resources He has entrusted to us), what might not be so clear is how the message applies to us. I mean, after all, we're not oppressing the poor or hoarding our riches or living excessively. Gracious me, we're not even rich!

Or are we...I checked numerous sources (Compassion International, UNICEF, WHO, Childinfo. org, Global Issues) just to be sure I wasn't misrepresenting or slanting the data. Here's the conservative numbers of who's rich and who's not:

Including food and shelter:

- 20% of the world's population live at or below $1.25 a day

- 50% of the world's population live at or below $2.50 a day

- 80% of the world's population live at or below $10.00 a day

I think it's safe to say my pets live better than over half the world's people. I think it's also safe to say I am rich. How about you?

And that God has entrusted these riches to me NOT so that:

- I can feel secure by hoarding.

- I can miss opportunities to pay people and help them.

- I can enjoy excess.

Instead, I can use my wealth to store up the TRUE riches in heaven, where I can enjoy them forever.

Do not lay up for yourselves treasures on earth, where moth and rust destroy and where thieves break in and steal, but lay up for yourselves treasures in heaven, where neither moth nor rust destroys and where thieves do not break in and steal. For where your treasure is, there your heart will be also. Matthew 6:19-21

Living Letters

Day 3

Be patient, therefore, brothers, until the coming of the Lord. See how the farmer waits for the precious fruit of the earth, being patient about it, until it receives the early and the late rains. You also, be patient. Establish your hearts, for the coming of the Lord is at hand. Do not grumble against one another, brothers, so that you may not be judged; behold, the Judge is standing at the door. As an example of suffering and patience, brothers, take the prophets who spoke in the name of the Lord. Behold, we consider those blessed who remained steadfast. You have heard of the steadfastness of Job, and you have seen the purpose of the Lord, how the Lord is compassionate and merciful. But above all, my brothers, do not swear, either by heaven or by earth or by any other oath, but let your "yes" be yes and your "no" be no, so that you may not fall under condemnation. James 5:7-12

These verses follow the admonition to the rich who are misusing their wealth and oppressing the poor. James is addressing the persecuted and distressed...the context is suffering.

Perhaps you and I are not being exploited and oppressed as many were that read this original letter and as many are persecuted for their faith even today. We might even feel uncomfortable putting ourselves in the same ballpark as those heroes. But all who are committed to the cause of Christ have experienced suffering to at least some degree. (This, by the way, is a litmus test of righteousness. If nothing in our lives causes enough of a stir to provoke at least some suffering, then we have reason to examine ourselves to see if truly we are in the faith.)

Suffering is not something we are eager for. In fact, we naturally want to alleviate it as soon as possible! It's not "popular" theology to teach that suffering is part of God's plan for His children. Not popular, but it's true. As we dig into the depths of the New Testament, we see that The Great Commission (Matthew 28:16-20) will not be completed without suffering, the suffering of those walking in obedience. For those times we find ourselves afflicted because our light is shining in someone's darkness, James has words of encouragement. Here's what he says:

- Be assured: God will avenge any wrong done to us. *"The coming of the Lord is at hand"* and when He comes, Revelation 22:12 comforts us that Jesus says, *"Behold, I am coming soon, bringing my recompense with me, to repay each one for what he has done."*

Because we know God is our avenger, we can accept what James exhorts us to do.

Let's leave it there for today.

Day 4

Be patient, therefore, brothers, until the coming of the Lord. See how the farmer waits for the precious fruit of the earth, being patient about it, until it receives the early and the late rains. You also, be patient. Establish your hearts, for the coming of the Lord is at hand. Do not grumble against one another, brothers, so that you may not be judged; behold, the Judge is standing at the door. As an example of suffering and patience, brothers, take the prophets who spoke in the name of the Lord. Behold, we consider those blessed who remained steadfast. You have heard of the steadfastness of Job, and you have seen the purpose of the Lord, how the Lord is compassionate and merciful. But above all, my brothers, do not swear, either by heaven or by earth or by any other oath, but let your "yes" be yes and your "no" be no, so that you may not fall under condemnation. James 5:7-12

How to handle suffering:

- Be assured: that God will repay right and wrong. Therefore…

- Be patient: The Greek word that James penned was not "regular old patience" like I strive to be when I am kept waiting longer than I like. This is a stronger word with a much different application. The word that we translate as "patient" here is "makrothumeo" which might better be rendered as "longsuffering." It means to bear up well under suffering, especially exercising kind patience and understanding towards people…even those causing the suffering.

As though he knew we might have hard time grasping this concept, James provides three examples of longsuffering to help us understand:

1. Farmers: When you have to rely on God's grace and provision to see your crop grow, you realize that you cannot control the elements you need in order to reach your goal. Patience and faith in waiting on the Lord to provide.

2. Prophets: Regardless of the consequences, these men of old spoke and lived God's truth. At great personal cost, they kept the faith. They ran the race. They finished the course.

3. Job: In the face of intense heartbreak and pain, he refused to cease from worshipping God. He served God for who He Is rather than what he could get from Him.

In order to be patient in the midst of oppression, to indeed suffer well, something is needful…

We will see tomorrow.

Living Letters

Day 5

Be patient, therefore, brothers, until the coming of the Lord. See how the farmer waits for the precious fruit of the earth, being patient about it, until it receives the early and the late rains. You also, be patient. Establish your hearts, for the coming of the Lord is at hand. Do not grumble against one another, brothers, so that you may not be judged; behold, the Judge is standing at the door. As an example of suffering and patience, brothers, take the prophets who spoke in the name of the Lord. Behold, we consider those blessed who remained steadfast. You have heard of the steadfastness of Job, and you have seen the purpose of the Lord, how the Lord is compassionate and merciful. But above all, my brothers, do not swear, either by heaven or by earth or by any other oath, but let your "yes" be yes and your "no" be no, so that you may not fall under condemnation. James 5:7-12

To victoriously handle suffering, we must:

1. Be assured: that God will repay right and wrong

2. Be patient: on His timing

And...

3. Be strengthened: James says we are to establish our hearts. The idea here is to set our hearts on Christ. "Establish" means our hearts, our minds, and our actions are firmly fixed on following Him.

4. Refuse to complain: What practical counsel Surely in the midst of suffering, we are tempted to complain! This would even be understandable, wouldn't it? Yet James says no. Don't grumble about what we are called to endure. Instead, Acts 5:41 provides the example we are to follow, *"Then they left the presence of the council, rejoicing that they were counted worthy to suffer dishonor for the name."*

5. Maintain a life of integrity: More practical counsel. When James says that our yes is to be yes and our no is to be no, he does so because, *"For out of the abundance of the heart the mouth speaks."* (Matthew 12:34) We are to live a life of such integrity that our words contain no deceit, no duplicity, and need no "propping up" by oaths, but are true enough to stand on their own merit.

May our prayer be that we will indeed be counted worthy to suffer for the name of Christ and when we do, may we remember James. And Peter:

And keep a good conscience so that in the thing in which you are slandered, those who revile your good behavior in Christ will be put to shame. For it is better, if God should will it so, that you suffer for doing what is right rather than for doing what is wrong. For Christ also died for sins once for all, the just for the unjust, so that He might bring us to God, having been put to death in the flesh, but made alive in the spirit. I Peter 3:16-18

Day 1

Is anyone among you suffering? Let him pray. Is anyone cheerful? Let him sing praise. Is anyone among you sick? Let him call for the elders of the church, and let them pray over him, anointing him with oil in the name of the Lord. And the prayer of faith will save the one who is sick, and the Lord will raise him up. And if he has committed sins, he will be forgiven. Therefore, confess your sins to one another and pray for one another, that you may be healed. The prayer of a righteous person has great power as it is working. Elijah was a man with a nature like ours, and he prayed fervently that it might not rain, and for three years and six months it did not rain on the earth. Then he prayed again, and heaven gave rain, and the earth bore its fruit. James 5:13-18

This passage is chock full of spiritual truth, and application. Here are some things I see in this passage:

• Prayer is called for in all situations: In tough times, pray. In good times, praise. In sickness, pray and get prayed over! (verses 13-14)

• Praying in community: Prayer is not a "magic potion" nor is it an attempt to persuade God to do something He doesn't want to do. But unmistakably there is power in praying together with God's people. Somehow God chooses to work through the prayers of the saints to release His power and work out His plan. Perhaps part of the design of praying together is that it builds bonds among people. Our hearts are knit together when our knees share the floor over a common concern. And, it takes humility to share our needs with others. And, where there is humility, God promises His grace.

• This passage does not preclude the use of medicine for healing: Very likely, the use of the oil here was for medicinal purposes and is portrayed as being administered in the name of the Lord, seeing Him as the ultimate healer. (verse 14)

• What about "*the prayer of faith*"? I do not believe this means that we can "claim" a verse and declare that God owes us the answer we want. "*The prayer of faith*" is one in accordance with God's will. And faith "*comes from hearing and hearing the Word of God.*" Verses 15-18 show the link between prayer, God's Word, and obedience. Not emotionally working ourselves into a certain belief. God's answers do not depend on how much we believe, but rather our belief rests on His Word. Elijah didn't get his prayers answered because he was a super saint. James makes sure to remind us that he was just like you and me, but he knew God's Word. And he knew what God said in Deuteronomy 28, "*The consequences of disobedience would be no rain. So when he prayed for God to withhold the rain, he was doing so in accordance with what God had already declared. And when the people repented and returned to the Lord, Elijah could proclaim God's promise of blessings for obedience...so he asked God to send the rain.*"

How are you praying today?

Living Letters

Day 2

We've spent a lot of days with our friend James. I hope you've fallen in love with God's Word through him...I especially hope that we've all learned to take the truth he shares from the pew to the pavement of our lives.

"Saving faith" shows up in how we live.

Or it's not "saving" us at all.

That's what James tells us.

Before we close out this epistle with the last two verses, let's take a brief power walk in review.

The theme of this entire book is succinctly spelled out in verse 20 of the second chapter, *"faith without works is dead (useless)."* We learned that James is not teaching salvation by works but rather demonstrating to us that genuine faith results in works.

And he pens an entire letter explaining how.

Can you list 6-8 ways that James has taught us that faith works?

Day 3

Here are some of the things we've seen about faith that works (list the verse/verses that contains this truth beside each one):

- Enables us to rejoice in trials because we have confidence that God is working all things for good

- Drives us to the throne for wisdom to know how to handle what comes our way

- Reminds us that God only gives good gifts, regardless of what the packaging looks like to us

- Transforms our hearts so that our personality becomes one that listens long and speaks short, and is slow to get angry because we know that anger won't accomplish what we desire

- Embraces God's Word, trusting it to conform us to the image of Christ

- Takes responsibility to care for those who can't take care of themselves

- Shows no favoritism in an attempt to gain personal benefit

- Delights in showing mercy instead of judgment

- Tames the tongue

- Demonstrates wisdom in behavior of peace, gentleness, deference, and good works

- Knows that our asking God to meet our desires works better than expecting others to do so

- Results in humility because we see the truth about who we are in relation to who He Is

- Does not criticize a brother

- Does not value riches nor trust in them

- Suffers well

- Prays in the midst of all circumstances

And, finally, the last two verses...

We'll unpack them tomorrow.

Day 4

My brethren, if any among you strays from the truth and one turns him back, let him know that he who turns a sinner from the error of his way will save his soul from death and will cover a multitude of sins. James 5:19-20

What is James's last demonstration of faith that works?

It's the same as he's already suggested. Love.

Just one more way that it manifests itself.

James closes his letter by urging us to love one another enough to feel responsibility for each other's spiritual wellbeing. No, he's not condoning being a busybody but he is saying we are our brother's keeper, and if one of us is straying, then the faith of the others should reach out to bring the one back.

That's not just James's idea. Peter said the same thing. (I Peter 4:8 *"Above all, keep fervent in your love for one another because love covers a multitude of sins."*)

And so did Solomon in Proverbs 10:12, *"Love covers all transgressions."*

So did Paul in I Corinthians 13:13, *"But now abide faith, hope, and love, these three, but the greatest of these is love."*

And so did Jesus.

"Teacher, which is the great commandment in the Law?" And he said to him, "You shall love the Lord your God with all your heart and with all your soul and with all your mind. This is the great and first commandment. And a second is like it: You shall love your neighbor as yourself. On these two commandments depend all the Law and the Prophets. Matthew 22:36-40

Amen.

Day 5

Therefore put away all filthiness and rampant wickedness and receive with meekness the implanted word, which is able to save your souls. But be doers of the Word, and not hearers only, deceiving yourselves. James 1:21-22

We've gone through this whole epistle. It's been a sweet time, getting to know our brother James and to attend to what he has to tell us. I think the whole book can be represented by these two verses above. They tell us that our faith isn't doing us any good unless we hear what God has to say and obey Him. We are transformed ("saved") by getting God's Word in us... and our faith is proven genuine when we do what that Word says to do.

Close out today by writing out at least three things that God has spoken to you about through this study of James...and how you are going to obey what He said.

Day 1

Are you in conflict with someone right now? Maybe it's your teenager, or your co-worker, someone at church or in the neighborhood, or maybe it's your spouse.

Ask yourself some questions about that...

What bothers you about that person? What is the source of the angst between you? What would you like to change about this relationship/that person?

Do you think things can get better?

This isn't about changing the other person to make this better. And it's not even so much a post about changing yourself...instead it's about the problem.

I continually surprise myself at how easily I get distracted from the real problem, and how quickly I can slip into thinking that my relational concerns are rooted in someone's quirks or issues or even their sin...or my own.

Those are not the root but rather the leaves and branches of the conflict.

Ephesians 6:12 spells out the problem clearly, *"For we do not wrestle against flesh and blood, but against the rulers, against the authorities, against the cosmic powers over this present darkness, against the spiritual forces of evil in the heavenly places."*

The root of the conflict between you and your child, you and your neighbor, you and your spouse is not the other person. And it's not you. It's not any person. It's spiritual, the spiritual forces of evil that wage war in the heavenly places against the saints. It's not a sci-fi movie... it's real.

The unseen powers of wickedness that temporarily rule over this world are the cause for the problems in your relationship, and the source for the conflicts that torment us. That's the enemy. That's who we need to battle...not the other person.

How easily we are deceived into blaming someone for the tension, the separation, or the pain that exists in our relationships. We battle the pride and selfishness and anger and greed of our friend, our child, our spouse...and ourselves.

And we keep losing. The conflict persists, intensifies, and breaks us apart, because we're fighting the wrong combatant!

We don't have to lose this war. We don't have to experience the casualties of conflict, but we do have to fight. Let's learn together.

Day 2

To win the battle, we need to know who the enemy is (we saw that yesterday) and we need to fight with the right weapons.

Whining, arguing, demanding, hoping for change—those are weapons indeed but they won't win the battle. We need to fight…with the right weapons.

For the weapons of our warfare are not of the flesh but have divine power to destroy strongholds. 2 Corinthians 10:4

Spiritual forces cannot be defeated with fleshly weapons.

Arguing, pleading, manipulating, and even counseling are insufficient (sometimes even more destructive) in our struggle against them.

We need divine power.

The weapons with which God has divinely equipped us are found in Ephesians 6. Verses 17-18 tell us, *"The sword of the Spirit, which is the Word of God. And pray in the Spirit on all occasions with all kinds of prayers and requests. With this in mind, be alert and always keep on praying for all the Lord's people."*

Two weapons. Divinely powered to destroy the real enemy in our relationships: prayer and God's Word.

No substitutes will effect the change we want, the peace we desire, or the blessings we seek.

Take a moment and ponder that relationship that is in such strife.

It's not their fault, or yours, but you can fix it.

Pray.

Pray God's Word over the problem, into the conflict, and onto victory.

Day 3

I believe that the enemy of our souls would like to lull us into thinking that once we are saved/ born again/receive Christ that the battle is over. He does a great job at his masterful deception and many of us live blindly unaware of the war against our souls. Now don't hear what I am NOT saying. Once we enter into a personal relationship with Christ, it is permanent. Nothing or no one can undo what Jesus did in adopting us as His own. The eternal security of the believer (the true believer) is confidently complete.

But that's not what I am talking about. I am talking about the attack on our souls, our minds, our emotions and wills that often leave us depressed, frustrated, powerless, and perplexed. We know that we are supposed to be joyful and peaceful and live a life of consistent triumph over sin. And yet, as we look in the mirror, we often see little difference in our life and that of the NON-believer. We don't know why that is so but we resolve to try a little harder, do a little better, and hope that next week and next month and next year will be a little better.

What's the deal?

Here's a clue from scripture...I Peter 2:11 says, "*Brethren, I urge you, as aliens and strangers to abstain from fleshly lusts, which wage war against the soul.*"

1. Remember that this world isn't my home. I should expect to feel out of place (as in an alien!) when looking to temporal things to fulfill me. Things that nonbelievers find joy in, even good things, can often leave me dissatisfied or disappointed.

2. What are "fleshly lusts"? Not only what you might think. While indulging in pornography certainly qualifies as "fleshly lust," by no means is it the only thing. "Fleshly" applies to whatever satisfies something other than my spirit. It might be physical appetite as in food or drink, or an emotional yearning such as praise or attention or achievement. "Lust" is exactly what you think... a longing for and a strong desire that causes us to set our heart on it.

3. So, if we don't stay away from these things, our soul will be under attack and in turmoil. Frustrated, unhappy, not at peace, empty-feeling. And James 4:1 adds that the attempt to satisfy these lusts will not only leave our own souls out of sorts, but it will also inevitably lead to stresses in our relationships with others. Conflicts and quarrels result when those lusts, uh, expectations, aren't satisfied? Oh yes.

OK, so we are to abstain from these fleshly lusts so as to avoid the perils of attack, but how? More tomorrow. For today, commit to practicing what you've already learned...fighting problems with prayer and God's Word. Tomorrow we learn how to avoid defeat in an attack.

Day 4

We cannot always avoid attack but we can place ourselves in the position for victory. James 1:21 explains, *"Therefore, putting aside all filthiness and all that remains of wickedness, in humility, receive the Word implanted which is able to save your souls."*

This is not about salvation but rather sanctification–transforming our souls into Christlikeness. It's getting rid of the darkness so that we do not give the enemy a place to gain entrance into our lives.

This verse tells us:

- Cease from anything we know to be wrong. Period. If something, some activity or pursuit popped into your head just now, that very well may be God's quiet voice urging you to cease.

- Humble ourselves. Ask for God's help, realize our propensity to fall, and recognize our constant need for His grace in order to obey Him.

- Receive the Word implanted. Major point. God's Word...we need to feast on it regularly and obey what it says. It will save, as in deliver, restore, repair, and protect our souls.

Suggestions for implementation: Be careful what you look at, listen to, and set your heart on. Music, media, mentors. Be careful.

Find a plan that will get God's Word into your life daily, commune with folks who are growing in their pursuit of Him, and be accountable to someone who is willing to hold you accountable.

Serve others. Consistently. Make right the things that are wrong, whether it is a relationship, decision, etc. Humble yourself. Wait on Him, confidently.

He wants you to win the war for your soul even more than you want to. (Where do you think the idea and the desire came from anyway?)

Day 5

Finally, be strong in the Lord and in the strength of his might. Put on the whole armor of God, that you may be able to stand against the schemes of the devil. For we do not wrestle against flesh and blood, but against the rulers, against the authorities, against the cosmic powers over this present darkness, against the spiritual forces of evil in the heavenly places. Therefore take up the whole armor of God, that you may be able to withstand in the evil day, and having done all, to stand firm. Stand therefore, having fastened on the belt of truth, and shaving put on the breastplate of righteousness, and, as shoes for your feet, having put on the readiness given by the gospel of peace. In all circumstances take up the shield of faith, with which you can extinguish all the flaming darts of the evil one; and take the helmet of salvation, and the sword of the Spirit, which is the Word of God, praying at all times in the Spirit, with all prayer and supplication. To that end keep alert with all perseverance, making supplication for all the saints. Ephesians 6:10-18

Yes, we are in a battle. Yes, it's hard. No, we cannot always avoid the battle but we can avoid defeat. That is God's plan for us. He wants us to fight...and win!

This passage explains how God equips us for victory, what we need to know in order to avoid defeat at the hands of the enemy. At the moment of our salvation, God made available to us tools for victory. An entire suit of armor, with exactly the pieces we need to protect our lives from defeat: a belt, shoes, breastplate, shield, and sword...all designed to help us stand. We just have to know how to employ them.

Over the next few days, we will look at the pieces of equipment God supplies to us, and how to use them for our victory. But first, I want us to focus on the most major aspects of spiritual warfare:

- The battle is real.

- We open ourselves up to defeat when we tolerate sin.

- We cannot always avoid the assault but we can avoid being defeated by it.

- God allows the battle for our good and His glory.

- The key to getting rid of the darkness of the enemy is to turn on the Light.

Let's get our armor on!

Day 1

Stand, therefore, having fastened on the belt of truth. Ephesians 6:14

The belt worn by these soldiers was not a skinny little fashion statement, not at all. It was a wide piece of strong leather, worn around the waist, and covering much of the ribs and abdomen area. Its three main purposes were: 1) to hold the breastplate securely, 2) as a place to stash weapons (sword and knife), and 3) a means whereby to tuck the tunic in to run unimpeded. Instead of being about fashion, it was definitely about function.

To begin with, let me state that I don't think the "belt of truth" is God's Word, although I certainly do believe that God's Word is truth! The reason why is because the sword is later identified as the Word of God and also because the belt HOLDS the weapons, rather than being a weapon itself. So, what is this belt? Let's look at the purposes of the soldier's belt and draw their spiritual parallels...

- Holding the breastplate securely: the breastplate is our righteousness, imputed to us because of Christ. The application, then, could be the TRUTH of who we are IN CHRIST. We are made righteous because of Him and this TRUTH gives us the confidence to approach the throne of grace to find help in the battle. Without the TRUTH of who we are IN CHRIST, we would be afraid to ask for His help (over and over and over) and would not have the grace and strength we need to win.

- A place to stash weapons: since our weapons are God's Word and prayer (see v. 18 - I am preempting things a bit!), TRUTH is needed to keep them ready for our use. The TRUTH that God's Word is divinely inspired ("*All scripture is breathed out by God and profitable for teaching, for reproof, for correction, and for training in righteousness.*" 2 Timothy 3:16), and the TRUTH that God answers the prayers of His children ("*I sought the LORD, and he answered me; he delivered me from all my fears.*" Psalm 34:4), prompts me to use these weapons in the battles that come my way. Again, there is confidence that comes from this TRUTH. Confidence that these weapons are not of the flesh but have divine power to destroy strongholds (2 Corinthians 10:4). In other words, relying on the TRUTH that God's Word and prayer will work!

- Tucking in the tunic so as to run without getting tangled up: I love this one. The belt of truth... training my mind to focus on what is true, not speculation or perception or vain imaginations. TRUTH. As in, a loved one is having tests run and focusing on that truth rather than what the results might be before they come in. As in, what someone actually said rather than drawing conclusions on what they meant and what that means for you. As in, accepting being wronged by someone and being willing to forgive rather than letting their offense define your relationship. This application of TRUTH helps us walk without stumbling, run without getting tangled up...in speculations, perceptions, and vain imaginations. Just walking in TRUTH.

The belt of truth helps us stand against the attacks of the enemy of our souls.

Day 2

Stand firm therefore, HAVING GIRDED YOUR LOINS WITH TRUTH, and HAVING PUT ON THE BREASTPLATE OF RIGHTEOUSNESS. Ephesians 6:14

The image evoked by this passage was a sight familiar to the readers of the day, of the Roman soldier dressed for battle. The breastplate was a heavy piece of metal, covering the front, back, and sides of the wearer in the chest area, providing protection for the vital organs. Without it, the soldier was completely vulnerable to the spears and arrows of the enemy.

How does that apply in the spiritual sense? The Christian is counted as completely righteous before God at the moment of personal salvation. Christ's perfection is credited to our account, instead of the sins and flaws and imperfections that actually define us. This righteousness is permanent and is completely without our effort. We just receive the free gift God offers through Christ.

The breastplate of righteousness, though, is something that we "put on." We participate in this covering of our heart. So I think this passage is not referring to the righteousness that is imputed to us at salvation but rather the practical, dynamic righteousness of living the life of faith. By that I mean the maintaining of our fellowship with God by being convicted of sin, confessing it, and then receiving the cleansing of all unrighteousness by the Holy Spirit. Putting on righteousness, living in obedience to His Word, and adjusting our lives to it. Confession. Repentance. Cleansing. Continuously.

We all seek to protect our hearts from injury but often we are tempted to resort to self-protection, withdrawal from potential pain, avoidance, denial, and defensiveness. These methods don't protect our hearts from injury but instead they harden it.

Being aware of our constant need for God to forgive us, change us, and give us grace is what protects our hearts successfully. It enables us to avoid defeat. It assures victory in the conflicts of this life, guarding our heart, for out of it flow the springs of life.

Day 3

And having shod your feet with the preparation of the gospel of peace. Ephesians 6:15

We've all been admonished to "walk a mile in their moccasins" in order to understand someone else's point of view. Good suggestion, but we are exhorted in scripture to walk in a different manner. Our feet are to be shod with the preparation of the gospel of peace. Let's unpack that verse...

First of all, this verse is in the midst of the passage sometimes referred to as "The Christian's Dress for Success"–putting on the armor of God so that we can successfully withstand the attacks of the enemy. What do shoes have to do with it?

Well, the writer of this epistle is drawing on a picture quite familiar to the readers of his day–that of the Roman soldier. The image evoked here would be of thick shoes, strapped onto the feet of the warrior. The bottom of the shoes would be studded with iron nails, which provided better traction on rugged terrain as well as protection from razor sharp spikes stuck in the ground as enemy traps. The shoes were strapped on with secure binding so that they wouldn't come loose in the battle.

The gospel of peace prepares the Christian to walk successfully in the battle, to endure the rugged trail, and to avoid injury from the traps set by the enemy. But how? This gospel of peace is not referring to our peace with God (that's taken care of by the breastplate of righteousness...but that's another post). No, the gospel of peace is referring to our relationship with others.

The counsel given here is that having peace with others is a key to victory in our walk of life. Peace, reconciliation, that is possible because we have peace with God ourselves.

When there is not peace with others, we are prone to stumble along the trail. To get cut by the spikes set out by the enemy of our souls. To be unable to walk or stand, sustaining injury. Practically speaking, this looks like bitterness towards a sister, hard-heartedness towards a neighbor, avoidance of a former friend, private pains of loneliness, feelings of rejection, depression over unmet needs, or isolation.

Maybe we need to strap on the shoes of peace and walk to someone today for reconciliation. If this brings a name or two to your mind, I hope you'll walk on, sister. Walk on. Victory is in sight for you, not to mention what it will do for your comrade.

Living Letters

Day 4

In all circumstances take up the shield of faith, with which you can extinguish all the flaming darts of the evil one. Ephesians 6:16

We've seen how God supplies the breastplate of righteousness to protect our heart, the belt of truth that gives us confidence in our relationships with God, ourselves, and others, and shoes of peace to walk out the gospel in the lives of those around us. What about the shield of faith? How exactly does it put out the flaming darts of the enemy of our soul?

The Roman warrior would have had a shield that was much larger than what we might think. Made of metal, it was three-sided and closer in size to a door than platter-size. Visualize how protective this would have been–its bearer could easily hide behind it and ward off arrows not only from the front but also from each side.

What's really interesting is that it was covered on the outside with leather that had been soaked in water. Those arrows shot by the enemy were not only often flaming with fire but also dripping with poison. The water-soaked leather diluted the poison, put out the fire, and kept the metal of the shield from becoming so heated that it burned the one behind it.

What is the parallel for the Christ-follower?

First, what is faith, and what is it NOT? Faith is not a positive thought or feeling. It is not the absence of doubt or fear. Rather, faith is confidence in an unshakeable God and His unfailing love for and never-wavering commitment to His saints. It's not the amount of faith that we have, but who our faith is in–omnipotent, omniscient, always loving, Holy, perfect, and Mighty God.

Faith is the assurance that leads to obedience. Because I know He loves me completely, I trust Him. Because I trust Him, I will do what He tells me to do in His Word. I love the way that old hymn puts it "Trust and obey." It's an inextricable link of faith and obedience, I "behave what I believe."

Faith–the assurance of things hoped for and the evidence of things not seen (Hebrews 11:1). That's what faith is. How do I get it? So faith comes from hearing, and hearing by the Word of Christ (Romans 10:17)

How do I *"take up"* this shield of faith? When the arrows of doubt and fear and temptation come at me, I "extinguish" them with God's Word. I hide behind His Word, not my own understanding. I don't rely on what I feel like or what seems to be true. I place my faith on what God says to me in His Word. If I ask Him for something and He says no, I don't assume that I "lacked faith" or that He didn't answer or that "this doesn't work." I respond to those suggestions with promises like the one in Psalm 84:11, *"No good thing does He withhold from those who walk uprightly."* If I didn't get what I asked for, then I know that, no matter what it seems like, that which I asked for was not a good thing. His Word assures me that He loves me and that ALL His ways are loving and faithful. His Word trumps my feelings every time. Faith… the assurance of things hoped for, the evidence of things not seen, a place for me to hide, and protection from the assault all around me.

Day 5

"...and take the helmet of salvation." Ephesians 6:17a

First, what is it? The helmet, obviously, protects the head. Our heads need protection because the mind is where the battle takes place. The helmet provided for the Christ-follower is "salvation." To understand this significance, let's consider the fact that salvation has three facets to it. The first is justification, God's declaration that a person is made acceptable to Him by grace through faith in Christ, receiving the Spirit of Christ. The second facet is sanctification, the process by which a Christ-follower is conformed to the image of Christ and the work of grace through the soul. The final aspect of salvation is glorification, when a believer enters eternity and is transformed in body to be immortal and incorruptible.

This protection of thought with regard to salvation gives the believer confidence that the relationship with God is secure, that God is indeed doing the work of transformation in one's life, and that one's eternal future is assured. Such confidence wards off the thoughts of doubt and fear and insecurity propelled by the enemy.

This helmet is also a reminder to the believer to renew one's mind through scripture, thus transforming one to the image of Christ...further protection from the darts of the devil. This commitment to mind renewal undergirds the confidence just mentioned.

One final thought on the helmet. The helmet referenced in this passage was one worn by the Roman soldier. It was made of metal and covered not only the head but also the face. Atop the helmet was a plume, a large colorful feather that identified the army to which the soldier belonged. Get the picture–in battle, you would know who your allies were by the color of the feather on their helmet. What message is conveyed to us through this feature on the helmet? A conspicuous lifestyle, one that clearly identifies us as a follower of Christ, offers great protection from the enemy in the battle.

Confidence that our salvation is assured + commitment to renew our minds + a conspicuous lifestyle that tells the world who we belong to = our helmet.

Living Letters

Day 1

We will wind up this section on the armor with one of the verses we began with:

And the sword of the Spirit which is the Word of God; with all prayer and petition, pray at all times in the Spirit, and with this in view, be on the alert with all perseverance and petition for all the saints. Ephesians 6:17-18

The best defense is a good offense. I've heard that (and its reciprocal) proclaimed often in my den during football season. The way to defeat an opponent is to score more points than they do. Duh.

That said, how do we "score points" against our enemy?

If you look at all the pieces of armor we've discussed so far, they are all defensive. The helmet of salvation, the breastplate of righteousness, the belt of truth, the shoes of peace, and the shield of faith all serve to protect us from assault. Defense. Then we get to the last pieces...the ones that enable us to be on the offensive...the ones that equip us to score.

And the sword of the Spirit, which is the Word of God, praying at all times in the Spirit, with all prayer and supplication. To that end keep alert with all perseverance, making supplication for all the saints. Ephesians 6:17-18

Do you see the two weapons listed there? Obviously, the sword, which scripture clearly explains is the Word of God. But don't miss the other one—prayer, God's word and prayer. That's how we attack the enemy. That's how we score points. That's how we win.

The weapons of our warfare, not just defensive and protecting us from attack, but also offensive, racking up victory against that which assails us.

God wants to do more than protect us from injury. He wants us to be victorious over the things that threaten our demise—unforgiveness, depression, bitterness, broken relationships, rebellion, greed, envy fear, and worry. And He's provided what we need to score. I hope we don't leave those weapons in the locker room. We need them on the field.

Day 2

Likewise the Spirit helps us in our weakness. For we do not know what to pray for as we ought, but the Spirit himself intercedes for us with groanings too deep for words. And he who searches hearts knows what is the mind of the Spirit, because the Spirit intercedes for the saints according to the will of God. And we know that for those who love God all things work together for good, for those who are called according to his purpose. For those whom he foreknew he also predestined to be conformed to the image of his Son, in order that he might be the firstborn among many brothers. And those whom he predestined he also called, and those whom he called he also justified, and those whom he justified he also glorified. Romans 8:28-31

As we prepare ourselves for battle everyday, this passage is so helpful. Remember, yes, we are weak. But God has given us the Spirit to help us in our weaknesses. And, yes, He exhorts to pray...but sometimes we don't even know what to pray. In those times, remember, the Spirit Himself is praying on our behalf as we cry out to Him in our weakness. He prays for us in perfection, always knowing what God's will is in every situation, always moving us towards fulfilling God's purpose.

And that purpose is that we become like Jesus.

God uses all things—good things, things that seem bad to us, hard things, even the battles He has us in—to fulfill that purpose, to make us like Jesus.

Let that sink into your soul today. God is at work, for your good and His glory, in your life. Let your purpose be to cooperate with what He has set out to do.

Day 3

And behold, a hand touched me and set me trembling on my hands and knees. And he said to me, "O Daniel, man greatly loved, understand the Words that I speak to you, and stand upright, for now I have been sent to you." And when he had spoken this word to me, I stood up trembling. Then he said to me, "Fear not, Daniel, for from the first day that you set your heart to understand and humbled yourself before your God, your words have been heard, and I have come because of your words. The prince of the kingdom of Persia withstood me twenty-one days, but Michael, one of the chief princes, came to help me, for I was left there with the kings of Persia, and came to make you understand what is to happen to your people in the latter days. For the vision is for days yet to come." Daniel 10:10-14

Daniel was fervently praying for answers and help and none came. Yet he persevered, trusting that God would respond. And, oh, how He did! God sent an angel to deliver a message to his servant Daniel. In the chapters that follow this encounter, God gave to Daniel a vision that reveals His plan for history. (I urge you to examine that vision for yourself. It is so very exciting, especially since we are in the opportune place to be able to look back and see the precise fulfillment of His revelation...and we can look forward in anticipation of His fulfilling the rest!) For today, let's just look at these few verses from Daniel 10 and marvel at the wonders of our mighty God! He sent a messenger—an angel to Daniel. Angels are created beings, spiritual beings without physical bodies that you and I can see...unless God chooses to put them in visible form to accomplish a mission or unless He opens our spiritual eyes for us to view them. In this case, we know that Daniel saw this angel! One moment he was praying his knees off and the next, he saw this messenger and received an explanation of what took so long. He was engaged in spiritual combat with another messenger—one that was also created and has a mission, but is opposed to the King of Kings.

Right now, at this very moment, an unseen war is being waged all around you and me. Just because we cannot see it does not make it any less true. (You cannot see electricity, can you? Or wind? But you can definitely see their effects! And if you are confident of their existence, you can harness their power for your benefit.) There are indeed wars going on all around us—wars that we cannot see, where the forces of God are wrestling with the forces of the enemy. Just like the angels of God are on a mission, so are these other messengers. Once, in eternity past, these beings were created to fulfill God's purposes and plans. Satan himself was one of these. Ezekiel 28:12-19 describes his past place of prominence before God...and his subsequent fall into eternal damnation. When Satan's pride corrupted him out of heaven, scripture reveals to us that one-third of God's angels—his "stars of heaven"—followed him in blind arrogance. These spiritual beings seek to prevent humans from coming to Christ, to frustrate the transformation into Christlikeness of those that do. For this reason, Ephesians 6 tells us that, *"our struggle (battle) is not against flesh and blood but against the rulers, against the power, and the world forces of darkness, against the spiritual forces of wickedness."* It's easy to forget that, isn't it? In our daily living, we can often get the enemy confused. We can think instead that it is our job or our church or our family. Sometimes we even think that God is our enemy! And when we get the enemy confused, we fight the wrong one, just like Satan wants us to. We wrestle against our circumstances or political parties or our spouse, hoping to make them change, hoping to "win" our way. But we see from Daniel that's the wrong war to wage, the wrong place to be.

Day 4

And behold, a hand touched me and set me trembling on my hands and knees. And he said to me, "O Daniel, man greatly loved, understand the words that I speak to you, and stand upright, for now I have been sent to you." And when he had spoken this word to me, I stood up trembling. Then he said to me, "Fear not, Daniel, for from the first day that you set your heart to understand and humbled yourself before your God, your words have been heard, and I have come because of your words. The prince of the kingdom of Persia withstood me twenty-one days, but Michael, one of the chief princes, came to help me, for I was left there with the kings of Persia, and came to make you understand what is to happen to your people in the latter days. For the vision is for days yet to come." Daniel 10:10-14

We saw yesterday that we must realize where the battle is so that we will fight the right one. Where was Daniel waging the war? On his hands and knees.

And that's where the answer came to him.

What was it about Daniel that caused God to grant favor to him, to have an angel deem him *"highly esteemed"*? What is it about Daniel that we should want to emulate?

Here is what I see:

- Humility: While it is true that we cannot earn God's favor, it is also true that He commits Himself to pour out His grace on the humble and to set Himself in opposition to the proud. Daniel is humble. Humble enough to pray, on his face. (He had to be brought UP to be on his hands and knees!) Before God, crying out, asking for answers, help, and strength. If we want what Daniel had (and we should), we have to know that being a person that God shows Himself to mightily begins with our recognition of our place before Him, our need of Him, and our faith in Him. Humility.

- Perseverance: If we are tempted to think that humility sounds like weakness, this trait will underscore that it is definitely not. This passage shows us that, yes, Daniel humbled himself to pray but he did more than that. He persevered when the answers didn't come. He didn't quit. He didn't claim, "well I tried but it didn't work" and then give up. He pressed on, apparently in the midst of an intense struggle. He might not have been able to see the battle being fought around him but he knew that his part was to keep praying and not give up.

- Resolve: I love this about Daniel–he had resolve. Scripture puts it this way, *"set your heart to understand."* This is not the first mention of Daniel's resolve; in the very first chapter of the same book, we read that *"Daniel made up his mind"* about his conduct and acted accordingly. Yes, God will accomplish His plan through whomever He chooses and yes, it's all grace working through those He chooses. But when we set our mind to obey Him, to seek to understand, and to humble ourselves before Him in desperate need of His grace, well, that's when He moves in response.

May we dare to be a Daniel today. May we fight the right battle and not give up too soon!

Day 5

When the servant of the man of God rose early in the morning and went out, behold, an army with horses and chariots was all around the city. And the servant said, "Alas, my master! What shall we do?" He said, "Do not be afraid, for those who are with us are more than those who are with them." Then Elisha prayed and said, "O Lord, please open his eyes that he may see." So the Lord opened the eyes of the young man, and he saw, and behold, the mountain was full of horses and chariots of fire all around Elisha. 2 Kings 6:15-17

I believe with all my heart that one of the activities in heaven is going to be for God to show us "behind the scenes" what was going on throughout our life. And then we will get to see how God protected us, guided us, and provided for us through His heavenly messengers. That is going to be so very exciting! I sort of imagine that I might sit down with Jesus with a heavenly bowl of popcorn in front of a screen stretched out across eternity and watch with heavenly eyes how the events of my life played out. And I'll not only be able to see things I've never seen before, but I also will view them through the lens of eternity...I'll be able to see what God was up to, how He was accomplishing His plan for me and through me. What a truly incredible showing that is going to be!

When I think about that, about what is going on around me that I cannot see, I find encouragement. Instead of feeling defeated by the battle I am in or discouraged by the attack I am under, I am strengthened by the assurance that God is fighting for me. And His warriors are stronger than those of the enemy.

Is there a battle going on in your life that has you scared, or at least worried? Maybe you feel panicked or even hopeless as a result of the attack. Maybe the enemy seems not only to outnumber you but also to be racking up victories at your expense. But the truth is, there is more that's for you than against you - you just can't see it when you're in the midst of the attack unless God opens your eyes.

Like Elisha, we just need to ask. And then God will open our eyes to see that He is at work on our behalf in a thousand different ways. He is preserving us, He is unfolding His plan, and He is not absent nor unwilling or unable to help. His warriors are all around us...ask Him to let you see with spiritual eyes what He is doing...how He is fighting for you...and the help He has provided.

And like the young servant, let that assuage your fear. Do not dismay. Do not give up. Help is here!

Day 1

Blessed are the poor in spirit, for theirs is the kingdom of heaven. Blessed are those who mourn, for they shall be comforted. Blessed are the meek, for they shall inherit the earth. Blessed are those who hunger and thirst for righteousness, for they shall be satisfied. Blessed are the merciful, for they shall receive mercy. Blessed are the pure in heart, for they shall see God. Blessed are the peacemakers, for they shall be called sons of God. Blessed are those who are persecuted for righteousness' sake, for theirs is the kingdom of heaven. Blessed are you when others revile you and persecute you and utter all kinds of evil against you falsely on my account. Rejoice and be glad, for your reward is great in heaven, for so they persecuted the prophets who were before you. Matthew 5:3-12

These verses, often referred to as "The Beatitudes," are part of a message Jesus delivered to His disciples as they sat on the side of a mountain. Most people call this whole message "The Sermon on the Mount."

In this passage, Jesus explains to His disciples what their lives are to look like as they follow Him (not how to obtain salvation–rather how to live as a believer). And He starts it off by telling them how to live in the place of greatest blessing. In fact, the Greek word He uses for "*blessed*" is "makriotes" and means fully satisfied, a state the ancient Greeks believed could only be attained by their gods.

We could say they sort of got it right, couldn't we? As Christians, we realize that complete happiness, full satisfaction, and highest blessing is only possible when we are indwelt by the Living God and living according to His plans.

That's what this section will be about–the "Be-Happy Attitudes." Not happy as a result of happenstance or circumstances but rather because of having our souls satisfied in Jesus.

We will look at each of these verses but for today, I want you probe this question, "Does God really want me to be happy?"

1. What do you really believe about that?

2. Are you happy?

3. Why or why not?

4. Is being happy a Godly pursuit?

Ask the Lord to show you over the next many days...

Living Letters

Day 2

Before we unpack the Beatitudes, we need to find God's answer to the question, "Does He want us to be happy?"

You probably figure the answer is "yes" but I want you to find it for yourself. Look up these verses and write what God shows you in each one.

- Matthew 7:11

- John 15:11

- Psalm 84:11

- Psalm 34:9-10

- Philippians 3:1

- John 13:17

- Romans 15:13

Does God want us to be happy?

YES! A thousand times, YES! The happiness He has for us is not fleeting self-satisfying comfort. It is far deeper and more fulfilling than that. His joy meets the deepest desires of the soul. And He designed us to pursue this satisfaction, to crave this happiness. It is the desire that only He can meet.

Seek it, we all shall do. The question is "in what." What does Deuteronomy 28:47-48 tell us about what happens if we do not pursue our joy in Him? If we don't find our joy in Him, our enemies will enslave us.

Close out today by embracing the truth that God is JOY and that in Him is the greatest, happiest, most secure satisfaction of your deepest desires. If you have a hard time sincerely believing that, read Mark 9:14-29 and cry out with that to our Father...I do believe; help my unbelief!

Day 3

Blessed are the poor in spirit, for theirs is the kingdom of heaven. Blessed are those who mourn, for they shall be comforted. Blessed are the meek, for they shall inherit the earth. Blessed are those who hunger and thirst for righteousness, for they shall be satisfied. Blessed are the merciful, for they shall receive mercy. Blessed are the pure in heart, for they shall see God. Blessed are the peacemakers, for they shall be called sons of God. Blessed are those who are persecuted for righteousness' sake, for theirs is the kingdom of heaven. Blessed are you when others revile you and persecute you and utter all kinds of evil against you falsely on my account. Rejoice and be glad, for your reward is great in heaven, for so they persecuted the prophets who were before you. Matthew 5:3-12

Although each verse stands alone as truth, this passage is best understood as a whole, how the different character traits fit with one another, progressing to deeper satisfaction in Him. Let's unpack the first one...

Blessed are the poor in spirit, for theirs is the kingdom of heaven.

Keep in mind that Jesus is not giving us the plan of salvation. (Just for a reminder, how are we saved? Ephesians 2:8-9 tells us.) Instead, He is describing what our lives look like as we follow Him as a result of salvation. This first attribute, though, is necessary on both sides of salvation. What does it mean?

"Poor in spirit" is not low self-esteem. The Greek word that we translate as "poor" here actually means destitute. It describes a helpless beggar, one who is completely unable to provide food for himself and must desperately cry to others for what he needs.

How in the world does this lead to happiness? Don't we need to feel good about ourselves to be happy?

NO!

In order to even enter the kingdom of heaven, to begin a relationship with Christ, we must realize our total depravity and our inability to save ourselves. That leads us to see Him as the only Savior; accepting our destitute state as what opens the way for us to receive Him.

And living in that state of awareness constantly is what enables us to depend on Him to meet all of our needs, including the desires of our heart...the path of happiness. This poverty of spirit is humility, and when we humble ourselves, God pours out grace upon us (I Peter 5:5).

The opposite of poverty of spirit is a mindset of independence and self-reliance, a lack of seeing one's need for God and His grace. These are the ones that God opposes. Not just that He does not help them, He opposes them–strong words indeed.

Day 4

Blessed are the poor in spirit, for theirs is the kingdom of heaven. Blessed are those who mourn, for they shall be comforted. Blessed are the meek, for they shall inherit the earth. Blessed are those who hunger and thirst for righteousness, for they shall be satisfied. Blessed are the merciful, for they shall receive mercy. Blessed are the pure in heart, for they shall see God. Blessed are the peacemakers, for they shall be called sons of God. Blessed are those who are persecuted for righteousness' sake, for theirs is the kingdom of heaven. Blessed are you when others revile you and persecute you and utter all kinds of evil against you falsely on my account. Rejoice and be glad, for your reward is great in heaven, for so they persecuted the prophets who were before you. Matthew 5:3-12

The first step on the continual path of happiness is that of humility. The more we constantly are aware of our need before Him, the more He meets us with grace. As we see ourselves for who we really are (not just when we are in need of saving grace, but all the way through the sanctification process!), our hearts are broken by our sin. We grieve our depravity...we mourn our sin. And Jesus said that is a key trait for blessedness.

Blessed are those who mourn, for they shall be comforted.

This verse is often used in sympathy cards for those who are bereaved. While that is a nice sentiment, I do not believe that is Jesus's intent here. Not everyone who loses someone in death will be comforted! But for those who mourn over sin, who are brokenhearted by the things that break God's heart, to those God will bring comfort.

How can "mourning" and "blessedness" go together? How can grieving be necessary for happiness?

Because when we grieve over our sin, we turn away from it. We cease to desire it. Instead, we long for holiness. We need to live in a constant state of an awareness of our sin. In order to be happy, we need to hate sin.

This puts us in the place for God to rush to our aid with grace, mercy, and comfort. He is our righteousness. He is our happiness.

Finish today by asking Him to show you your sin. Prepare to take some time to listen as He speaks.

And wait for His glorious comfort.

Day 5

Blessed are the poor in spirit, for theirs is the kingdom of heaven. Blessed are those who mourn, for they shall be comforted. Blessed are the meek, for they shall inherit the earth. Blessed are those who hunger and thirst for righteousness, for they shall be satisfied. Blessed are the merciful, for they shall receive mercy. Blessed are the pure in heart, for they shall see God. Blessed are the peacemakers, for they shall be called sons of God. Blessed are those who are persecuted for righteousness' sake, for theirs is the kingdom of heaven. Blessed are you when others revile you and persecute you and utter all kinds of evil against you falsely on my account. Rejoice and be glad, for your reward is great in heaven, for so they persecuted the prophets who were before you. Matthew 5:3-12

Humility, broken-heartedness over sin, what do we find next on the path of happiness?

Blessed are the meek, for they shall inherit the earth.

Let's start with the promise, then the condition. *"For they shall inherit the earth"*–what does that mean? This is a reference to ruling with Christ when He sets up His kingdom here on earth.

How unlike the economy of the world this is, where power is associated with being driven and dominant, not meekness.

What is meekness, anyway? It is unfortunate that our word "meekness" rhymes with "weakness" because that is often the connotation it has. Wimpy. Subservient. Pushover. But that is not at all what Jesus is conveying here. The picture He paints with the words He chose is that of a powerful horse...restrained. It's strength under control, not passive indifference.

Meekness is the inward attitude that accepts whatever happens without resisting or disputing because its heart trusts in God's loving sovereignty. Confident of God's power and love, meekness does not fight against circumstances–or people–that seem to bring unpleasantness. Meekness trusts, meekness accepts, and meekness waits.

And God rewards meekness with power.

Numbers 12:3 tells us, *"Now the man Moses was very meek, more than all people who were on the face of the earth.   Moses went from being a cowardly, angry murderer to being the most meek man alive."*

And God placed in his hands the care of all His people. Wow. Meekness yields power indeed.

How, then, do we get to be meek?

Humble ourselves, mourn over our sin, abide in Him, and He produces meekness (Galatians 5:22-23).

Day 1

Blessed are the poor in spirit, for theirs is the kingdom of heaven. Blessed are those who mourn, for they shall be comforted. Blessed are the meek, for they shall inherit the earth. Blessed are those who hunger and thirst for righteousness, for they shall be satisfied. Blessed are the merciful, for they shall receive mercy. Blessed are the pure in heart, for they shall see God. Blessed are the peacemakers, for they shall be called sons of God. Blessed are those who are persecuted for righteousness' sake, for theirs is the kingdom of heaven. Blessed are you when others revile you and persecute you and utter all kinds of evil against you falsely on my account. Rejoice and be glad, for your reward is great in heaven, for so they persecuted the prophets who were before you. Matthew 5:3-12

Let's review the progression found along the path of happiness (not, mind you, the path TO happiness but rather the path OF happiness).

Poverty of spirit, or humility, leads us to mourn over our sin. In our broken-heartedness, God brings comfort. He gives grace. As we experience His grace, we trust Him, regardless of what enters our life. We know He is working all things for His glory and our good and we meekly accept whatever He does. This leads to:

Blessed are those who hunger and thirst for righteousness for they shall be satisfied.

Hunger and thirst are physical longings that must be satisfied in order for life to be sustained, over and over again. That's the word picture Jesus chooses to convey this spiritual truth–the path of blessedness is a longing for God's expectations and desires to be fulfilled in our lives. It is a desperate craving that supersedes all other desires in our lives. Not thinking we have to earn His favor–no, that was settled forever at Calvary. God graciously bestows His favor upon all that accept Jesus's gift of salvation. Rather, this desire is born out of a need to feed our spirit. A delight in trusting Him, obeying Him, serving Him, worshipping Him above all else...and finding that He delights in satisfying this longing because He put it there to begin with!

It's like my dear mother-in-law's amazingly delicious chocolate peanut butter cookies–the more we eat, the more we want! The more we long to be like Christ, the more righteousness He bestows...and the more we hunger for it. The more He satisfies our longing, the more righteousness we desire and the greater our hatred of sin. This is the process of sanctification!

How do we get this hunger? First of all, we ask Him for it, and He will gladly grant our request. But we need to also know that our part to stoke the hunger for righteousness in our spirits is to fast from the substitutes that the world offers. Try some sort of fast for a period of time–maybe three weeks or so from whatever the Lord is whispering in your heart right now. Do you need to fast from Facebook? Or TV? Or chocolate? Ask Him. Then listen.

Then prepare to get really really hungry...for Him!

Day 2

Blessed are the poor in spirit, for theirs is the kingdom of heaven. Blessed are those who mourn, for they shall be comforted. Blessed are the meek, for they shall inherit the earth. Blessed are those who hunger and thirst for righteousness, for they shall be satisfied. Blessed are the merciful, for they shall receive mercy. Blessed are the pure in heart, for they shall see God. Blessed are the peacemakers, for they shall be called sons of God. Blessed are those who are persecuted for righteousness' sake, for theirs is the kingdom of heaven. Blessed are you when others revile you and persecute you and utter all kinds of evil against you falsely on my account. Rejoice and be glad, for your reward is great in heaven, for so they persecuted the prophets who were before you. Matthew 5:3-12

The steps on the path of happiness…poverty of spirit, which evokes mourning over our sin. This produces a meekness in us, and a hunger to be righteous like Christ. This righteousness that Christ forms in us doesn't just take place on the inside—it shows up on the outside, in our lives! The righteousness of Christ is most seen in how we treat others.

Blessed are the merciful, for they shall receive mercy.

What is mercy? Mercy is more than a feeling of pity; rather it is action that alleviates the consequences of sin, especially to those who cannot help themselves. The sin might be of the one needing mercy or it might be just a result of living in this fallen world. Here are three ways mercy is manifested in the lives of those who follow Christ: (as you read the verses, ask the Lord to show you specific opportunities for you to show mercy this week—and list them here):

- Read James 2:15-16 - mercy meets physical needs

- Read Colossians 3:12-16 - mercy meets the need of forgiveness

- Read Matthew 7:1-5, Luke 6:36-38 - mercy withholds judgment of others

Being merciful is a result of being righteous and that brings the highest state of joy—blessedness. I am all in for that, aren't you?

One last bit of motivation. Read James 2:12-13.

I need all the mercy I can get. How 'bout you?

Day 3

Blessed are the poor in spirit, for theirs is the kingdom of heaven. Blessed are those who mourn, for they shall be comforted. Blessed are the meek, for they shall inherit the earth. Blessed are those who hunger and thirst for righteousness, for they shall be satisfied. Blessed are the merciful, for they shall receive mercy. Blessed are the pure in heart, for they shall see God. Blessed are the peacemakers, for they shall be called sons of God. Blessed are those who are persecuted for righteousness' sake, for theirs is the kingdom of heaven. Blessed are you when others revile you and persecute you and utter all kinds of evil against you falsely on my account. Rejoice and be glad, for your reward is great in heaven, for so they persecuted the prophets who were before you. Matthew 5:3-12

Blessed are the pure in heart, for they shall see God

The first two things to see as we unpack this phrase are the words *"pure"* and *"heart."* This word that we translate as *"pure"* is the Greek work "katharos." It specifies a certain type of purity–not something that is pure in its natural state, but rather it is pure as a result of having been cleansed. Moreover, the verb tense is that of continual action, repeated over and over. What a great truth this conveys! Blessedness comes from not only realizing our need for Christ but also in confessing our sins before Him on a regular basis. Letting the light of His Word show us our sin and then submitting ourselves to His cleansing.

And that word *"heart"*? Well, the heart is the center of affection; it directs all our behavior. When that is pure–cleansed by the Lord–our lives are not governed by what we think will please ourselves but rather what is in the best interests of others and what would best honor our Lord.

And the result of such cleansing, such purity of heart? To see God. Not only in the sense of being before Him in eternity but also the spiritual discernment to see and understand the character of God now. To view all that happens through the lens of God's goodness and sovereignty and love. To see His hand at work in our lives and to know Him…to KNOW Him. And to experience intimacy and communion with Him.

Purity of heart and seeing God.

Yes.

Let's go before Him right now. Read Psalm 119:18 and Psalm 25:4-6 and ask that He would open our eyes.

Day 4

Blessed are the poor in spirit, for theirs is the kingdom of heaven. Blessed are those who mourn, for they shall be comforted. Blessed are the meek, for they shall inherit the earth. Blessed are those who hunger and thirst for righteousness, for they shall be satisfied. Blessed are the merciful, for they shall receive mercy. Blessed are the pure in heart, for they shall see God. Blessed are the peacemakers, for they shall be called sons of God. Blessed are those who are persecuted for righteousness' sake, for theirs is the kingdom of heaven. Blessed are you when others revile you and persecute you and utter all kinds of evil against you falsely on my account. Rejoice and be glad, for your reward is great in heaven, for so they persecuted the prophets who were before you. Matthew 5:3-12

Blessed are the peacemakers, for they shall be called sons of God.

What does it mean to be a peacemaker?

The need for peace implies a conflict! And that is surely the case. There is conflict among nations and peoples and there is conflict between God and man. Being a peacemaker means that we bring reconciliation, first of all, between God and man. Leading unbelievers to Christ is the foremost example of being a peacemaker.

Peacemaking also involves resolving conflict between individuals (or even countries, but today we will settle for individuals). Peacemaking is not pacifism or mediation (that's peace-faking). Rather, peacemaking is using our words and our actions to resolve conflicts in such a way that relationships are not only sustained but are actually strengthened.

Read James 3:13-18 and remember what we learned from that passage about making peace.

What does it mean to be called sons of God? The product of being a peacemaker is more than just resolving peace. It is a powerful truth—the Greek word for "sons" here is not the word "teknos" used for a child; rather it is the word "huios" which indicates maturity and likeness of the father. Do you get what Jesus is saying here? When we do this peacemaking thing, it will be publicly evident that we are like our Father. We will show ourselves to be mature and strong in the faith...His likeness will be seen in us!

Ask the Lord to speak to you right now about opportunities for you to make peace...and then obey Him.

And you will hear heaven declare, "she surely looks like her Dad!"

Day 5

Blessed are the poor in spirit, for theirs is the kingdom of heaven. Blessed are those who mourn, for they shall be comforted. Blessed are the meek, for they shall inherit the earth. Blessed are those who hunger and thirst for righteousness, for they shall be satisfied. Blessed are the merciful, for they shall receive mercy. Blessed are the pure in heart, for they shall see God. Blessed are the peacemakers, for they shall be called sons of God. Blessed are those who are persecuted for righteousness' sake, for theirs is the kingdom of heaven. Blessed are you when others revile you and persecute you and utter all kinds of evil against you falsely on my account. Rejoice and be glad, for your reward is great in heaven, for so they persecuted the prophets who were before you. Matthew 5:3-12

Blessed are those who are persecuted for righteousness' sake, for theirs is the kingdom of heaven. Blessed are you when others revile you and persecute you and utter all kinds of evil against you falsely on my account. Rejoice and be glad, for your reward is great in heaven, for so they persecuted the prophets who were before you.

Persecuted? Are you kidding me? Seems like all those previous character traits (humility, hating sin, meekness, righteousness, mercy, purity, peace) would make the world love us and long to hang out with us! Persecuted? Reviled? Lied about? Whoa Nelly that sounds awful–and on top of that, I am supposed to rejoice and be glad? No way!

Yes way.

Today we are just gonna focus on the suffering that comes as a result of being righteous. First, look up 2 Timothy 3:12. What does that tell you to expect?

In fact, I would go so far as to say that if you and I aren't experiencing at least SOME type of persecution, we are in deep trouble. Check out Luke 6:26 and write down what that says:

We need to check out our anchor and see where it's holding, because righteous living will bring persecution. Period. Make no mistake about it, sister, the darkness hates the light and it deeply desires to extinguish it.

OK, so we should expect to be persecuted if we want to live like Jesus, but to rejoice about it? Isn't that a bit insane? Nobody likes to be rejected or lied about or mistreated! Except for when we know it's because of Jesus! When we suffer because of godliness we can choose gladness for two reasons: Matthew 5:10 and Matthew 5:12.

Because it is evidence that we belong to Christ and because such suffering holds so much promise of reward that we should leap and jump for joy! One day, one glorious day, it will be so very much worth it that we will actually wish we had suffered more.

That is amazing. So very like our God!

Day 1

But even if you should suffer for righteousness' sake, you will be blessed. Have no fear of them, nor be troubled, but in your hearts honor Christ the Lord as holy, always being prepared to make a defense to anyone who asks you for a reason for the hope that is in you; yet do it with gentleness and respect, having a good conscience, so that, when you are slandered, those who revile your good behavior in Christ may be put to shame. For it is better to suffer for doing good, if that should be God's will, than for doing evil. I Peter 3:14-17

Now that we know we are to rejoice when we suffer for righteousness' sake, what are some things that can help us do that?

Look up the verses listed below in addition to the passage above and see what you find:

- I Peter 2:13-20

- I Peter 2:21-23

Did you discover encouragement there? Through the Apostle Peter, Jesus exhorts us not to give up. He is cheering us on against intimidation and fear and urging us to keep our hearts free from pride or anger. He reminds us to stay alert and look for ways to gently answer those who oppose us, and to defend His reputation–not our own. Remember how Christ suffered and let His integrity and lack of reviling be our example. Keep trusting that God will judge righteously...evil will be punished and righteousness will be rewarded.

In these days of violence and corruption, where evil seems to triumph and righteousness is made to look like lies, do not despair. Do not fear. Do not quit and do not forget that God is still on the throne. He is still King of Kings and Lord of Lords.

And He will be victorious.

I am glad I am on His side!

Day 2

And have you forgotten the exhortation that addresses you as sons? "My son, do not regard lightly the discipline of the Lord, nor be weary when reproved by him. For the Lord disciplines the one he loves, and chastises every son whom he receives." It is for discipline that you have to endure. God is treating you as sons. For what son is there whom his father does not discipline? If you are left without discipline, in which all have participated, then you are illegitimate children and not sons. Besides this, we have had earthly fathers who disciplined us and we respected them. Shall we not much more be subject to the Father of spirits and live? For they disciplined us for a short time as it seemed best to them, but he disciplines us for our good, that we may share his holiness. For the moment all discipline seems painful rather than pleasant, but later it yields the peaceful fruit of righteousness to those who have been trained by it. Hebrews 12:5-11

Yesterday we contemplated suffering as a result of righteous living. Good stuff. But sometimes, suffering is not because we are living right but rather because we have chosen wrong. In those times, God disciplines us...and it hurts.

What can we learn about those times that can encourage us? This passage in Hebrews will help...

First, look at verse 5. What does the writer remind us of there? It reminds us that we are sons (and daughters!). When we disobey the Lord, He disciplines us. Think about it–if you are at a restaurant and the kid at the next table is throwing an awful fit, do you step in and correct him? Of course not, we don't discipline a kid that isn't ours! (And if someone else did try and intervene in that situation, well, Mama bears everywhere would be on him like white on rice!) In the same way, the times we disobey and experience consequential discipline is an encouragement because it proves we belong to the Lord. And if someone can live in flagrant disobedience for a prolonged period of time without the Lord's discipline, well, that would make me question whose kid they are!

Next, what does the discipline of the Lord show us? That He loves us. I'll bet you're like I am in that you don't enjoy correcting your children and meting out consequences. But we do it because we love our kids, and we don't want them to continue wrong behavior. We know that an undisciplined child turns out to be a bratty adult. An adult that didn't receive appropriate discipline as a child is not only difficult to be around but he/she never reaches full life potential. It's actually a tragedy. So, as good parents, we subject ourselves to the temporarily unpleasant task of disciplining our children because we know that such action will eventually reap great benefit to this one we love so much.

On that note, the last encouragement about discipline is that it bears good fruit. We learn very quickly that certain choices bring certain results and that drives our behavior. Discipline keeps us from sin–which reaps a harvest of happy holiness in our lives!

No one likes the present tense of discipline. But, take heart, if we will let it train us, we will enjoy its peaceful fruit forever. Amen!

Day 3

Beloved, do not be surprised at the fiery trial when it comes upon you to test you, as though something strange were happening to you. But rejoice insofar as you share Christ's sufferings, that you may also rejoice and be glad when his glory is revealed. I Peter 4:12-13

We've looked at suffering that Christians experience because they are living righteous lives. Oftentimes, the darkness lashes out at us because it hates the Light. We also pondered the suffering that comes into our lives because God is disciplining us and training us to live righteously and holy. We will take encouragement from the truth that such discipline assures us of who we belong to and that He loves us and is correcting us for our blessing.

But sometimes, we suffer just because we live in a fallen world. Not everything is a result of our wrong choices or the reaction of the darkness. Sometimes, we experience suffering because this world is broken. And scripture wants to be sure we understand that such suffering is part of "the abundant life" that Jesus promised. Not all cancer gets cured. Not every kid turns out to be a superstar. Not every accident gets circumvented. Not all believers enjoy financial luxury. And, contrary to what some so-called Christians would have you believe, Jesus never promised us that would be the case. In fact, He warned us just the opposite. He said to expect difficulties and trials and heartache. He said that was normal, not unusual.

But, again, He says to rejoice. To the extent that we share in these sufferings–these same hurts and disappointments and mistreatments that Jesus experienced–to that extent, we rejoice. We will have the opportunity for His glory to be revealed.

Does God send the suffering? Well, that's the million-dollar question. God is not the author of evil (I John 1:5). But make no mistake about it, He is sovereign. He is completely able to prevent any evil or misfortune or unhappiness from ever gracing the life of a believer. And sometimes, He does! In those times, we are quick to see His benevolent hand and give Him praise.

But sometimes, it seems, He does not. Babies die. Mommies get cancer. Hard-working dads lose their jobs. Missionaries get killed in tsunamis…or die as martyrs. Where is God then? Why does it look like He didn't show up at those times?

I do not have a quick word that can sufficiently explain it all so easily. Not at all.

But I ask you, I ask us, in those times of suffering when there is no explanation that suffices or no reason that brings peace, I ask us to trust Him. To know that His purposes are good and they supersede those of the enemy who wills evil. Trust that He is walking through the fiery trial with us, comforting us, equipping us, and sustaining us. Remember that others are watching to see how we handle it and this is our opportunity to show what a treasure He is.

And one day, one glorious day, that suffering will secure for us the eternal weight of glory (2 Corinthians 4:17,18). Amen.

Day 4 - Sermon on the Mount

You are the salt of the earth, but if salt has lost its taste, how shall its saltiness be restored? It is no longer good for anything except to be thrown out and trampled under people's feet. You are the light of the world. A city set on a hill cannot be hidden. Nor do people light a lamp and put it under a basket, but on a stand, and it gives light to all in the house. In the same way, let your light shine before others, so that they may see your good works and give glory to your Father who is in heaven. Matthew 5:13-16

You are the salt of the earth, but if salt has lost its taste, how shall its saltiness be restored? It is no longer good for anything except to be thrown out and trampled under people's feet.

If you're on a low sodium diet, you might be inclined to think that salt is bad and to be avoided. So this passage would seem odd and out of place. Let's take a look at the context in which it was written and understand what salt meant to the listeners in Jesus's day...

Salt was very valuable. In fact, it was often the means of payment for day laborers (ever heard the term " a man worth his salt" to describe a good worker?). Unlike the table salt we are accustomed to using at dinner today, salt in Bible times was found in varying degrees of purity and therefore had differing uses accordingly. The general purposes of salt were medicinal (kill germs), preservative (prevent decay), and seasoning. When salt had begun to lose its saltiness—its savor—it was then strewn over the ground as a path covering.

That's the context in which Jesus's listeners would have received the admonition to be salt. As His followers, we are to be salty—to provide healing in the lives of others, to stop the spread of corruption in the world, and to make others thirsty for Jesus by tasting our lives. If we stop being salty, we lose out on these opportunities and just get walked on.

What are some specific ways this week that you and I can be salt with savor? Can we provide a listening ear to a hurting friend and encourage her to seek God's solutions to her pain? Can we contact our congressman and take a stand against abortion? Maybe we can become a foster family for a child that otherwise would be alone. Or let our unbelieving neighbor see the joy we have in serving them...for Him.

As we end today, I want to point out one more thing. These verses are often read in isolation and that's fine. But notice the impact they have when we realize they follow what Jesus just said about rejoicing when we experience persecution. The placement of this passage is not a coincidence. Divine inspiration put them in exactly this place...maybe Jesus is making the point the way we respond to unjust treatment is an opportunity to impact the world...to be salt and light...or not...

Day 5

You are the salt of the earth, but if salt has lost its taste, how shall its saltiness be restored? It is no longer good for anything except to be thrown out and trampled under people's feet. You are the light of the world. A city set on a hill cannot be hidden. Nor do people light a lamp and put it under a basket, but on a stand, and it gives light to all in the house. In the same way, let your light shine before others, so that they may see your good works and give glory to your Father who is in heaven. Matthew 5:13-16

You are the light of the world. A city set on a hill cannot be hidden. Nor do people light a lamp and put it under a basket, but on a stand, and it gives light to all in the house. In the same way, let your light shine before others, so that they may see your good works and give glory to your Father who is in heaven.

Light. What do we know about light?

That it dispels darkness. The two cannot occupy the same space. Darkness tries to overtake the light but light always wins. If there is light in a place—even small or faint—then there cannot be darkness there.

Light also provides direction; it illumines the path we walk. Not only direction, but also confidence and security, when we can see where we are going. And warmth, light brings warmth.

Ponder those things as we unpack this passage…

The word translated as *"light"* here is the Greek word *"phos."* This is the light of the sun, not the moon or light from fire. This is significant because the light from the sun is neither kindled nor quenched and this is the same word that Jesus used in John 8:12 when He describes Himself as *"the light of the world."* Pretty obvious that He wants us to connect that He is our source for this light—in fact, it is HE who shines through us to scatter the darkness, to light up the way to go, and to offer warmth and security.

And like a city is "set"—placed deliberately—on a hill where it will be visible to all, our lives are not to be hidden. Like the purpose of a lamp is to be put in a place where it can be seen so that it can do what it is designed to do, so our lives should be on display. But a word of caution here—Jesus is very clear that the purpose of the light is not to call attention to itself but rather to glorify our Father, the source from which our light comes.

Where is your light shining today? Have you foolishly hidden your light with deeds of darkness or from cowardly fear? Let me suggest, as Jesus says, to let our lights shine first within our own homes…to give light to all who are in the house.

WEEK 42 - RELATIONSHIPS

Day 1

You have heard that it was said to those of old, "You shall not murder; and whoever murders will be liable to judgment." But I say to you that everyone who is angry with his brother will be liable to judgment; whoever insults his brother will be liable to the council; and whoever says, "You fool!" will be liable to the hell of fire. So if you are offering your gift at the altar and there remember that your brother has something against you, leave your gift there before the altar and go. First be reconciled to your brother, and then come and offer your gift. Come to terms quickly with your accuser while you are going with him to court, lest your accuser hand you over to the judge, and the judge to the guard, and you be put in prison. Truly, I say to you, you will never get out until you have paid the last penny. Matthew 5:21-26

At first glance, it might seem as though Jesus is saying here to do away with the Old Testament law and replace it with His New Testament teaching. *"You have heard...but I say"* is repeated after this passage at least six times just in the next few verses!

Let's see if that is indeed what the scriptures say, as the very best commentary on scripture is always scripture itself. In other words, look at the Bible as a whole. Know that it does not contradict itself ever; if you find a passage where it seems to, then dig in some more until the meaning is clear because scripture corroborates itself, not contradicts!

First, look up a few verses from where we are in Matthew 5 to verses 17-19. What is Jesus saying here?

What is 'the Law' that is referred to here? The commands that God gave Moses for the Israelites–these are found in the Old Testament books of Exodus and Leviticus primarily.

Since that clearly tells us that Jesus is not giving instructions that conflict with the Law of Moses, we have to dig deeper and see what *"you have heard...but I say"* means. Read Galatians 3:21-26 to see the purpose of the Law:

So the purpose of the Law is to show us the holiness of God and to reveal to us our inability to meet His standards...and therefore we see our need for a Savior. Between the time of the giving of the law and the appearance of Jesus, people faced the same desperate need that we have today–that of how to bridge the gap between God's holiness and our sin. Since they, like us, could not ever keep the law, their leaders added their own interpretations (*"you have heard"*) in an attempt to make themselves feel better about reaching a standard of holiness. In these statements, Jesus is explaining the intent of the law...and showing how only He can change a heart and provide the grace that fulfills the requirements of God's holiness.

Day 2

You have heard that it was said to those of old, "You shall not murder; and whoever murders will be liable to judgment." But I say to you that everyone who is angry with his brother will be liable to judgment; whoever insults his brother will be liable to the council; and whoever says, "You fool!" will be liable to the hell of fire. So if you are offering your gift at the altar and there remember that your brother has something against you, leave your gift there before the altar and go. First be reconciled to your brother, and then come and offer your gift. Come to terms quickly with your accuser while you are going with him to court, lest your accuser hand you over to the judge, and the judge to the guard, and you be put in prison. Truly, I say to you, you will never get out until you have paid the last penny. Matthew 5:21-26

To get a refresher on the law, read Exodus 20:1-18. This contains what we commonly call "The Ten Commandments" and is what the subsequent ordinances and ceremonial laws are based upon. It is quite easy to deceive ourselves and think we are keeping these commands—not guilty of murder or adultery and no statues of idols lying around. But Jesus's words pierce straight into our spirits and we see the deeper intent of the law...and we realize our innocence is not so sure at all.

This passage takes Exodus 20:13 and explains it. What is the command given here?

We would all agree that murder (not self-defense or accidental killings but murder) is wrong and deserving of punishment. But it sounds like Jesus is equating that with anger and insults! Can it be?

Let's dig deeper. Look up these passages and then let's answer some questions together.

- James 4:1-2

- Matthew 12:34-37

- James 3:6

What causes murder?
What is revealed by our words?
What is the seat of behavior?

This command that Christ explains shows us clearly that murder is hideous because it contradicts the value God places on life...because HE is LIFE. Only God has the right to the power of life and death, and to murder is to put ourselves in God's place. Calling someone a "fool" devalues him in an attempt to elevate ourselves as judge. That is never to be our place.

And He issues a warning—Jesus is telling us that our heart is what directs our actions and that because murder begins with anger in the heart, that is where we must deal with it. It's serious business.

Close out today with some encouragement and read Romans 8:3-4.

Day 3

You have heard that it was said to those of old, "You shall not murder; and whoever murders will be liable to judgment." But I say to you that everyone who is angry with his brother will be liable to judgment; whoever insults his brother will be liable to the council; and whoever says, "You fool!" will be liable to the hell of fire. So if you are offering your gift at the altar and there remember that your brother has something against you, leave your gift there before the altar and go. First be reconciled to your brother, and then come and offer your gift. Come to terms quickly with your accuser while you are going with him to court, lest your accuser hand you over to the judge, and the judge to the guard, and you be put in prison. Truly, I say to you, you will never get out until you have paid the last penny. Matthew 5:21-26

So if you are offering your gift at the altar and there remember that your brother has something against you, leave your gift there before the altar and go. First be reconciled to your brother, and then come and offer your gift. Come to terms quickly with your accuser while you are going with him to court, lest your accuser hand you over to the judge, and the judge to the guard, and you be put in prison. Truly, I say to you, you will never get out until you have paid the last penny.

SO–Jesus links the warning of anger towards a brother with the need to restore a relationship. And He underscores the importance of right relationships by prioritizing it above giving gifts at church! Wow!

The first thing that jumps out at me here is "*that your brother has something against you.*" Note that it does not say, "if you have wronged your brother." In other words, is someone offended with you, in spite of the fact that you do not feel you have done anything wrong? Is there a relationship that is strained or in disrepair? As in–if you rounded the aisle at Publix and bumped your buggy into a certain someone, would your stomach knot up? Would theirs?

If any person came to mind, then I think it is clear what Jesus is saying. Before you put your tithe in the plate on Sunday or keep nursery on Wednesday or any of the things you do that are a gift of service to Him, go to your brother or sister. Even if (especially if!) you feel like you are in the right. Go to that person. Not to defend yourself but rather to demonstrate that you value the relationship–and them–greatly. Listen to their heart...and their hurt. Be willing to absorb their pain and anger; be willing to be misunderstood, even if it costs you. Take the high road, as my husband says, take the high road. If given the opportunity, explain yourself but be very careful. Such "explanation" often sounds like "defense" to the hearer. So be very careful here. You don't want to do more damage.

The goal is to restore the relationship, not to prove you're right.

Value the other person.

Jesus does.

Day 4

If possible, so far as it depends on you, live peaceably with all. Romans 12:18

The last couple of days have dealt with relationships from the standpoint of our own hearts. We know that Jesus wants us to take the responsibility and the initiative for being right with others. We know that our relationship with others is a barometer for our relationship with Him. And so we strive to keep our heart right towards others and to pursue restoration when there is a breach.

But sometimes, no matter what we do, things just don't work out well. The fissure remains. The angst persists.

That is hard.

One of the many reasons I love God's Word so much is that it is really applicable. Not theoretical or idealistic. It goes from the pew to the pavement and stands the test. Well.

That's what happens in this verse in Romans. Look at it again, "*if possible* (because sometimes it isn't)–*so far as it depends on you* (relationships are not one-sided: two people are involved)." God knows that sometimes things can't be restored. The other person might be unwilling no matter what we try, or unreachable, or even dead. So, He wants us to know, we can still be at peace. When we've done all He says to do, when we can stand before His throne with confidence that we have forgiven and obeyed and pursued, then He says, "Be at peace, my daughter. Rest, my child. You have been faithful in what I called you to...all is well."

If you have such a relationship, or even know of one, pray right now. Ask the God of peace to speak to your heart. And rest.

Amen.

Day 5

Beloved, never avenge yourselves, but leave it to the wrath of God, for it is written, "Vengeance is mine, I will repay, says the Lord." To the contrary, "if your enemy is hungry, feed him; if he is thirsty, give him something to drink; for by so doing you will heap burning coals on his head." Do not be overcome by evil, but overcome evil with good. Romans 12:19-21

Just one more thought to close out this week on relationships–how to respond when we are wronged. Goodness knows we are going to be!

God is very clear about how we are to behave–do not seek revenge. Do not strive to inflict harm or injury as payment for an injury received or a wrong suffered. Maybe we wouldn't go so far as to inflict bodily harm to someone that had hurt us (or our child–bless their heart!) but what about doing damage to their reputation, or their happiness, or their self-esteem? What about withholding forgiveness from them and at least giving them the cold shoulder?

Yeah, well, that's another story.

Well, actually, the rest of the story is that God says not only are we not to seek revenge but He instructs us to go out of our way to do good to the perpetrator!

Whaaaaaaaaaat?

Yes. What.

I used to think that God was telling us to do good to our enemies and in so doing, we would bring pain on them–burning coals on the head. Sounds awful, doesn't it? And I was motivated by that! Well, sure, if this is going to hurt them for hurting me, well, I'll be glad to be "nice" to them! Burn 'em up, Lord!

Wrong.

That is not what God is saying at all. The picture here is that of a person with a pan of coals on his head, taking them from his own fire to light a fire for another.

See what God is saying now? By showing kindness to those who have wronged us, we are taking the light of His love–the truth of the gospel–to them in hopes that the embers of His love that we share will kindle His love in the heart of one who is cold to His love.

That's the gospel.

That's what Jesus does for us.

That's what He wants us to do for others.

Day 1

Beware of practicing your righteousness before other people in order to be seen by them, for then you will have no reward from your Father who is in heaven. "Thus, when you give to the needy, sound no trumpet before you, as the hypocrites do in the synagogues and in the streets, that they may be praised by others. Truly, I say to you, they have received their reward. But when you give to the needy, do not let your left hand know what your right hand is doing, so that your giving may be in secret. And your Father who sees in secret will reward you. "And when you pray, you must not be like the hypocrites. For they love to stand and pray in the synagogues and at the street corners, that they may be seen by others. Truly, I say to you, they have received their reward. But when you pray, go into your room and shut the door and pray to your Father who is in secret. And your Father who sees in secret will reward you. "And when you pray, do not heap up empty phrases as the Gentiles do, for they think that they will be heard for their many words. Do not be like them, for your Father knows what you need before you ask him. Matthew 6:1-8

Beware of practicing your righteousness before other people in order to be seen by them, for then you will have no reward from your Father who is in heaven

It's hard not to seek affirmation from people, isn't it? We think we are great about obeying the Lord and then we have to be careful to check our hearts and be sure that our motive is to please Him, not to impress others!

Read Galatians 1:10 and note what it says:

Our approval must come from God, not man. In this section of the Sermon on the Mount, Jesus covers three types of righteous acts that can be done with unrighteous agendas: giving, praying, and fasting. He is instructing us that these are important facets of our spiritual life, that we should be active in doing these activities, and that there are blessings (rewards!) in doing them! WOW–can you even believe that God is going to reward us for obeying Him? But we digress...back to practicing our righteousness before men.

How like the enemy of our souls to try to deceive us, divert us, and distract us from the joy of obedience by tempting us to "look good" so that others will praise us! Jesus is quite aware of this temptation so He warns us "beware."

Can you think of a time you have given or prayed or even fasted so that someone else would affirm you?

Day 2 - Giving

"Thus, when you give to the needy, sound no trumpet before you, as the hypocrites do in the synagogues and in the streets, that they may be praised by others. Truly, I say to you, they have received their reward. But when you give to the needy, do not let your left hand know what your right hand is doing, so that your giving may be in secret. And your Father who sees in secret will reward you. Matthew 6:2-4

God is very clear in His Word that His people are to give. Look up these verses for some of those instructions and note what you learn:

- Deuteronomy 15:7-11

- Proverbs 11:24-25

- Malachi 3:8-12

- 2 Corinthians 9:1-12

Did it stand out to you that God promises great blessing to us when we are obedient in giving?

If the enemy can't stop our giving, then he at least wants to thwart the blessing. So he tempts us to give in order to be noticed by others: a name on a plaque or in a bulletin, a public word of thanks from the pastor or ministry leader, or admission into a certain "donors list."

And if that is what motivates our giving, well, Jesus says we need to understand that it will be the only reward we get.

Pretty temporary. Quite fleeting. Paltry.

Let's aim for higher than that...the praise of God himself!

Day 3 - Praying

"And when you pray, you must not be like the hypocrites. For they love to stand and pray in the synagogues and at the street corners, that they may be seen by others. Truly, I say to you, they have received their reward. But when you pray, go into your room and shut the door and pray to your Father who is in secret. And your Father who sees in secret will reward you. And when you pray, do not heap up empty phrases as the Gentiles do, for they think that they will be heard for their many words. Do not be like them, for your Father knows what you need before you ask him." Matthew 6:5-8

Is Jesus prohibiting praying out loud before others?

No, He's not. He Himself prayed publicly so this cannot possibly be His warning. No, He is telling His listeners (and us) to beware about our motivation. And to reveal to us that prayer is communion between God and the individual, so intimacy is required. Even when we are "leading others in prayer" or speaking a blessing over our food in public, we must remember that the object of our communication is God. Not to impress others with our spirituality. When the bulk of our praying is done in private, we are blessed, transformed, and rewarded. And *"your Father who sees in secret will reward you"* when we pray with the awareness that we have come into the presence of our holy and powerful God and when we are worshipping Him in spirit and in truth…that is prayer. And that changes us. We learn as we practice praying to align ourselves with His Word, to desire what He desires, and to ask for His will, not our own.

What about the *"empty phrases"* mentioned here, or *"meaningless repetition"* as some translations put it? What does Jesus mean with that? The issue here is not persistence—there are numerous places where Jesus exhorts us to pray without ceasing, to pray and not give up, and to keep on asking. So "repetition" does not imply perseverance. Instead, Jesus is telling us not to use words and phrases that are merely that—just words and phrases without a consciousness of intimacy with the Father. Sometimes, we honestly might as well be reciting nursery rhymes for as much meaning as some of our prayers have in them! In fact, the verses containing what is sometimes called "The Lord's Prayer" were not meant to be repeated thoughtlessly as though they contain a magic formula for prayers. Instead, we learned earlier when we went through this passage that this is a model prayer, a guide for coming into the presence of God and seeking Him.

Prayer—a vital component of our relationship with God. Not a stage for flaunting our piety before others.

One last thought on how God sees our prayers. Just for fun, read Revelation 5:8 and 8:3-4 and note what you learn there:

Day 4 - Fasting

And when you fast, do not look gloomy like the hypocrites, for they disfigure their faces that their fasting may be seen by others. Truly, I say to you, they have received their reward. But when you fast, anoint your head and wash your face, that your fasting may not be seen by others but by your Father who is in secret. And your Father who sees in secret will reward you. Matthew 6:16-18

Just like with giving and praying, Jesus is communicating to us that these are the activities of His followers: when you give, when you pray, when you fast. Not "if." Clearly we are to be active in these pursuits, and in these passages Jesus tells us how, when, and where to do them!

Just as with the other spiritual disciplines of praying and giving, fasting is to be directed towards God Himself, not people. It evokes a spiritual giggle to think about how we can draw attention to ourselves when fasting—looking so haggard and pathetic from the lack of food that we make it obvious to those nearby that we are spiritual giants. Hungry giants, but giants all the same!

Let's take a couple of days to examine fasting. I think it is likely a much-neglected discipline (at least it is in my life!) so it warrants a bit more attention here.

Look up these passages and note what you learn from them about fasting. Tomorrow we will see how we can apply these truths to our personal lives.

- Daniel 6:18

- Daniel 9:3

- Daniel 10:2-3

- Matthew 4:1-2

- Esther 4:16

- Ezra 8:21-23

- Acts 13:2-3

- Acts 14:23

- Isaiah 58:1-12

Day 5 - Fasting

And when you fast, do not look gloomy like the hypocrites, for they disfigure their faces that their fasting may be seen by others. Truly, I say to you, they have received their reward. But when you fast, anoint your head and wash your face, that your fasting may not be seen by others but by your Father who is in secret. And your Father who sees in secret will reward you
Matthew 6:16-18

Let's dig in and see what fasting is, why we are to do it, and how to do it.

- What: Fasting is abstinence. Usually from food but it can be from anything. (OK so it should be something we find desirable or helpful–if I declare I am fasting from housework, that doesn't cut it).

- Why: God calls us to fast so that we can pull back from the routine preoccupations of our body or soul in order to gain greater intimacy with Him. Fasting is an opportunity for deeper, more serious communion with the Lord because we are denying ourselves the pleasures we are accustomed to and therefore able to focus more intently on Him. Specific situations can give rise to a need to fast: deep sorrow, serious illness, a need for wisdom or guidance, the desire for God's help and protection, spiritual warfare. Just like giving and praying, though, fasting can be done with a selfish motivation in our hearts–to be noticed and admired by others.

- How: With a heart to seek God and know Him, to commune deeply with Him–not to manipulate Him to meet our demands nor to fulfill a superficial need for recognition by others.

Spend the rest of your time with the Lord today asking Him how He wants you to apply what you have learned about fasting. Perhaps He will direct you to a regular time to abstain from food each week. (Just FYI - I usually follow the Jewish tradition of fasting from evening meal to evening meal when doing a daily fast). Or He may whisper to you that you should fast from social media or technology for a time. (Just beware of proclaiming your fast in a self-righteous FB post–that would sort of defeat the purpose!)

Ask Him. He will speak to you. He desires rich fellowship with each of us...He will respond.

Write out what you hear Him say.

Then obey Him.

Day 1

Do not lay up for yourselves treasures on earth, where moth and rust destroy and where thieves break in and steal, but lay up for yourselves treasures in heaven, where neither moth nor rust destroys and where thieves do not break in and steal. For where your treasure is, there your heart will be also. Matthew 6:19-21

The command here is clear, something to do and something not to do: do not lay up treasures on earth and do lay up treasures in heaven. We can glide right over this directive and figure that we are doing OK since we give to church and often other ministries.

Let's not let ourselves off so easily...

First thing to notice is that "treasure-storing" is exclusive. Whatever we lay up in one place, means that it cannot be stored in the other. So Jesus says to choose well–He wants us to be intentional about our investments. The treasures that we lay up here are not secure, no matter how well protected we might think they are. Conversely, the treasures that are laid up in heaven cannot be stolen or decayed–they are literally eternally secure.

To start us off, what is a treasure? The dictionary says is it something (or someone) that we prize and value, something we consider worth our time, attention, and energy.

Three questions:

- What does it mean to lay up treasures on earth?

- What does it mean to lay up treasures in heaven?

- How can we follow this command?

While the first question needs to be answered on a personal level, let's look at it together. How are we laying up earthly treasures? Is it our homes and their contents? Our portfolio? Our appearance?

To answer the second question, look up these verses and see what they say about treasure:

- Isaiah 33:6

- Matthew 19:21

- 2 Corinthians 4:7

How can we follow this command? By understanding that earth is not our home–heaven is. What we treasure is a fruit of our repentance (Luke 3:8-14). If you want to love what Jesus loves, start putting treasure in His home. Your heart will follow your treasure.

Day 2

The eye is the lamp of the body. So, if your eye is healthy, your whole body will be full of light, but if your eye is bad, your whole body will be full of darkness. If then the light in you is darkness, how great is the darkness! "No one can serve two masters, for either he will hate the one and love the other, or he will be devoted to the one and despise the other. You cannot serve God and money. Matthew 6:22-24

These verses seem to not be connected. In fact, it seems as though verse 24 belongs with yesterday's passage! But, in fact, they are all connected. They explain and expound on one another. Let's unpack them...

"The eye is the lamp of the body"—what does a lamp do? It provides light. So does the eye—it shines the way for us to walk. So if our eye is "healthy," we walk in light. However, if our eye is "bad," we walk in darkness.

One additional clue to understanding this passage is to see more about *"the eye"* in Matthew 20:15. What does that tell us about *"the eye"*?

This means that if our eye is fixed on or desires earthly treasures instead of embracing and valuing the mercy we have received from God, then we will be full of darkness...of evil. The "bad eye" desires earthly treasures, and focuses on what we don't have instead of what we do have...and that fills us with darkness.

But the good eye sees God and His ways as the great treasure in life. The good eye does not serve the urge to accumulate wealth because the good eye knows that our heart cannot be divided—we will either serve and value God, or we will serve and value money.

Chances are, this passage makes us uncomfortable. We hope it applies to those folks who are richer than we are and we convince ourselves that we are just being wise and careful with our money.

I don't know what guidelines to offer you. I do not know how much is enough, how much is too much, or what is being wise or foolish. Here's all I can offer—when we get to heaven, it won't matter how much we left on earth but only what we sent on ahead.

And we will be so glad for all we gave away; probably wishing we had given more.

I guess the universal principle is to ask the Lord if we need eye surgery to change our bad eye to a good one.

Day 3

Therefore I tell you, do not be anxious about your life, what you will eat or what you will drink, nor about your body, what you will put on. Is not life more than food, and the body more than clothing? Look at the birds of the air: they neither sow nor reap nor gather into barns, and yet your Heavenly Father feeds them. Are you not of more value than they? And which of you by being anxious can add a single hour to his span of life? And why are you anxious about clothing? Consider the lilies of the field, how they grow: they neither toil nor spin, yet I tell you, even Solomon in all his glory was not arrayed like one of these. But if God so clothes the grass of the field, which today is alive and tomorrow is thrown into the oven, will he not much more clothe you, O you of little faith? Therefore do not be anxious, saying, "What shall we eat?" or "What shall we drink?" or "What shall we wear?" For the Gentiles seek after all these things, and your Heavenly Father knows that you need them all. Matthew 6:25-32

As you read through this passage, remember what it follows–Jesus's exhortation to lay up treasures in heaven rather than on earth. He is responding to our tendency to feel more secure with trusting our lives to what we can see rather than what we cannot see. We more easily occupy our minds with what we can touch and do and see. And when we move outside that comfort zone, we can get anxious.

So Jesus gestures to the birds in the trees nearby and the beautiful lilies in the adjacent field to encourage His disciples...and us...not to worry. And not just about college funds and retirement portfolios but even down to the most basic of life's necessities–what to eat or drink or wear. He says do not even worry about those.

And the reason not to worry is twofold - one, because being anxious does not accomplish one single positive thing. Only negative, unproductive byproducts result from anxiety. Physical ailments, tangled emotions, and clouded thinking are some of the consequences of anxiety. But the greatest harm done by worry is the effect it has on our hearts. Worry is the greatest deterrent to giving because it is based on the illusion that earth is our home. Conversely, when we trust instead of worrying, something happens to the heart that increases its capacity for joy, for eternal joy.

The other reason not to worry is because faith in God is way more sure than faith in what we can see! And Jesus demonstrates that by calling our attention to the birds and flowers that are taken care of so faithfully, so beautifully, so abundantly. God is trustworthy. Fear is faith in the enemy; He bids us to let our faith in Him displace our fear.

Here's an assignment for today–stop by Publix and purchase a bouquet of lilies. Leave them on your bathroom counter so that each morning and evening you can be reminded of how well our Heavenly Father takes care of you.

And to exercise that trust this week, give something unexpected to bless someone. The bigger the better!

Day 4

But seek first the kingdom of God and his righteousness, and all these things will be added to you. Therefore do not be anxious about tomorrow, for tomorrow will be anxious for itself. Sufficient for the day is its own trouble. Matthew 6:33,34

"Replacement theology" is a fancy term that helps us understand that we can't successfully rid our hearts of the undesirable things unless we replace them with something desirable. So, in order not to worry or fear we need to actively focus on seeking God's kingdom instead. It is not helpful to tell our soul not to be anxious, but if we direct our energy to seeking God and His righteousness, we will find that fear displaced. Jon Bloom of Desiring God puts it this way, "Fear for tomorrow kills our faith for today. So, having faith for today often means killing fear for tomorrow."

Satan wants to rob us of joy today by getting us to stress out over an imaginary tomorrow. He whispers (or sometimes shouts!) "what if this" and "what if that" and he even taunts us with pain from the past, tempting us to think we know what tomorrow will bring, and it's not good. Why should we believe him? He doesn't know what tomorrow holds! His plans for us are death!

Jesus gently says, "No, do not be controlled by the fear of tomorrow." God only gives us grace for today. Yes, we will have troubles (John 16:33) but God gives us the power we need to live in peace and joy today. Not for tomorrow until it becomes today.

Fear for tomorrow not only robs us of the joy for today, it also diverts our energy from pursuing the work to build God's kingdom. When our hearts are occupied with protecting ourselves against an imaginary future, we are not free to enjoy God's gracious provision and direction for today. In essence, Jesus is saying, "You be focused on the works I have prepared for you to do for today and let me take care of all you need to do them!"

This can sound idealistic and "easy to say, hard to do." Jesus doesn't want that to be true for you and me. He wants our reality to be one of daily resting in His sufficient grace. He never promises to give us all that our greedy hearts think we want (see Philippians 4:12 and simultaneously praise His name for this truth!), but He does promise all the grace we need for joy and strength today. He promises grace for abundance and grace for need, grace for joy and grace for grief, grace for unexpected gifts and grace for painful disappointments, and grace for life and grace for death. Jesus gives us all we need and we can trust Him.

It takes practice. A choice on our part to transfer our cares to Him and divert our energy to obeying what He calls us to daily. But, just like we get better at playing the piano when we practice daily, so we will get better at trusting when we resolve to trust...and obey.

Close by reading I Peter 5:7 and rejoicing in that great truth.

Day 5

Rejoice in the Lord always; again I will say, rejoice. Let your reasonableness be known to everyone. The Lord is at hand; do not be anxious about anything, but in everything by prayer and supplication with thanksgiving let your requests be made known to God. And the peace of God, which surpasses all understanding, will guard your hearts and your minds in Christ Jesus. Philippians 4:4-7

We will finish out this week on anxiety with this most wonderful passage. Read through it at least three times and then list at least four things these verses tell us to do in order to combat worry.

•

•

•

•

I wish we were sitting across from one another, sharing a TAB and a piece of chocolate so you could share with me what you found! (You can email me, if you want to. I'd totally love that. chamfam@bellsouth.net) Did you find four things? I'll bet you found five!

Here's what I see God says to do in the fight against anxiety: rejoice in Him; rejoice in Him some more; be restrained and patient (instead of impetuous and out of control, jumping to all sorts of conclusions that are usually wrong); pray and pray specifically; thank God for His provision.

Let's unpack them:

• Rejoice in the Lord: Worry cannot occupy a heart that is rejoicing. We might not have circumstances to rejoice over but there is always cause to rejoice in the Lord. Beginning with His free gift of salvation to His abundant grace and faithfulness, to our ultimate eternity with Him, there is an inexhaustible list of reasons to rejoice in Him.

• Let your reasonableness be known to everyone: Do we stop and think about how our worry perpetuates worry, even fueling it in the lives of others? When we react with fear, wring our hands over "what if," and pretty much work ourselves into a frenzy, we do not solve the worry problem at all. So we need to stop it. Now.

• But in everything by prayer and supplication with thanksgiving let your requests be made known to God: Instead of worrying, pray. Specifically. Sounds almost trite, doesn't it? But how often do we neglect this command and just jump straight to panic? It's almost like we don't believe prayer has any impact! Pray. Pray about anything and everything. Tell God your requests—and trust that His answer (yes or no or wait) is the absolute best for you. Pray and remember what all He has already done, responding with thanksgiving.

And what happens? Peace. Peace that cannot be understood. Peace that will protect us from worry.

Day 1

Rejoice in the Lord always; again I will say, rejoice. Philippians 4:4

Have you ever stopped to realize that "joy" is a command for those who follow Christ? Being joyful isn't "icing on the cake" for Christians–Jesus intends it to be our way of life!

So He repeatedly instructs us accordingly; in this one letter to the believers at Philippi, the apostle Paul tells us, *"Finally, my brothers, rejoice in the Lord. To write the same things to you is no trouble to me and is a safeguard for you,"* (Philippians 3:1). In numerous other places in scripture He reveals to us that joy is not just His hope for us, but it is His intentional design. A few weeks ago, we looked up several verses on this very thing but let's review just a few now to remind ourselves that joy is not only possible in Christ, it is commanded! As you read these passages, note what they have to say about joy:

- John 10:10

- Romans 15:13

- John 13:17

- John 15:11

Yes, God's plan is for our joy. But what is joy? Is it happiness? Is it the happy endings that fairy tales are made of? Is it a facet of some personalities, an enthusiasm?

Let's dig in and see what we can learn about joy…

Joy is a feeling (yes, a feeling) of gladness that is brought about by being satisfied and content. Even in the midst of great sorrow, it is possible to have great joy.

The word we translate as "joy" from the original Greek text is "chairo." Its literal translation indicates a lamb skipping and jumping, carefree and happy. It is significant to note that this word comes from another Greek word "charis" which is usually translated as "grace." The meaning of "charis" is "the divine influence upon the heart"; it is the power God gives us to not only obey but to even want to in the first place! The fact that "chairo" is related to this word indicates that joy is a direct result of God's grace. Apart from Him, there can be no genuine joy. And in Him, there is joy overflowing!

Ladies, let's be real. There is a lot of pressure on us to be joyful. We know that is God's plan for us and we also know that we have tremendous influence on the joy of those around us (as in "if mama ain't happy, ain't nobody happy"!) Sometimes, we just do not have joy.

This week and next, we are going to sit at His feet and get equipped to be joyful women. You with me?

Day 2

I know that I will remain and continue with you all, for your progress and joy in the faith, so that in me you may have ample cause to glory in Christ Jesus, because of my coming to you again. Only let your manner of life be worthy of the gospel of Christ, so that whether I come and see you or am absent, I may hear of you that you are standing firm in one spirit, with one mind striving side by side for the faith of the gospel, and not frightened in anything by your opponents. This is a clear sign to them of their destruction, but of your salvation, and that from God. For it has been granted to you that for the sake of Christ you should not only believe in him but also suffer for his sake, engaged in the same conflict that you saw I had and now hear that I still have. Philippians 1:25-30

So we have established already that God's plan is for us to have joy. The next thing we need to see is found in this passage. It is a bit obscure so read through it a couple of times. Do you see in the first verse how Paul desires their growth (*"progress"*) and joy? He urges them to live a life worthy of the gospel, standing firm and without fear. Now dig into that last verse—there we see that not only progress in the faith, but also joy, is a fight!

Yes, dear sister, it is indeed a fight to maintain our joy in the Lord. On the one hand, that probably doesn't surprise you! In each of our lives, we undoubtedly have times where we do not experience joy. In spite of how we all long to be happy, sometimes it seems to elude us. We can even spiral down into depression and despair, seemingly helpless.

On the other hand, though, perhaps we do not give enough thought to the fact that maintaining our joy is a struggle. We have to fight to win our joy because Satan opposes us at every turn. His mission to steal, kill, and destroy includes his being in direct conflict with our joy. That is why he sends every obstacle imaginable into our path; these are his attempts to steal our joy.

Therefore, today's truth is for us to resolve to be good soldiers, to fight victoriously for joy, to stand firm in the hope that this is not only possible but also desirable. Evaluate yourself for a moment. Do you feel joy? Would those that live and work around you describe you as a joyful person? If yes, then hooray and hallelujah! Dig deeper into the well of salvation and know that God's joy for us is an endless source. You cannot plumb the depths of His joy!

However, if that does not describe you, if you feel depressed or even just empty, then what may be needed is a resolve to fight. Instead of seeking to be happy, ask the Lord to help you fight. Confess your disobedience to His command to rejoice in Him and turn your energy to combat training.

The first step to being a good soldier of Jesus…worship!

When we turn our eyes to the glory of God and Christ, the enemy scatters.

Close out your time today by singing aloud a hymn of praise. Or at least turn on some worship music!

Day 3

He was a murderer from the beginning and does not stand in the truth because there is no truth in him. Whenever he speaks a lie, he speaks from his own nature for he is a liar and the father of lies. John 8:44b

This verse is of course describing Satan. Jesus is explaining that we must be on guard against what comes from Satan's mouth because he speaks lies. We must be so careful not to put our trust in what he whispers because it will lead us into places of captivity and destruction.

Perhaps his most favorite tactic with those who follow Christ is to take scripture and twist it or add to it in some way. If we do not firmly know what truth looks like, we can be deceived into thinking that what he is saying to us is truth. Know this, dear sisters, most of Satan's attacks are against the character of God. He doesn't want us to know what God is like because he is fully aware that to know God is to love Him, to worship Him, to follow Him. So it is his mission to lie about God's character–His goodness, His holiness, His love, His faithfulness–so that we will base our behavior on a lie.

One particularly widespread lie is to make God seem like the Cosmic Kris Kringle.

Satan takes the truth of John 15:7 and tries to make it sound like "make a wish and God will make it come true!" Look up that verse and see what part he leaves out:

What do you think that passage means?

How do you think Satan makes it sound instead?

The enemy wants us to believe that God is our genie in a bottle, the giant Cosmic Kris Kringle to indulge our requests and get whatever we want "in His name." You can see how this leads to destruction! We have all seen people use this lie as justification for sin–"God wants me to be happy so this must be OK for me to do." And we have all seen, perhaps even experienced, the pain of doubt and dismay that comes when we ask God for something that we desperately want...and it doesn't come to pass as we hoped.

Just like Satan planned.

No, dear sister, God is not the Cosmic Kris Kringle. He is not promising us that we can have whatever we want so that we will be happy. Over the next couple of days, we will see the truth of who He is. For today, I want to be sure you immerse yourself into the truth of John 15:7. When we abide in–settle in, remain in, find our life in, receive–His words, this results not only in a change of behavior but also in a change in desire. We want what He wants...and that is what we ask for.

Read through John 15:7 again. Confess to the Lord that He is not the Cosmic Kris Kringle and ask Him to help you abide in Him. So that what you ask will be what He wants to give.

It's an exciting way to live, my friend!

Living Letters

Day 4

If Satan (whom I like to refer to as "The Defeated One") can't deceive you with the idea that God is our Cosmic Kris Kringle, then he might attempt to make you believe He is the Cosmic Killjoy. Instead of seeing God for who He really is, Satan lies to tell us we will have to forfeit all our hopes and dreams and desires to follow Jesus. He often uses the line, "God doesn't want me to be happy, He wants me to be holy." Oh, my, this is such a lie! Let's look at what happens to us when we act on this lie and then we will dwell on the truth:

Matthew 5:8 says, *"This people honors Me with their lips but their heart is far from Me."*

What that means is that we cannot continue to serve God with our whole heart if we see it as a duty of drudgery. Living a life of "martyrs" to joy will not only surely kill our joy but it will eventually develop a spirit of criticism, cynicism, and bitterness. We might say "the right things," the "spiritual" things, but if our heart is not satisfied in Christ, if it doesn't match what our lips are saying, we will not sustain "spiritual" behavior. Sooner or later, our actions will catch up to our heart.

Thankfully God does not want us to live this way! He is not the Cosmic Kris Kringle but He is also not the Cosmic Killjoy! Look up these two passages and write out what the Lord shows you in them:

* Deuteronomy 28:47-48

* John 5:40

Girlfriend, we are designed by God to have joy. Not just any joy–fullness of joy! And we are programmed from conception to seek to have that desire satiated. If we don't find it in Christ, we cannot help but continue to seek it elsewhere. In things that not only do not fully satisfy, they will actually enslave us. When our Heavenly Father tells us "no" it is not because He is killing our joy, but rather because He is keeping us from settling for less than what He has for us.

No longer let us fall for Satan's lies: God is neither Cosmic Kris Kringle nor Cosmic Killjoy–He is The Cosmic King! Lasting happiness comes when we see Him in the glory of His sovereignty and His love, and gladly arrange our lives around Him.

Bow before the King right now and pour out your heart. If you have thought of Him as "killjoy," requiring you to live as a martyr, tell Him the truth. (He knows it anyway–you just need to get it out of your heart!) Then soak yourself in His majesty, His power, and His goodness. He loves you!

Day 5

Though the fig tree should not blossom, nor fruit be on the vines, the produce of the olive fail and the fields yield no food, the flock be cut off from the fold and there be no herd in the stalls, yet I will rejoice in the Lord; I will take joy in the God of my salvation. Habakkuk 3:17-18

Joy. Not just any joy but joy that will sustain us when times are hard.

We spend a lot of time speculating "what if." What if I lose my job or what if that test result shows cancer? What if my children rebel or what if I never get to be a wife or a mom? What if my friendships betray me, or the car repairs are more than I have in the bank or my marriage dissolves? What will I do if this happens or that? And we can spiral down into despair over these imaginings if we are not careful.

Most of the time, our speculations never materialize beyond our imagination. And we do well to remember to "think only" on truth, not speculations!

But what about those times when the worst possible thing does happen? What about when the diagnosis is bad, the loss comes, or the dreaded fear becomes reality? What then?

The prophet Habakkuk covers that for us. He says even in times of great loss–no food, no source of sweet pleasure, not even any potential for income–it is possible to have joy. Habakkuk reminds us that our welfare, even our very existence, is not dependent on fig trees or olives or livestock, or paychecks or relationships or elected officials. Our existence, our joy, and our security is found in the self-existent I AM.

Knowing Him and His glory is the source of our joy and security. Even if all the circumstances of our lives should turn out to be the worst we could imagine, there is still cause for joy because God is in control and His purposes are love. He cares for us in our heartbreaks and He provides hope for us in our despair. Knowing Him–in the midst of suffering and disappointment–will sustain us. Knowing that He is faithful and worthy of our trust produces joy. Contentment. Satisfaction.

Even in the midst of great pain and loss.

When we resolve to rejoice in the God of our salvation even in, especially in, the midst of great fear and sad valleys, then we will find great strength. We will be able to say with the prophet Habakkuk, "*And He has made my feet like hinds feet and makes me walk on high places.*"

WEEK 46 - JOY: WHAT IF YOU DON'T HAVE JOY?

Day 1

Ahab told Jezebel all that Elijah had done, and how he had killed all the prophets with the sword. Then Jezebel sent a messenger to Elijah, saying, "So may the gods do to me and more also, if I do not make your life as the life of one of them by this time tomorrow." Then he was afraid, and he arose and ran for his life and came to Beersheba, which belongs to Judah, and left his servant there. But he himself went a day's journey into the wilderness and came and sat down under a broom tree. And he asked that he might die, saying, "It is enough; now, O Lord, take away my life, for I am no better than my fathers." And he lay down and slept under a broom tree. And behold, an angel touched him and said to him, "Arise and eat." And he looked, and behold, there was at his head a cake baked on hot stones and a jar of water. And he ate and drank and lay down again. And the angel of the Lord came again a second time and touched him and said, "Arise and eat, for the journey is too great for you." And he arose and ate and drank, and went in the strength of that food forty days and forty nights to Horeb, the mount of God. I Kings 19:1-8

Sometimes after the highs of our lives (wonderful blessings or even great spiritual victories as was the case with Elijah), we experience quite undesirable lows. How gracious of our God to include in His Holy Word this story of Elijah's journey from depression back to joy! Tucked into the book of I Kings is a prescription that we can use in our fight for joy. Let's see what is included in this passage...

Here's the background: Elijah, prophet of God, was witness and catalyst to a mighty display of God's glory. He invited the prophets of the false god Baal to a showdown between their god and the one true God. I hope that in eternity, God will pull back the curtain of time to let us witness this amazing event where God shows those misguided people who He is! Talk about a blaze of glory! (For the details, check out I Kings 18.)

In spite of this great victory, Elijah is human. And that means he is susceptible to doubt and fear. He falls prey to the temptation to fear what man could do to him (or in this case, a woman!) and he subsequently doubts God's care for him. In this state, he runs away from the problem, hides out, and prefers death to living this way. God shows such tender mercy to him! Instead of telling him to straighten up and face things like a man, God is so gentle, so kind, and so compassionate. Look up Psalm 103:13-14 for a reminder of how God sees us.

This passage above has a message for us about our own tendency to dip into depression. First, don't be taken off guard. Know that we are all vulnerable in this way and be intentional about resting in Him always, especially in the aftermath of those "mountaintop experiences."

But if you find yourself in the valley, take a page out of Elijah's story. Take care of your body. Sometimes the most spiritual thing we can do is to take a nap! We are physical beings, not just spiritual ones! And when our bodies are exhausted or ill, that can definitely take a toll on our spirit.

Day 2

Beloved, I urge you as aliens and strangers to abstain from fleshly lusts, which wage war against the soul. I Peter 2:11

Be of sober spirit, be on the alert. Your adversary, the devil, prowls about like a roaring lion, seeking someone to devour. I Peter 5:8

In the quest for joy, we are looking at some things that can be obstacles on our path. Yesterday we saw that scripture teaches us we are physical beings as well as spiritual and sometimes a sickness in our body can negatively impact our spirits. Today we are looking at two other roadblocks and how to re-route around them: sin and Satan.

Since we spent a lot of time recently on the enemy, let's not give him any more space except just to remember that he is out to get us. He definitely wants to steal our joy, but don't fret, he cannot do one single thing to you unless he has God's permission. And God will only grant the permission if He has a higher purpose. If you are experiencing the attacks of the enemy, don't forget that he doesn't want you to find total satisfaction in the Lord. He wants you to think you need something in addition to Him in order to be happy. And remember, also, that we ourselves grant Satan access to us when we allow sin to remain in our lives.

Sin. Gratifying the desires of the flesh. What seems like it will bring joy, actually wages war against our soul. We sin because we choose to. We choose sin because we want it. And we want it because it holds a deceitful promise of joy.

And it doesn't deliver on its promise.

The re-route to this obstacle is simple: stop sinning! If you are not experiencing the joy of your salvation, then listen to the Holy Spirit as you ask Him to reveal any sin that is there. It is the absolute mercies of God that He allows us to be miserable and to experience the loss of joy when we sin! Sin brings death and God is LIFE.

As far as the other roadblock, Satan, well, read the verses just after I Peter 5:8. Basically, God tells us through the apostle Peter to toughen up. Don't feel sorry for yourself–plenty of others have gone through the same things as you (and worse) and remained faithful.

Resist him, firm in your faith, knowing that the same kinds of suffering are being experienced by your brotherhood throughout the world. And after you have suffered a little while, the God of all grace, who has called you to his eternal glory in Christ, will himself restore, confirm, strengthen, and establish you. 1 Peter 5:9-10

Run to Him. Seek Him. Trust Him. Worship Him.

Sing Him a song and rest in Him. Stand firm in what you know to be true.

Sadness will flee.

Day 3

For we do not want you to be unaware, brethren, of our affliction which came to us in Asia, that we were burdened excessively, beyond our strength, so that we despaired even of life.
2 Corinthians 1:8

We have seen roadblocks on the route to happiness–sickness, sin, and Satan. Today let's look at another one: stuff.

Let's face it: "stuff" happens. Stuff happens like devastating circumstances that threaten to bury us in despair or maybe instead a slow leak that subtly but surely siphons off our joy and we find ourselves suddenly empty. What do we do about this kind of stuff? Can we still make it to joy even in the midst of stuff?

Scripture says yes!

First, when it comes to the stuff of devastating circumstances, 2 Corinthians 1 gives us two tips that reroute us around this obstacle to joy. Verses 9-11 tell us, *"Indeed, we felt that we had received the sentence of death. But that was to make us rely not on ourselves but on God who raises the dead. He delivered us from such a deadly peril, and he will deliver us. On him we have set our hope that he will deliver us again. You also must help us by prayer, so that many will give thanks on our behalf for the blessing granted us through the prayers of many."*

Do you see the tips that Paul encourages here?

He says that he and his companions felt like dying. Their stuff was so burdensome that they felt they could not take it, even to the point of preferring death to life. Things were bad. Maybe you've been at that same point, or perhaps you are even now.

Then you can find encouragement in the example of Paul. He didn't quit. He didn't remain in despair. He knew the truth–he could not rely on himself but he could rely on God. He trusted God, who can raise the dead, to pull him out of such a dark place of despair. He was not telling us that God will never let His children go through things that result in death–instead he is saying that even with the threat of death, even when things are so bad we would rather die, God is able to deliver us from despair. That is the deadly peril from which we need escape! And the key that unlocks that door is trust. Trust in God.

But that isn't all that Paul did and that's not all he encourages us to do.

He reached out to his friends and asked for their prayers. So many times we are reluctant to ask people to pray for us but that goes against the example here. We miss the power unleashed by the prayers of others and, perhaps more importantly, we rob them of the blessing of giving thanks when they see God answer!

And, for the rest of the story...did Paul's trust in God and the prayers of his friends result in his return to joy? Check out 2 Corinthians 7:4 and see what you think!

Day 4

And he told them many things in parables, saying: "A sower went out to sow. And as he sowed, some seeds fell along the path, and the birds came and devoured them. Other seeds fell on rocky ground, where they did not have much soil, and immediately they sprang up, since they had no depth of soil, but when the sun rose they were scorched. And since they had no root, they withered away. Other seeds fell among thorns, and the thorns grew up and choked them. Other seeds fell on good soil and produced grain, some a hundredfold, some sixty, some thirty. He who has ears, let him hear." Matthew 13:3-9

As for what was sown among thorns, this is the one who hears the Word, but the cares of the world and the deceitfulness of riches choke the Word, and it proves unfruitful. As for what was sown on good soil, this is the one who hears the Word and understands it. He indeed bears fruit and yields, in one case a hundredfold, in another sixty, and in another thirty. Matthew 13:22-23

Sometimes the stuff that threatens our joy is made up of devastating circumstances such as untimely death, desperate financial need, extreme persecution, or relational loss. Devastating circumstances indeed that push us to the point of despair.

But what about the "slow leaks" that siphon off our joy, that creep up on us a degree at a time until all of a sudden we are empty and desperate, seemingly without warning?

The above passage seems to apply here. Let's unpack it...

First, remember from Galatians 5:22 that joy is fruit, evidence that the Holy Spirit is unleashed in our lives, and we are walking according to His dictates. When joy is not present, that must mean that the Holy Spirit is being hindered in some way. Matthew 13:22 gives us the key we need to understand this. The lack of fruit (joy) is caused by the choking weeds that nullify the seed (the Word) that was sown in the soil (the heart). These thorns? They are the cares of the world and the deceitfulness of riches. That is what often chokes out our joy.

What cares of the world are robbing you of joy? Matthew 6:25-34 tells us not to be burdened by the cares of the world! Maybe for you and me, it's not so much where the next meal is coming from but how to get it on the table! Let us trust God with every detail of our lives so that we do not have our joy drained out of us, a thimbleful at a time!

And what about the deceitfulness of riches? That surely is a trap! Remember 1 Timothy 6:8-11 tells us, *"If we have food and clothing, with these we will be content. But those who desire to be rich fall into temptation, into a snare, into many senseless and harmful desires that plunge people into ruin and destruction. For the love of money is a root of all kinds of evils. It is through this craving that some have wandered away from the faith and pierced themselves with many pangs. But as for you, O man of God, flee these things. Pursue righteousness, godliness, faith, love, steadfastness, gentleness."*

Jump right over the obstacles of cares of the world and the deceitfulness of riches as you instead pursue Christ!

Living Letters

Day 5

My people have changed their glory for that which does not profit. Be appalled, O heavens, at this; be shocked, be utterly desolate, declares the Lord, for my people have committed two evils: they have forsaken me, the fountain of living waters, and hewed out cisterns for themselves, broken cisterns that can hold no water. Jeremiah 2:11-13

Obstacles to joy on the road to happiness: sickness, sin, Satan, stuff...and what else?

Substitutes.

Our "*glory*" is our essence, what we are "worth." The prophet Jeremiah warns us that we will be tempted to sell ourselves (our glory) for that which is worthless–that which does not profit. Can you think of ways we do that? CS Lewis is famous for saying "we are far too easily pleased." In other words, we settle for what we think will make us happy (a new house, a more fit self, a relationship, status in the eyes of others) instead of longing for the fountain of living waters, God Himself.

Is God saying we cannot have any of these things? Not at all. Look up James 1:16-17 and I Timothy 6:17 and note what you think about things in our lives other than Christ.

God gives good gifts, doesn't He? So that we can richly enjoy them, absolutely! Where we get in trouble is when we long for the gifts instead of the giver. But nothing is a suitable substitute. Nothing else brings lasting joy.

Joy is only found in one place.

You will make known to me the path of life; in YOUR presence is fullness of joy; in YOUR right hand there are pleasures forever. Psalm 16:11

Why do we bother to look anywhere else?

End our time together today by visualizing yourself before the throne. Bask in His holiness, His love, and His majesty. Praise Him with a song–especially out loud!

Day 1

As a deer pants for flowing streams, so pants my soul for you, O God. My soul thirsts for God, for the living God. When shall I come and appear before God? My tears have been my food day and night, while they say to me all the day long, "Where is your God?" These things I remember, as I pour out my soul: how I would go with the throng and lead them in procession to the house of God with glad shouts and songs of praise, a multitude keeping festival. Why are you cast down, O my soul, and why are you in turmoil within me? Hope in God; for I shall again praise him, my salvation and my God. My soul is cast down within me; therefore I remember you from the land of Jordan and of Hermon, from Mount Mizar. Deep calls to deep at the roar of your waterfalls; all your breakers and your waves have gone over me. By day the Lord commands his steadfast love, and at night his song is with me, a prayer to the God of my life. I say to God, my rock: "Why have you forgotten me? Why do I go mourning because of the oppression of the enemy?" As with a deadly wound in my bones, my adversaries taunt me, while they say to me all the day long, "Where is your God?" Why are you cast down, O my soul, and why are you in turmoil within me? Hope in God; for I shall again praise him, my salvation and my God. Psalm 42

There will inevitably be times in our walks with the Lord where we feel dry. Times when we cannot shake the discouragement or even apathy, times when we wonder where God is and why our relationship feels empty. How I praise God for His glorious empathy for us! He does not leave us in this desert to find our way back to Him on our own and alone! In the treasure of His Word, He gives us the truth and grace we need to survive the desert and also to return to the fountains of living water. The psalms are a vivid example that God validates the importance of our emotions; He gives us the psalms to help us express, shape, and sanctify our emotions. In this psalm, the writer reveals to us that he is in heartbreaking and devastating circumstances. He feels abandoned by God and pummeled by his enemies. Even though he is fighting to hold onto hope, the end of the psalm doesn't tell us that he has gotten out of the hole completely. What a refreshment that is to any of us who have battled discouraging times, who have felt empty and hopeless, who have wondered if God had walked away. And we know that there is no quick fix to this! Such truthful transparency in scripture is rich and so helpful to us! Here's what we can take away from this passage:

- The psalmist knows deep down that what he really longs for is intimacy with God, and that circumstances cannot be responsible for his joy (verse 1).

- He does not deny the pain he feels. It's as though he is expressing the healthy need to "get it all out" but he wisely realizes that the only healthy place to pour it out is before the Lord.

- In spite of some understandable emotional hyperbole (verses 6,7,9,10), the psalmist recalls the faithfulness of God and his joy in Him (verse 4), and keeps focusing his heart towards his only hope.

Next time we feel down or dry, let's commit to read and re-read Psalm 42 until we feel hope creeping in!

Day 2

Fret not yourself because of evildoers; be not envious of wrongdoers! For they will soon fade like the grass and wither like the green herb. Trust in the Lord, and do good; dwell in the land and befriend faithfulness. Delight yourself in the Lord, and he will give you the desires of your heart. Commit your way to the Lord; trust in him, and he will act. He will bring forth your righteousness as the light, and your justice as the noonday. Be still before the Lord and wait patiently for him; fret not yourself over the one who prospers in his way, over the man who carries out evil devices! Refrain from anger, and forsake wrath! Fret not yourself; it tends only to evil. For the evildoers shall be cut off, but those who wait for the Lord shall inherit the land. In just a little while, the wicked will be no more, though you look carefully at his place, he will not be there but the meek shall inherit the land and delight themselves in abundant peace.
Psalm 37:1-11

Fret not yourself because of evildoers; be not envious of wrongdoers! For they will soon fade like the grass and wither like the green herb. Trust in the Lord, and do good; dwell in the land and befriend faithfulness.

If we forget to look up instead of looking around us, we can surely get bothered...even to the point of envy. Have you ever felt like that old adage "nice guys finish last" was true? All around us we can see evidence of folks whose lives don't honor the Lord and they seem to be doing just fine! Even better than we are, truth be told. And it is just plain irritating, if we're honest about it!

"Do not fret" is more than just "don't worry." It includes the bubbling up of resentment and worry, which is what we can tend toward when we sense a lack of fairness. When those who are doing wrong seem to be winning, well, we often experience what we'd like to call "righteous anger" but deep down we are just plain mad. Why doesn't God do something about this? Why does He let it continue instead of giving them what they deserve? This psalm reminds us not to fret. Do not let that resentment evolve into anger. Don't do it. Here's why...

Instead, he urges us to trust the Lord. One day, God will set it all aright. Each one of us will receive the payment we are due. For those who don't know him, any pleasure or ease they experienced on this earth will be a distant memory. Gone like summer's grass in winter. Gone. Trust the faithfulness and integrity of the Lord. He is going to set it all straight one day.

And since we can trust Him to give the wrongdoers what they are entitled to, we can also know that we can trust Him to reward us for the good done for Him. Since our righteousness is from Christ, we will not have to pay the debt of sin we owe. But even beyond that, we will also receive rewards! So, He urges us through this passage and others to trust His faithfulness, and to do good and know that He who sees everything will reward us. Wherever we are is our opportunity to be faithful in doing good to those He has placed around us.

Today, ask Him to open your eyes to what you can do to bless others. Turn focus away from those that seem to be breaking the rules and still winning. Dwell in the land–don't try to escape unpleasant circumstances–and befriend faithfulness. Beginning today.

Day 3

Fret not yourself because of evildoers; be not envious of wrongdoers! For they will soon fade like the grass and wither like the green herb. Trust in the Lord, and do good; dwell in the land and befriend faithfulness. Delight yourself in the Lord, and he will give you the desires of your heart. Commit your way to the Lord; trust in him, and he will act. He will bring forth your righteousness as the light, and your justice as the noonday. Be still before the Lord and wait patiently for him; fret not yourself over the one who prospers in his way, over the man who carries out evil devices! Refrain from anger, and forsake wrath! Fret not yourself; it tends only to evil. For the evildoers shall be cut off, but those who wait for the Lord shall inherit the land. In just a little while, the wicked will be no more, though you look carefully at his place, he will not be there but the meek shall inherit the land and delight themselves in abundant peace.
Psalm 37:1-11

Delight yourself in the Lord, and he will give you the desires of your heart

Yesterday we learned not to fret but instead to do good, trusting in the Lord. Practically, we do that by looking up instead of looking around. Look up to God. Trust who He is and what He is doing. In fact, delight yourself in the Lord, and He will give you the desires of your heart.

When we let our minds dwell on those evildoers, we fret. We become resentful and angry. But when we trust that God is sovereign and good, we experience a freedom to do good and leave the consequences up to Him. We can then continue to keep our heart turned toward Him and enjoy the treasure of who He is. Our heart is quieted before Him in worship.

Then, you know what happens? He gives us what we long for! When we delight in Him, we find that our deepest desire has been Him all along! When we were focused on the evildoers, we were deceived about what we really wanted. We thought it was some temporary pleasure or some fleeting fulfillment, but that was not the truth.

Sometimes this verse is manipulated to make us think that God is our genie in a bottle—that we can get whatever our little heart desires by conjuring up some feeling of delight towards Him. That's blasphemy. And baloney! God has created us so that we will seek to fill up the longings of our soul. All that we do is an attempt to get this satisfaction! Much of the time, we are "far too easily pleased," as CS Lewis says.

It's when we delight in Him that we find He is what we really want.

The best way to delight in Him is to feast on His Word. Meditate on it. Memorize it. And mind it!

Finish today by reading Psalm 84.

Day 4

Fret not yourself because of evildoers; be not envious of wrongdoers! For they will soon fade like the grass and wither like the green herb. Trust in the Lord, and do good; dwell in the land and befriend faithfulness. Delight yourself in the Lord, and he will give you the desires of your heart. Commit your way to the Lord; trust in him, and he will act. He will bring forth your righteousness as the light, and your justice as the noonday. Be still before the Lord and wait patiently for him; fret not yourself over the one who prospers in his way, over the man who carries out evil devices! Refrain from anger, and forsake wrath! Fret not yourself; it tends only to evil. For the evildoers shall be cut off, but those who wait for the Lord shall inherit the land. In just a little while, the wicked will be no more, though you look carefully at his place, he will not be there but the meek shall inherit the land and delight themselves in abundant peace.
Psalm 37:1-11

Commit your way to the Lord; trust in him, and he will act. He will bring forth your righteousness as the light, and your justice as the noonday. Be still before the Lord and wait patiently for him;fret not yourself over the one who prospers in his way, over the man who carries out evil devices!

Do not become worried or angry over the prosperity of evildoers. Focus instead on the goodness of God. Entrust yourself to Him and do good to all (even the evildoers) wherever God has placed you. Immerse yourself in the worship of the Lord; fill up your heart with His wonder and be delighted with His goodness. You will find your deepest longings satisfied in Him.

As you experience His trustworthiness, commit your way to Him.

The word "*commit*" seems like it means to promise or dedicate oneself to another person or cause. But the Hebrew word that we translate as "*commit*" is "galai" and has an interesting dimension to its meaning. It means "to roll oneself upon." What a rich truth this word choice conveys! The psalmist is explaining the "don't worry" of the earlier verse by telling us that we are to transfer our burdens from our shoulders to the Lord's! That we can rely on, entrust ourselves to, put our plans in the hands of, the only one who can be trusted to take care of us. That's the same idea expressed in I Peter 5:7, "*casting all your anxiety on Him because He cares for you.*"

Entrust your future, your reputation, and your life plan. Commit your health concerns, your parenting stresses, and your marriage state. Roll onto the Lord that problem with your friend, that shortfall in your finances, that mistreatment by your boss. Instead of acting according to our female nature to fix things ourselves (or at least to do something about it!), we trust God to act. We believe that He is at work on our behalf in spite of what we can see—in His time, in His way.

And we will find that He will shine His light on things. He will expose what is wrong and bring to light the truth...in His time.

But He will not act if we get in His way. We have to roll our burdens onto Him and leave them there for Him to handle as He sees best.

What burdens are you holding onto today?

Day 5

Fret not yourself because of evildoers; be not envious of wrongdoers! For they will soon fade like the grass and wither like the green herb. Trust in the Lord, and do good; dwell in the land and befriend faithfulness. Delight yourself in the Lord, and he will give you the desires of your heart. Commit your way to the Lord; trust in him, and he will act. He will bring forth your righteousness as the light, and your justice as the noonday. Be still before the Lord and wait patiently for him; fret not yourself over the one who prospers in his way, over the man who carries out evil devices! Refrain from anger, and forsake wrath! Fret not yourself; it tends only to evil. For the evildoers shall be cut off, but those who wait for the Lord shall inherit the land. In just a little while, the wicked will be no more, though you look carefully at his place, he will not be there but the meek shall inherit the land and delight themselves in abundant peace.
Psalm 37:1-11

Refrain from anger, and forsake wrath! Fret not yourself; it tends only to evil. For the evildoers shall be cut off, but those who wait for the Lord shall inherit the land. In just a little while, the wicked will be no more, though you look carefully at his place, he will not be there but the meek shall inherit the land and delight themselves in abundant peace.

Psalm 37 offers us the contrast of the woman who worries and the woman who trusts. We see in this passage that fretting leads to evil. Worrying, anger, resentment, strife. But the woman who trusts in the Lord will be at peace regardless of the circumstances. She will trust in God's sovereign goodness and not be tempted to manipulate people or events to suit her own agenda.

What are some ways we can be a fretful woman?

By trusting our emotions rather than the Lord. By making decisions based on desires, which seem paramount but later prove to be temporary. By seeking to establish ourselves as important in the eyes of others instead of finding our significance and security in Jesus.

Through this psalm, God is urging us to stop fretting, to cease from our anger over things that we do not like. He warns us that evil is inevitable when we give in to our emotions; we will become fearful in addition to fretful.

But meekness–that attitude which trusts that God is not only loving and faithful but also that He is in control–such a spirit enables us to be calm in the midst of storms and to have courage in the midst of battle. A woman like this is not controlled by emotions or hormones or circumstances, but instead she is secure and stable and consistent…always trusting that God is good and that He is for her.

What does it mean to *"inherit the land"*? One day, those who are meek will rule this world with Christ.

Did you get that? How faithfully we live in this life has an impact on what we will do in eternity…

WEEK 48 - ETERNAL REWARDS

Day 1

And just as my Father has granted Me a kingdom, I grant you that you may eat and drink at my table in my kingdom and you will sit on thrones judging the twelve tribes of Israel. Luke 22:29-30

Blessed are the meek for they shall inherit the earth. Matthew 5:3

This is not an often-taught topic and that is such a shame, because these truths have the potential for unlimited impact on our eternity. So much so that the choices and priorities of our everyday living will be drastically changed.

First, let's be sure that we know that we are not talking about how to be saved. Look up Titus 3:5-7 and write out the basis of our salvation:

That settles that!

However, that does not mean that our behavior here on earth after salvation does not have a bearing on how we spend eternity! Not where, mind you, but how. After life on earth as we know it is done, God's glorious plan includes putting His people (that would be you and me!) in positions of authority, ruling and reigning with Christ. (Does that make you gasp? Me, too!) He has much work to be done that we cannot even imagine and He is going to put us in charge...

Read Matthew 25:14-30 and Luke 19:11-27. I know that is a lot to read today but do not skim over it. Even if you think it is familiar to you.

Dear sister, God gave us gifts and opportunities that He expects us to use for Him. He wants us to multiply what He has graciously given and He will reward us in direct proportion to what we have done with what He has given us. Not everyone will receive the same commendation from Him. In fact, it is clear from these passages that if we do not use what God has placed in our care to honor Him, then we will suffer loss. No, we do not lose our salvation but we will lose the reward He has for us, including the opportunity to serve Him most fully in eternity.

Those are sobering thoughts. Spend some time now asking Him what He wants you to do with the truth He has shown.

Day 2

So whether we are at home or away, we make it our aim to please him. For we must all appear before the judgment seat of Christ, so that each one may receive what is due for what he has done in the body, whether good or evil. 2 Corinthians 5:9-10

It is unspeakably amazing that God chooses to reward us for serving Him! Let us always remember that His rewards are purely a reflection of His generous grace and not our worthiness.

Today, let's ponder some of the details of His generosity...

This verse is written to believers, not all people. It refers to a magnificent display of God's glory where the followers of Christ are evaluated for their works done on earth. (Remember, this is not about testing us for salvation! It is testing our works!)

The Greek word that we translate as *"judgment seat"* is "bema." In the Greek athletic games of this time, the bema was the place where judges determined and publicly honored the winners of the contests. The Apostle Paul uses this word to explain to us that Jesus will test our works and reward us accordingly.

Look up each of these scriptures and write out what you see there:

- Proverbs 24:12

- Ecclesiastes 12:13-14

- Matthew 10:26

- Matthew12:36-37

- I Corinthians 3:8

- Revelation 2:25-29

- Revelation 22:12

Clearly, there will be an accounting in heaven of how we lived our lives on earth.

Day 3

For no one can lay a foundation other than that which is laid, which is Jesus Christ. Now if anyone builds on the foundation with gold, silver, precious stones, wood, hay, straw— each one's work will become manifest, for the day will disclose it, because it will be revealed by fire, and the fire will test what sort of work each one has done. If the work that anyone has built on the foundation survives, he will receive a reward. If anyone's work is burned up, he will suffer loss, though he himself will be saved, but only as through fire. I Corinthians 3:11-15

We know from previous days that we will receive rewards for our labor. Just because God is incredulously generous! But how is He going to measure them out, what will He do to determine our reward? This passage further explains the evaluation process. Our works will be tested by fire. Fire burns up some materials but it refines others by removing the impurities. Some of the works that we do will make it through that fire but others will not. That is a sobering truth.

These verses describe two different sets of materials: wood, hay, straw and gold, silver, precious stones. One group is easily obtained, commonplace, and cannot withstand the fire. The other group is very valuable–they require effort to obtain and cannot only withstand the fire but actually be refined by it.

What is the fire? Look up Jeremiah 23:29 and Isaiah 30:27 to find the answer:

Girlfriends, our God is a consuming fire. Were it not for His mercies, we all would be consumed in the presence of His throne! On that day, the works of our lives will be revealed and tested. They will be exposed to the holy fire of His presence. Going into the fire, it will not be evident what materials comprise our works, but once they come out, it will be quite obvious! Not only will the fire burn up the worthless things, but it will also do something else.

Have you ever done something for the Lord but maybe your attitude was a little off? Or you found yourself wanting some praise for it? Or maybe you detected some pride way down deep? Well, bless our amazing God, He will use the fire to burn those impurities off the works of ours that are valuable and make them perfectly pure! That is a glorious truth!

What are the things that will come out as gold, silver, and precious stones? I am not an expert on God's choice of building materials but I have some thoughts to share. Tomorrow. ☺ In preparation for that, look up these verses and note what you learn from them. Don't worry about putting the puzzle together yet; just glean truth from these verses.

- John 15:16

- Galatians 5:22-23

- Luke 8:11

- Ephesians 4:11-16

- I Corinthians 4:5

Day 4

You did not choose me, but I chose you and appointed you that you should go and bear fruit and that your fruit should abide, so that whatever you ask the Father in my name, He may give it to you. John 15:16

But the fruit of the Spirit is love, joy, peace, patience, kindness, goodness, faithfulness, gentleness, self-control; against such things there is no law. Galatians 5:22-23

Jesus didn't leave us clueless about what He says is valuable; here we see exactly what His purpose is for us as His followers: to bear fruit. Think for a moment, what is the chief characteristic of fruit? Not that it is sweet and tastes good, but botanically speaking, the chief characteristic of fruit is that it contains seeds! And then we have the next clues...

Now the parable is this: The seed is the Word of God. Luke 8:11

And he gave the apostles, the prophets, the evangelists, the shepherds and teachers, to equip the saints for the work of ministry, for building up the body of Christ, until we all attain to the unity of the faith and of the knowledge of the Son of God, to mature manhood, to the measure of the stature of the fullness of Christ, so that we may no longer be children, tossed to and fro by the waves and carried about by every wind of doctrine, by human cunning, by craftiness in deceitful schemes. Rather, speaking the truth in love, we are to grow up in every way into him who is the head, into Christ, from whom the whole body, joined and held together by every joint with which it is equipped, when each part is working properly, makes the body grow so that it builds itself up in love. Ephesians 4:11-16

Put all those thoughts together and what do you see?

The way we "*build well,*" the way we live a life that produces gold, silver, and precious stones is to live out our love for God by loving others, specifically by helping others grow in their walk with Him. He provides our building materials in the forms of His gifts and opportunities. Then we appropriate His grace and operate in His strength, and He produces His fruit in us as we serve Him. It produces the love, joy, peace, patience, kindness, goodness, gentleness, and self-control that spill out as we build up the body for Him. It might be a word of encouragement to a weary young mom or a generous gift of money to missions. It could be teaching His Word to first graders on Sundays or singing lullabies to your babies. Maybe it's rebuking a sister in sin or feeding the homeless. The key elements I think are work done for the body of Christ, based on the truth of His Word, done in His strength and for His glory.

One last thought—what insight do we gain from I Corinthians 4:5?

Day 5

Therefore do not pronounce judgment before the time, before the Lord comes, who will bring to light the things now hidden in darkness and will disclose the purposes of the heart. Then each one will receive his commendation from God. I Corinthians 4:5

Why does God promise us rewards in heaven for what we do for Him on earth? It sounds practically scandalous, doesn't it? As though being with Jesus isn't enough? What else could we possibly want or need?

Not one thing. Truth. Not one thing more will we possibly want. So, why?

I will never even pretend to know the mind of God but I think perhaps He has given us some insight into a reason behind His preposterous generosity. To motivate our right behavior!

When my kids were little, I wanted them to love to read. I knew that it would be so beneficial to them! They would learn so much, it would sharpen their minds in all other areas, and plus, I knew they would enjoy it if I could just get them to do it! I knew I could require it of them (I am their teacher, after all!) or demand that they read, but I knew that would not work for the long haul. And I knew that we often resent the things we have to do, even if those things are good things. So God gave me an idea–appeal to the self-serving nature in us all! You got it–bribe them to do what I wanted them to do and what I knew would bless them! I devised a reward system for reading: Book Bucks. I compiled a list of books I wanted them to read for each age and assigned point values to each book. (The more I wanted them to read it–such as missionary biographies- the more points I gave.) Upon completion of each book, I awarded paper money–book bucks–that they could save and then trade in for prizes.

It worked like a charm! They were now motivated to read and did so cheerfully because they knew they were "earning" coveted prizes like Beanie Babies, trips to DQ with Dad, or no kitchen duty for a week! And, you know what happened? They grew to love to read. All on their own. Over time, the reward ceased being the Book Bucks and became the reading itself.

Maybe, just maybe, that's what God is doing with our rewards. He is motivating us to the behavior He desires for us, to the acts of selflessness and kindness and service that will deepen and bless our lives right now–just because He is generous. And He loves us. Wow.

One last thought–what do we do with these rewards of gold and silver and precious stones once we get them? I am not sure. We won't "need " them in heaven. But since He gives them to us, there must be a purpose.

Here's a thought, look up these passages: I Corinthians 3:9-15 and I Peter 2:5. What do you notice in both these passages?

Maybe we take our treasures and decorate the walls! Perhaps it is the fire-tested works of the saints that will adorn the walls of the city on that day!

WEEK 49 - WORKS OF A BELIEVER

Day 1

For we are his workmanship, created in Christ Jesus for good works, which God prepared beforehand, that we should walk in them. Ephesians 2:10

I have a painting hung above the fireplace in my basement. It depicts an old barn in a hay field, done in browns and beiges. To the discerning art critic, it probably wouldn't merit a great deal of attention. Likely no one in sophisticated circles would long to own it.

But to me, it is priceless. I would never give it away or even sell it to the highest bidder. To me, it is beautiful and irreplaceably treasured.

Not because the scene is so beautiful or because it is so rare, but because of who painted it and gave it to me.

A friend, who became so dear to me in college and then moved to the mission field, tried her hand at painting before she left. She found she had a good bit of talent for it and she completed a few pieces, just for fun. One such piece is displayed in my den, a precious reminder of one I love so very much.

The painting is valuable because of who made it.

Regardless of what the art experts may think about my painting, I know beyond a shadow of doubt they may cast upon it that this painting is of inestimable value.

Girlfriends, it's the same for you and me. We are His workmanship. The master designer has conceived and created us according to His flawless plan. We must not listen to the amateur art critics who try to speak into our lives, those who judge us according to temporal standards and find us lacking. Our design is not only intentional…it is also good. We are of infinite value because of who made us. We are His workmanship, created in Christ Jesus.

Unlike my precious painting, however, the designs of the master are not created to just hang around and get looked upon. We have been created with purpose. Purpose that is not incidental but rather priority–for good works, which God prepared beforehand, that we should walk in them.

Let's be about discovering what those are for each day.

Day 2

The one who receives a prophet because he is a prophet will receive a prophet's reward, and the one who receives a righteous person because he is a righteous person will receive a righteous person's reward. And whoever gives one of these little ones even a cup of cold water because he is a disciple, truly, I say to you, he will by no means lose his reward. Matthew 10:41-42

Sometimes we are tempted to compare ourselves to others and we usually come up lacking, especially in the spiritual realm. We look at missionaries and ministers and others who seem to be doing lots more for God than we consider ourselves as doing, and we label ourselves inferior.

That's not how God's economy works.

First, know that His economy works according to His character and that He is unfathomably generous and loving! So whatever rewards we receive from Him are first of all because He is lavish in His giving!

Next, notice what He considers significant—our heart. Loving and ministering to others is what He values, no matter what the scope of the deed seems to be!

Lastly, know that every single thing we do that has any eternal value whatsoever is only possible because of His grace working through us.

Read each of these verses and list what is treasure-worthy in God's sight:

- Luke 14:12-14

- Matthew 5:10-12

- Matthew 6:1-18

- Matthew 19:29

We will do this last one together since we began with it today: Matthew 10:41-42

The last verse is a bit easier to grasp—giving even a cup of cold water to a little one can have eternal significance. A cup of cold water in Jesus's day took some effort. No dispenser on the front of the fridge! It required a trip to the well and drawing it out, so it seems that the acts that require us to go to some trouble for those who appear insignificant are the ones Christ values. Verse 41 takes some thought, but perhaps it is conveying the truth of the body working together in order to function well. *"Receiving a prophet"* is on the same level as a prophet—when we serve so as to enable others to do what God has called them to do, we are then participating in their work as well.

What a glorious truth!

Day 3

Now there are varieties of gifts, but the same Spirit; and there are varieties of service, but the same Lord; and there are varieties of activities, but it is the same God who empowers them all in everyone. To each is given the manifestation of the Spirit for the common good. I Corinthians 12:4-7

We are created in Christ Jesus for good works. God already has a mission for us and He has already equipped us with gifts specifically suited to accomplishing that which He has prepared for us to do.

It is irrelevant if we think we are gifted because the truth says that we are. Every follower of Christ is endowed with a variety of gifts that are to be employed in a variety of services. And the purpose in every single life is for the good of God's people.

What are these gifts that He has imparted to us?

Having gifts that differ according to the grace given to us, let us use them: if prophecy, in proportion to our faith; if service, in our serving; the one who teaches, in his teaching; the one who exhorts, in his exhortation; the one who contributes, in generosity; the one who leads, with zeal; the one who does acts of mercy, with cheerfulness. Romans 12:6-8

For to one is given through the Spirit the utterance of wisdom, and to another the utterance of knowledge according to the same Spirit, to another faith by the same Spirit, to another gifts of healing by the one Spirit, to another the working of miracles, to another prophecy, to another the ability to distinguish between spirits, to another various kinds of tongues, to another the interpretation of tongues. All these are empowered by one and the same Spirit, who apportions to each one individually as he wills. I Corinthians 12:8-11

What are the ones you see listed in each passage?

Ask the Lord to speak to your heart about how He has gifted you and especially how He wants you to utilize those gifts for Him. Write out what you hear Him say.

Day 4

Now you are the body of Christ and individually members of it. And God has appointed in the church first apostles, second prophets, third teachers, then miracles, then gifts of healing, helping, administrating, and various kinds of tongues. Are all apostles? Are all prophets? Are all teachers? Do all work miracles? Do all possess gifts of healing? Do all speak with tongues? Do all interpret? But earnestly desire the higher gifts. And I will show you a still more excellent way. I Corinthians 12:28-31

The Apostle Paul exhorts us to not only know that we have gifts, but especially to accept them as God's tools for serving Him.

Then, in a flash of realization that we humans tend to focus on the gift instead of the purpose of the giver, he urges us on. The gifts are not what we are to long for.

If I speak in the tongues of men and of angels, but have not love, I am a noisy gong or a clanging cymbal. And if I have prophetic powers, and understand all mysteries and all knowledge, and if I have all faith, so as to remove mountains, but have not love, I am nothing. If I give away all I have, and if I deliver up my body to be burned, but have not love, I gain nothing. I Corinthians 13:1-3

Let's not get so caught up in what our special gifts are that we neglect the reason we have them—to love others. We can speak impressive words and do impressive things even to the point of sacrifice but if there is not love, it all means nothing. Instead, we are just making a bunch of meaningless noise.

We must ask ourselves, in our service to Him, is it with love?

Take the test:

Love is patient and kind; love does not envy or boast; it is not arrogant or rude. It does not insist on its own way; it is not irritable or resentful; it does not rejoice at wrongdoing, but rejoices with the truth. Love bears all things, believes all things, hopes all things, and endures all things. Love never fails. I Corinthians 13:4-8

Day 5

Pursue love, yet earnestly desire spiritual gifts. I Corinthians 14:1

This verse immediately follows Paul's exhortation of love. I love this! He instructs us on the gifts of the Spirit, he warns us not to value them above love, and then he ends with more urging to employ those gifts–just do it in love!

Notice the same urging in verse 12, *"So also you, since you are zealous of spiritual gifts, see to abound for the edification of the church."*

The gifts God has given us are not for our own pride but rather for the good of the body. Read Romans 12:3-6 and write that passage out:

Where are you employing the gifts He has given you? How well are you doing so with love?

Write out a commitment to Him regarding your gifts.

Day 1

Do you not know that those who run in a race all run, but only one receives the prize? Run in such a way that you may win. I Corinthians 9:24

I have fought the good fight, I have finished the course, I have kept the faith. 2 Timothy 4:7

You have earned an "Atta Girl!" You've hung in there–we've almost completed a year's worth of study. Way to go, girlfriend!

I am writing this during the 2016 Summer Olympics and I have had an absolute blast watching these athletes compete. (Side note: so many of them have testified of their faith in Christ. Glory to God, that is the most exciting part ever!) As I vicariously run and swim and spike the volleyball through them, I have been reminded over and over again how talented they are, how hard they must train, and what sacrifices are necessary in order for them to compete.

But mostly I think about what I consider to be the most important thing that goes into making Olympic champions.

Not talent or training or trading pleasure for workouts.

Perseverance. Or call it endurance, tenacity, or steadfastness. It's the ability to not give up, to keep doing what needs to be done even when it's hard or the results are not readily apparent. Hanging in there.

Story after story surfaces of athletes who fell short of success...but they kept trying. Oh, there are some stories of unbelievable talent and surreal abilities, but the ones that inspire us are those who had to overcome great obstacles in order to win. Those with odds stacked against them but they just wouldn't quit. Persevered. Endured. Would not give up.

Those are the stories that give us hope for our own story, that encourage us to keep doing what we know to do even when it's hard. And to try a little harder when giving up seems easier.

Living for Jesus is hard; the Apostle Paul describes it as a fight. Let us resolve to be able to say that we fought the good fight, finished well the course, and that we ran for the prize. Tomorrow we are going to take a look at some of those prizes, but I want us to ponder one last thought for today. Look up Hebrews 12:1. This verse encourages us to run with endurance, having set aside things that entangle and ensnare. But look at the beginning of the verse–what is the reason we are to run well?

Since we have so great a cloud of witnesses.

Scripture does not elaborate on who those witnesses are but I believe they are both heavenly and earthly people. I believe this is telling us that those who have gone before us are cheering us on, encouraging us to finish well, and also that there are others all around us watching our lives. When we hang in there, it helps them to know they can do the same. When we quit... well, we give them permission to quit as well. Will those that are watching you find you faithful?

Day 2

In the future is laid up for me the crown of righteousness which the Lord, the righteous Judge, will award to me on that day, and not only to me, but also to all who have loved His appearing.
2 Timothy 4:8

It almost feels greedy to long for crowns in heaven, doesn't it? Being with Jesus, forever away from the effects of sin and eternally in the presence of love and joy is more than enough to satisfy us completely! And yet, scripture repeats the promise of rewards, of treasure, and of crowns over and over and over. God is scandalously generous to us!

Before we check out the passages on crowns, take a moment and read Hebrews 11:6. What does this verse say about rewards?

So that means that desiring rewards is evidence of faith and obedience! Hebrews 12:2 tells us that Jesus endured for what? Rewards!

Now I do not know exactly what these rewards will be like. Our visions are so earthly and God's plans are so greatly divine! But we can dig out some clues from His Word that give us some insight into what He has in store for us. Let's dig....

What do we know about a crown? That it is a symbol of authority and honor. This lets us know that we will be honored to receive them in eternity and that His purposes for us include reigning with Him. (I know–it's almost preposterous to even consider myself ruling with Jesus but I'm just repeating what He says!) God inspired two different words to be used in His Word that give us further clues; we translate both of them as "crowns" but the Greek here is very helpful in distinguishing between them. The Greek word "diadem" designates the highest royalty and every time this word is used in scripture, it is only for Jesus. Hallelujah and amen! He will always be the one on the throne beside the Father. But in His generous grace towards us, He has laid up "stephanos" crowns–these are awarded to winners. Sort of like Olympic medals maybe! But they are not medals, they are definitely crowns, symbols of authority.

There seem to be different types:

- 1 Corinthians 9:24 indicates a victor's crown for those who finish well.

- I Thessalonians 2:19 describes what is sometimes called a soul winner's crown.

- I Peter 5:2-4 tells us of a crown of glory–a shepherd's crown–for those who faithfully teach the Word of God and lead by the example of their own lives.

- 2 Timothy 4:3-8 describes a crown of righteousness for those who, amidst adverse circumstances, never give up but faithfully long for Jesus to return.

- Revelation 2:10 assures us that those who pay the ultimate price for their faith will be rewarded with a special crown–the martyr's crown.

I am just sitting here grinning widely, thinking about how gorgeous you are gonna look in your crown!

Day 3

For you have need of endurance, so that when you have done the will of God you may receive what is promised. Hebrews 10:36.

We need endurance all the time. We need it in times of pain and difficulty, so as not to give up. We need it in times of temptation, so that we won't give in. We need it when we are weary of the battle and no sign of victory is in sight. We need endurance in prayer when the answers are not coming…and when the answer comes and it is "no." We need it when the attacks of the enemy are so very real and frightening that we feel defeat is inevitable. We need it when we feel that no one notices–or cares–about our battles and our pain. And we need it in times of prosperity so that we won't give away our faith and find our pleasure in that which will not satisfy truly. We need endurance, the consistent satisfaction in knowing Christ and making Him known, all the time.

How can we endure to the end, how can we persevere throughout the valleys and mountains of life? Probably lots of things are helpful but I want to focus on a couple today and more over the next two days.

- Absolute confidence in the love and sovereignty of God: Knowing beyond a shadow of a doubt, regardless of what goes on all around me, that God is simultaneously 100% love and 100% sovereign is a great faith-builder in my life. Without this confidence, I am tempted to fear or dismay or even become bitter when things seem to not be going "according to plan." With this certain assurance, I am able to trust it's not important what things "seem like." Instead, I am relying on God's sovereign love to work all things for His glory and my good. That helps me persevere, waiting to receive what has been promised.

- Consistent times with the Lord, on a daily basis: I can know all the right things, believe all the right truth, but without a steady, regular commitment to times of prayer and Bible study, I will inevitably stumble and fall away. Consistent time with the Lord strengthens our souls.

Read Romans 15:4 and see what how it exhorts us:

Daily handling of the sword of the spirit makes us better warriors. Read Ephesians 5:16-19 and see how this urges us towards perseverance:

Finally, read Romans 10:17 and see what builds our faith:

Day 4

Two are better than one because they have a good return for their labor. For if either of them falls, the one will lift up his companion. But woe to the one who falls when there is not another to lift him up. Furthermore, if two lie down together they keep warm but how can one be warm alone? And if one can overpower him who is alone, two can resist him. A cord of three strands is not quickly broken. Ecclesiastes 4:9-12

Assurance that God is sovereign and completely loving over all the affairs of the world, and my own personal life, is crucial to our perseverance. So is our commitment to consistent times in the Word and in prayer.

But there is something else that we must not overlook.

Other believers. We need other believers in our lives.

God designed us to need other believers. He programmed into our spiritual DNA the necessity of connection with others. Having other people as integral parts of our lives is frequently what keeps us persevering in the race. Our performance is enhanced (*"because they have a good return for their labor"*). We have someone to help us when something trips us up, and we have a source of encouragement to keep our heart from becoming cold and hard.

We need other people.

But these encouragers, these strengtheners, need to share our faith. *"A cord of three strands is not quickly broken,"* tells us there is a presence of a third strand in the cord of these valuable relationships–that of the Holy Spirit. Without Him, these friendships will not help us persevere in our faith.

There need not be only one special person to fulfill this role; often the Lord provides several people who each meet different needs in our life. (Indeed, beware of expecting one person to satisfy all your relational needs. That is quite suffocating and will likely destroy the friendship!) Have lots of mentors from whom you learn and many genuine friends with whom you mutually invest.

You may be thinking that sounds great! I'd love that, but I don't have even one friend like that. Ask the Lord, sweet sister, ask the Lord to supply what you need. Remind yourself of the truth in these verses:

- James 1:17

- Matthew 7:11-12

Living Letters

Day 5

And He put a new song in my mouth, a song of praise to our God; many will see and fear and trust in the Lord. Psalm 40:3

We have need of endurance. In order to receive what has been promised, we must persevere.

This week we have seen not only the importance of that, but also how to obtain it–trusting God's power and complete goodness, spending consistent time in prayer and His Word, and inviting and including other people into our life.

One more key that helps us not give up.

Read the above verse again and then these next ones and see what you think is one more element of endurance:

- Matthew 5:16

- I Peter 2:12

- I Thessalonians 1:6-8

- Hebrews 12:1

We started the week off with this thought. Running our race with endurance…because others are watching us. Yes, we need other people…and they need us.

Many times we are kept from quitting because we are reminded that we are an example to someone else. Somebody is looking at the we live and work and raise our kids, the way we talk and serve and care for others, and the way we celebrate and grieve and respond to adversity. We need to finish well because, mark it down, somebody is watching.

Somebody is watching to see if we quit when God's answer is no. Somebody is watching to see if we slip away from Christ when things seem to be going so well that we don't appear to need Him. Somebody is watching to see if we will remain faithful when He takes His gifts away.

Somebody is watching…will we be found faithful?

Day 1

Be imitators of me, as I am of Christ. 1 Corinthians 11:1

A few years ago, a sweet and generous friend invited my kids and me to spend a few days with her and hers at her beach house. Being at the beach is my happy place so, of course, I leapt at the chance. Because of an earlier commitment, I couldn't leave at the same time as my friend. Being the wise and compassionate friend that she is, she was not content to leave me to my senses. She took her husband's mobile GPS system, made sure it was programmed for their favorite route, and insisted I use it to get there. She's a gem, for sure.

I packed up my two youngest, as well as a buddy for my very youngest, and set out long after dark. I don't like to drive unfamiliar routes in the dark and especially not in the pouring rain. But I plugged that system in and focused only on its instructions. Turns out, there are several ways to reach this place, and a few tricky, unclear turns to make. But with this handy-dandy device, I was able to follow the tried and true route without mishap. I felt more confident and a lot less worried than if I would have had to navigate the journey with just my instincts. Not once did I consider it arrogant or presumptuous of my generous friend to suggest I use her pre-programmed GPS. Not once did I think of declining her offer and just winging it. Not once did I presume to be better off on my own. Instead, I was immensely grateful and fastidious to follow it precisely. I knew she'd been there a hundred times before and she knew the best way. Even if it wasn't easy in the dark with rain pouring and three other lives depending on my ability to stay out of the ditch, I knew I could make it if I just followed the instructions. Since I couldn't follow her car directly, I could instead follow the path she laid out for me. She showed tremendous compassion and concern to see to it I had a path to follow.

Why, then, are we so reluctant to do the same in life? Instead of telling someone a season or so behind us "just follow me, I can help you get there," we get down in the ditch with them and agree that it's a hard place to be. In an effort to maintain humility, we parade all our failures, whine about our woes, and insist everything is just impossible. We need instead to be people worth watching and trusting enough to emulate. Not perfection–just someone that would say, "you can imitate me because I am imitating Christ." Someone willing to be scrutinized...because they weren't afraid of what would be found. Someone willing to be examined because their reputation was of no concern–only Christ's. Someone willing to be followed because they were willing to follow.

Granted, it's hard to be a "human GPS." We're liable to make a wrong turn or project an ETA incorrectly, and that might cause some angst to whoever is watching our screen. But just as Mike Mulligan and his steam shovel Mary Anne, in that classic children's favorite, worked harder and faster because people came to watch–maybe the same will be true of us. Maybe just knowing that someone else is imitating us, we'll be more careful to imitate Christ...instead of expecting to be excused for laziness or error or stumbles.

Day 2

If you are like I am, you might be tempted to feel overwhelmed as you try to be what God calls us to be. We've learned a lot of great stuff from God's Word, to be sure, but it's also tempting to think of all the mistakes and failures in the past. Not to mention fearing an inability to live up to being the wise woman of God that we long to be.

So here's our verse for today:

For we walk by faith and not by sight. 2 Corinthians 5:7.

Hallelujah! If I look at myself and my circumstances, I am discouraged and defeated. But when I walk by grace through faith–the same way I trusted Him for salvation–my walk is established and abundant.

Practically speaking, how do we walk by faith? Well, first let's look at what it means to walk by sight. Walking by sight means that I am governed by my emotions (or hormones!) or my circumstances. To walk by faith is the antithesis of that–my behavior is not dictated by what I feel like or what is happening around me. Instead, I obey what His Word tells me to do...I am controlled and empowered by His Spirit within me. The life of faith is one of obedience–to Him.

Trust and be confident that He is at work within you, perfecting you, and at work around you to accomplish His plan. He wants us to be whole even more than we want it for ourselves (Philippians 1:6, Romans 8:25-30)!

What is He speaking to you about today? When you quiet your heart before Him, what is He telling you to do? To share a good word with a neighbor? To forgive someone who has wronged you? To give generously? To cease from a certain activity, even if it's not a sinful one? To reconcile with a family member or a friend?

It seems counterintuitive but when we walk by sight, we are unsteady, weak, uncertain, and easily thrown off course. But when we walk by faith, we are sure, confident, strong, and effective.

Close today by reading Colossians 2:6-7 and ask the Lord to help you walk by faith and not by sight. Then believe Him when He says He will do just that.

Day 3

Your kingdom is an everlasting kingdom, and your dominion endures throughout all generations. The Lord is faithful in all his words and kind in all his works. The Lord upholds all who are falling and raises up all who are bowed down. The eyes of all look to you, and you give them their food in due season. You open your hand; you satisfy the desire of every living thing. The Lord is righteous in all his ways and kind in all his works. The Lord is near to all who call on him, to all who call on him in truth. He fulfills the desire of those who fear him; He also hears their cry and saves them. The Lord preserves all who love Him, but all the wicked He will destroy. My mouth will speak the praise of the Lord, and let all flesh bless His holy name forever and ever. Psalm 145:13-21

Read over this passage a couple of times and let its truth sink into your soul. God is everlasting, from eternity past to eternity future. He is forever in both directions of the number line. He is always faithful and all His works are righteous and kind—regardless of what it looks like to me. He catches us when we stumble and restores us when we are broken. He hears us when we cry, what a comfort! He will one day destroy those who have stubbornly remained in their wickedness but He will keep forever those who love Him.

Focus now on one phrase in the middle of the passage, *"You satisfy the desire of every living thing."* Can you grasp the significance of that truth? We think we long for security, so we seek it in obtaining money. We think we need love, so we pin all our hopes onto relationships with friends or family. We think that if we were famous enough or attractive enough or popular enough that our ache for significance would be content.

But what we really desire is only to be satisfied in Him. The longings of our heart can only be gratified in who He is. When we settle for anything else, we will be disappointed, frustrated, and even angry. We find ourselves demanding from people and things and situation a joy that can only be delivered by our creator.

Day 4

Blessed is the man who walks not in the counsel of the wicked, nor stands in the way of sinners, nor sits in the seat of scoffers; but his delight is in the law of the Lord, and on his law he meditates day and night. He is like a tree   planted by streams of water that yields its fruit in its season, and its leaf does not wither. In all that he does, he prospers. The wicked are not so, but are like chaff that the wind drives away. Psalm 1:1-4

I want that *"prospering in all he does"* and *"yielding fruit"* and *"not withering"* part, don't you? How can we become women like this? Instead of ones that get blown away by the winds of life?

Here's what this psalm exhorts:

- Not following wrong counsel: Sounds simple and straightforward, doesn't it? But it's not. Wrong, wicked counsel is everywhere. Magazines, well-intentioned friends, talk shows, and blogs :) It's extremely easy to find (and to follow). It's harder to learn and to discern wise counsel from the wicked—to recognize lies in contrast to God's ways, and then to obey it. But that's what successful women learn to do.

- Loving the truth and the ways of God: Making God's Word a priority in terms of time and treasure, studying it, and finding joy in it. It's a challenge to find the time to do this in the midst of all our demands. But successful women learn that this is the key to meeting all those demands. Just like we eat because we're hungry, not because we have to—successful women feast on the Word of life.

When these things characterize a life, that person will be full of life—vibrant and constantly nourished by life-giving water. This life will be like a strong tree that won't be torn down by strong winds. Its leaves won't dry up when the heat bears down.

Instead, this life will be a source of fruit for those around it. Rich. Abundant. Prosperous.

One last thought...this fruit is borne *"in its season."*

Fruit is borne in one season but it's been planted and fertilized and nurtured throughout preceding ones.

May we be ones that are tending to our vines so that the season of fruit production will be rich.

Day 5

But Jesus said, "They need not go away; you give them something to eat." They said to Him, "We have only five loaves here and two fish." And He said, "Bring them here to me." Matthew 14:14-18

These verses are from a familiar story. Jesus was teaching to a crowd of folks (as in 5000+) and it got time to eat. No Chick-fil-A was nearby and Jesus had compassion on the people. I expect He was hungry, too! So He told His disciples to feed them.

You know what happened. They were perplexed at His request because they didn't have anything to eat themselves, much less enough to feed this hungry bunch. Then a little boy, scripture calls him "a lad" in the Gospel of John, offers what he has–five barley loaves and two fish.

I wonder if the disciples scoffed at him. Silly boy, to think that such a paltry portion could make a dent in what was needed to take care of all these people! Indeed it was a pitifully meager offering, a mustard seed provision in the face of a mountain of need.

But in Jesus's hands, it became so much more. Miraculously, it multiplied to be not just what was needed, but even more. So much more that 12 baskets of leftovers were gathered after everyone had eaten *"as much as they wanted,"* John tells us.

Twelve baskets. Ya think that number was a coincidence?

I don't. I believe God provided one for each of the 12 perplexed disciples to pick up and marvel at what God can do with what we have to offer.

Maybe you are feeling like the disciples did. You might be facing a mountain of need and no provision is in sight. People may want from you more than you have to give. Offer Jesus what you do have. Even if you feel inadequate or insufficient or just plain lacking, offer it anyway. Trust Him to meet the need…in such a way that He and only He gets the glory.

Oh, and one more thought. Did you ever wonder who packed that lunch?

With everything in me, I believe it was his Mom–a Mom who raised a lad with a heart to share, the confidence to offer, and the willingness to sacrifice. She saw the purpose of her parenting as packing one lunch to feed an entire crowd. I believe it was a Mom whose boy knew that in the hands of Jesus, there is no such thing as "too little."

WEEK 52 - OBEDIENCE

Day 1

"Not everyone who says to me, 'Lord, Lord,' will enter the kingdom of heaven, but the one who does the will of my Father who is in heaven. On that day many will say to me, 'Lord, Lord, did we not prophesy in your name, and cast out demons in your name, and do many mighty works in your name?' And then will I declare to them, 'I never knew you; depart from me, you workers of lawlessness.' Everyone then who hears these words of mine and does them will be like a wise man who built his house on the rock. And the rain fell, and the floods came, and the winds blew and beat on that house, but it did not fall, because it had been founded on the rock. And everyone who hears these words of mine and does not do them will be like a foolish man who built his house on the sand. And the rain fell, and the floods came, and the winds blew and beat against that house, and it fell, and great was the fall of it." And when Jesus finished these sayings, the crowds were astonished at his teaching, for he was teaching them as one who had authority, and not as their scribes. Matthew 7:21-28

"Not everyone who says to me, 'Lord, Lord,' will enter the kingdom of heaven, but the one who does the will of my Father who is in heaven. On that day many will say to me, 'Lord, Lord, did we not prophesy in your name, and cast out demons in your name, and do many mighty works in your name?' And then will I declare to them, 'I never knew you; depart from me, you workers of lawlessness'"

It's the last week of our year together and I've loved having you along for the journey. The time in His Word has been sweet. We've learned a lot of truth, and seen glimpses of the glory of God all along the way. But sweet times, great truth, and glory revealed are incomplete without one thing.

Obedience.

We can read all about the holiness and power of God, and even hear what He wants us to do, but if we don't obey Him, then, well, the question has to become—do we even know Him?

In this passage, we see that on that day, there will be many who have done good works. And from the outside looking in, it would seem to us that those works have been in Jesus's name. But Jesus warns us here that we must not presume that to be true. Just because we or anyone else talks a good talk and seems to do a lot for Jesus, does not mean there is salvation. That is a scary thought.

What, then, is the difference?

Obedience to the Son—obedience which comes because we love and treasure Christ above all else, above selfish ambitions and conveniences and desires.

Let's check our own hearts. What do we treasure most of all?

Day 2

"Everyone then who hears these words of mine and does them will be like a wise man who built his house on the rock. And the rain fell, and the floods came, and the winds blew and beat on that house, but it did not fall, because it had been founded on the rock. And everyone who hears these words of mine and does not do them will be like a foolish man who built his house on the sand. And the rain fell, and the floods came, and the winds blew and beat against that house, and it fell, and great was the fall of it." And when Jesus finished these sayings, the crowds were astonished at his teaching, for he was teaching them as one who had authority, and not as their scribes. Matthew 7:24-29

The way we can know that we belong to Jesus is not by a past event but rather by our present and continuous obedience. That is not to say, of course, that we will never stumble ever again! But what Jesus is saying here is that one who does not just call Him Lord, but rather is characterized by obeying Him, is the wise one—the one that knows Him and obeys what He says to do.

And the life of one who obeys Him will be different from the one who does not.

Notice these two in this passage—the wise man and the foolish man. The rain and the floods and the winds came into each of their lives. Just because we follow Christ in obedience does not exempt us from the difficulties of life. We should not expect our days to be all sunshine, no problems, or all wishes granted when we trust Christ. In fact, He tells us plainly that we should expect trouble and persecution instead! But when problems come, when the diagnosis is cancer, or the finances are drained dry, or the relationship will not mend, then we can expect a difference.

When a life is not based on obedience to His commands, the difficulties of life will cause our "house" to fall. What we built so carefully will crumble into pieces.

Perhaps the greatest tragedy of this is the phrase *"great was the fall of it."* The repercussions from a "house" falling apart are that it affects not only the builder but also so many others.

But a life built on the Rock—one that habitually obeys His Word—will stand even as the storms of life assail it. And many can find protection in that house because it will not fall.

What is your life built on?

Day 3

Has the Lord as great delight in burnt offerings and sacrifices, as in obeying the voice of the Lord? Behold, to obey is better than sacrifice, and to hearken than the fat of rams. For rebellion is as the sin of divination, and stubbornness is as iniquity and idolatry. I Samuel 15:22

Sometimes we know what to do about a certain situation but we don't want to do it. So we substitute another action that appears "sacrificial" in an attempt to appease God...and assuage our guilty conscience. It might be any number of things–perhaps God is speaking to us about our finances, and instead of obeying what He says to do, we volunteer to keep the nursery. Or maybe the opposite is true–perhaps God is calling us to serve somewhere and instead we want to write a check!

Maybe He is telling us to abstain from some habit but we ignore that and try to do something "big" for Him instead. Or we might refrain from a big step of faith, telling ourselves that we should be content with wherever we are at the moment.

The rebuke from the prophet Samuel to King Saul is recorded above and he tells us plainly that obedience is the lifeblood of one who follows Christ. Disobedience is serious, not trivial at all. Here we learn that God labels disobedience as rebellion. And a stubborn heart is actually idolatry because it places the desires of self (pleasure, approval of others, power or fame, material gain) above the commands of God.

But obedience, ah, obedience is the opposite of this! Obedience honors God because it acknowledges His right to the throne! God delights in the obedience of His people because it glorifies Him as God. And because He is always good, always loving, we can know that obedience to His commands is the path to blessing for us!

Sometimes we act like obedience is soooooo hard, too hard in fact, but that is a lie. God's commands are not too hard. Deuteronomy 30:11 says, *"This commandment which I command you this day is not too hard for you."* And 1 John 5:3 says, *"This is the love of God, that we keep his commandments. And his commandments are not burdensome."*

Also, let's remind ourselves that whatever God tells us to do is for our own joy. So He is really delighting in us when He tells us to obey. Deuteronomy 10:12–13 says, *"And now, Israel, what does the Lord your God require of you, but to fear the Lord your God, to walk in all his ways, to love him, to serve the Lord your God with all your heart and with all your soul, and to keep the commandments and statutes of the Lord which I command you this day for your good."*

Has the Lord as great delight in burnt offerings and sacrifices, as in obeying the voice of the Lord? Behold, to obey is better than sacrifice, and to hearken than the fat of rams. For rebellion is as the sin of divination, and stubbornness is as iniquity and idolatry. I Samuel 15:22

Day 4

For I know the plans I have for you, declares the Lord, plans for welfare and not for evil, to give you a future and a hope. Jeremiah 29:11

As the Father has loved me, so have I loved you. Abide in my love. If you keep my commandments, you will abide in my love, just as I have kept my Father's commandments and abide in his love. These things I have spoken to you, that my joy may be in you, and that your joy may be full. John 15:9-11

Dear sister, do you believe these words? Do you believe that God's plans for you are good, and full of hope and promise? Will you trust Him that the greatest joy is to be found in obeying His commands and resting in His love for you?

Do not listen to the lies that can so subtly creep in to our hearts–lies that make us think our appearance is of extreme importance, or that happiness can be found in a beautiful home or a comfortable bank account, or that God's plans are punitive and spartan in order to make us "do better."

I so want you to build your life on the truth. The truth that God is good and all His ways are loving and faithful. The truth that His way is indeed narrow and few are those that find it but oh my, how worth it! The truth that God loves you and me more deeply than we can ever fathom and that it is His glorious desire to have us with Him for eternity so that we can experience the riches of His love forever.

The enemy is always lying to us about God's glory and His dwelling place. Resolve not to fall victim to his schemes. Test every thought against the scriptures. Trust only His Word and not your own thoughts and certainly not your feelings! Search out His truth, dig for it like diamonds, desire it above all else, and trust it alone.

What is one example from your own life of a lie you have believed?

What is the truth you need to replace it with?

The power of His Word performs its work in us who believe (I Thessalonians 2:13).

Day 5

We ought always to give thanks to God for you, brothers, as is right, because your faith is growing abundantly, and the love of every one of you for one another is increasing. 2 Thessalonians 1:3

We've made it, a whole year of enjoying the beauty and glory of God's Word together. I wish I could look next to me on my sofa and see your dear face. I would reach over and hug you so tight and let you know I am so proud of you. I'm so thankful that we got to do this journey together. Sister, it has been my utmost joy and honor to do this alongside you! I hope you feel the same.

I'd love to hear from you. I'd love to know how your life absorbed these treasures and what God did in you and those around you as a result of your time in His Word. Would you let me know? Please? My email address is chamfam@bellsouth.net. It would make my day to know how you're doing and where you plan to go from here.

Don't stop—stay in His Word. Let it dwell richly in you and experience the growth of your faith. As you do, your life will show the evidence of His love pouring through you. Blessing others, making new disciples, meeting needs, growing His Kingdom, and being filled with the glorious knowledge of our Lord.

If you haven't already tackled the Bible reading plan, resolve to do it now. Read through the entire Bible and see what you learn that you've never known before. You will not be able to contain your joy, I promise!

Keep seeking Him. Keep enjoying Him. Keep obeying Him.

He is coming back soon.

I'll see you at home—our forever home! Hallelujah and amen!

Sample Bible Reading Plan

(check online for other schedules, such as chronological or daily selections from Old and New Testaments)

Jan 1: Gen 1-3	Jan 30: Ex 36-38	Feb 28: Deut 3-4
Jan 2: Gen 4-7	Jan 31: Ex 39-40	Mar 1: Deut 5-7
Jan 3: Gen 8-11	Feb 1: Lev 1-4	Mar 2: Deut 8-10
Jan 4: Gen 12-15	Feb 2: Lev 5-7	Mar 3: Deut 11-13
Jan 5: Gen 16-18	Feb 3: Lev 8-10	Mar 4: Deut 14-16
Jan 6: Gen 19-21	Feb 4: Lev 11-13	Mar 5: Deut 17-20
Jan 7: Gen 22-24	Feb 5: Lev 14-15	Mar 6: Deut 21-23
Jan 8: Gen 25-26	Feb 6: Lev 16-18	Mar 7: Deut 24-27
Jan 9: Gen 27-29	Feb 7: Lev 19-21	Mar 8: Deut 28-29
Jan 10: Gen 30-31	Feb 8: Lev 22-23	Mar 9: Deut 30-31
Jan 11: Gen 32-34	Feb 9: Lev 24-25	Mar 10: Deut 32-34
Jan 12: Gen 35-37	Feb 10: Lev 26-27	Mar 11: Josh 1-4
Jan 13: Gen 38-40	Feb 11: Num 1-2	Mar 12: Josh 5-8
Jan 14: Gen 41-42	Feb 12: Num 3-4	Mar 13: Josh 9-11
Jan 15: Gen 43-45	Feb 13: Num 5-6	Mar 14: Josh 12-15
Jan 16: Gen 46-47	Feb 14: Num 7	Mar 15: Josh 16-18
Jan 17: Gen 48-50	Feb 15: Num 8-10	Mar 16: Josh 19-21
Jan 18: Ex 1-3	Feb 16: Num 11-13	Mar 17: Josh 22-24
Jan 19: Ex 4-6	Feb 17: Num 14-15	Mar 18: Jud 1-2
Jan 20: Ex 7-9	Feb 18: Num 16-17	Mar 19: Jud 3-5
Jan 21: Ex 10-12	Feb 19: Num 18-20	Mar 20: Jud 6-7
Jan 22: Ex 13-15	Feb 20: Num 21-22	Mar 21: Jud 8-9
Jan 23: Ex 16-18	Feb 21: Num 23-25	Mar 22: Jud 10-12
Jan 24: Ex 19-21	Feb 22: Num 26-27	Mar 23: Jud 13-15
Jan 25: Ex 22-24	Feb 23: Num 28-30	Mar 24: Jud 16-18
Jan 26: Ex 25-27	Feb 24: Num 31-32	Mar 25: Jud 19-21
Jan 27: Ex 28-29	Feb 25: Num 33-34	Mar 26: Ruth
Jan 28: Ex 30-32	Feb 26: Num 35-36	Mar 27: 1Sam 1-3
Jan 29: Ex 33-35	Feb 27: Deut 1-2	Mar 28: 1Sam 4-8

Mar 29: 1Sam 9-12	Apr 30: 1Chron 1-2	Jun 1: Job 1-4
Mar 30: 1Sam 13-14	May 1: 1Chron 3-5	Jun 2: Job 5-7
Mar 31: 1Sam 15-17	May 2: 1Chron 6	Jun 3: Job 8-10
Apr 1: 1Sam 18-20	May 3: 1Chron 7-8	Jun 4: Job 11-13
Apr 2: 1Sam 21-24	May 4: 1Chron 9-11	Jun 5: Job 14-16
Apr 3: 1Sam 25-27	May 5: 1Chron 12-14	Jun 6: Job 17-20
Apr 4: 1Sam 28-31	May 6: 1Chron 15-17	Jun 7: Job 21-23
Apr 5: 2Sam 1-3	May 7: 1Chron 18-21	Jun 8: Job 24-28
Apr 6: 2Sam 4-7	May 8: 1Chron 22-24	Jun 9: Job 29-31
Apr 7: 2Sam 8-12	May 9: 1Chron 25-27	Jun 10: Job 32-34
Apr 8: 2Sam 13-15	May 10: 1/2Chron 28-1	Jun 11: Job 35-37
Apr 9: 2Sam 16-18	May 11: 2Chron 2-5	Jun 12: Job 38-39
Apr 10: 2Sam 19-21	May 12: 2Chron 6-8	Jun 13: Job 40-42
Apr 11: 2Sam 22-24	May 13: 2Chron 9-12	Jun 14: Ps 1-8
Apr 12: 1King 1-2	May 14: 2Chron 13-17	Jun 15: Ps 9-16
Apr 13: 1King 3-5	May 15: 2Chron 18-20	Jun 16: Ps 17-20
Apr 14: 1King 6-7	May 16: 2Chron 21-24	Jun 17: Ps 21-25
Apr 15: 1King 8-9	May 17: 2Chron 25-27	Jun 18: Ps 26-31
Apr 16: 1King 10-11	May 18: 2Chron 28-31	Jun 19: Ps 32-35
Apr 17: 1King 12-14	May 19: 2Chron 32-34	Jun 20: Ps 36-39
Apr 18: 1King 15-17	May 20: 2Chron 35-36	Jun 21: Ps 40-45
Apr 19: 1King 18-20	May 21: Ezra 1-3	Jun 22: Ps 46-50
Apr 20: 1King 21-22	May 22: Ezra 4-7	Jun 23: Ps 51-57
Apr 21: 2King 1-3	May 23: Ezra 8-10	Jun 24: Ps 58-65
Apr 22: 2King 4-5	May 24: Neh 1-3	Jun 25: Ps 66-69
Apr 23: 2King 6-8	May 25: Neh 4-6	Jun 26: Ps 70-73
Apr 24: 2King 9-11	May 26: Neh 7	Jun 27: Ps 74-77
Apr 25: 2King 12-14	May 27: Neh 8-9	Jun 28: Ps 78-79
Apr 26: 2King 15-17	May 28: Neh 10-11	Jun 29: Ps 80-85
Apr 27: 2King 18-19	May 29: Neh 12-13	Jun 30: Ps 86-89
Apr 28: 2King 20-22	May 30: Est 1-5	Jul 1: Ps 90-95
Apr 29: 2King 23-25	May 31: Est 6-10	Jul 2: Ps 96-102

Jul 3: Ps 103-105	Aug 4: Is 31-35	Sep 5: Ezek 21-22
Jul 4: Ps 106-107	Aug 5: Is 36-41	Sep 6: Ezek 23-24
Jul 5: Ps 108-114	Aug 6: Is 42-44	Sep 7: Ezek 25-27
Jul 6: Ps 115-118	Aug 7: Is 45-48	Sep 8: Ezek 28-30
Jul 7: Ps 119:1-88	Aug 8: Is 49-53	Sep 9: Ezek 31-33
Jul 8: Ps 119:89-176	Aug 9: Is 54-58	Sep 10: Ezek 34-36
Jul 9: Ps 120-132	Aug 10: Is 59-63	Sep 11: Ezek 37-39
Jul 10: Ps 133-139	Aug 11: Is 64-66	Sep 12: Ezek 40-42
Jul 11: Ps 140-145	Aug 12: Jer 1-3	Sep 13: Ezek 43-45
Jul 12: Ps 146-150	Aug 13: Jer 4-6	Sep 14: Ezek 46-48
Jul 13: Prov 1-3	Aug 14: Jer 7-9	Sep 15: Dan 1-3
Jul 14: Prov 4-6	Aug 15: Jer 10-13	Sep 16: Dan 4-6
Jul 15: Prov 7-9	Aug 16: Jer 14-17	Sep 17: Dan 7-9
Jul 16: Prov 10-12	Aug 17: Jer 18-22	Sep 18: Dan 10-12
Jul 17: Prov 13-15	Aug 18: Jer 23-25	Sep 19: Hos 1-7
Jul 18: Prov 16-18	Aug 19: Jer 26-29	Sep 20: Hos 8-14
Jul 19: Prov 19-21	Aug 20: Jer 30-31	Sep 21: Joel
Jul 20: Prov 22-23	Aug 21: Jer 32-34	Sep 22: Amos 1-5
Jul 21: Prov 24-26	Aug 22: Jer 35-37	Sep 23: Amos 6-9
Jul 22: Prov 27-29	Aug 23: Jer 38-41	Sep 24: Oba-Jonah
Jul 23: Prov 30-31	Aug 24: Jer 42-45	Sep 25: Micah 1-7
Jul 24: Ecc 1-4	Aug 25: Jer 46-48	Sep 26: Nahum 1-3
Jul 25: Ecc 5-8	Aug 26: Jer 49-50	Sep 27: Hab-Zeph
Jul 26: Ecc 9-12	Aug 27: Jer 51-52	Sep 28: Haggai 1-2
Jul 27: Solomon 1-8	Aug 28: Lam 1-3:36	Sep 29: Zech 1-7
Jul 28: Is 1-4	Aug 29: Lam 3:37-5	Sep 30: Zech 8-14
Jul 29: Is 5-8	Aug 30: Ezek 1-4	Oct 1: Malachi 1-4
Jul 30: Is 9-12	Aug 31: Ezek 5-8	Oct 2: Matt 1-4
Jul 31: Is 13-17	Sep 1: Ezek 9-12	Oct 3: Matt 5-6
Aug 1: Is 18-22	Sep 2: Ezek 13-15	Oct 4: Matt 7-8
Aug 2: Is 23-27	Sep 3: Ezek 16-17	Oct 5: Matt 9-10
Aug 3: Is 28-30	Sep 4: Ezek 18-20	Oct 6: Matt 11-12

Oct 7: Matt 13-14	Nov 8: John 9-10	Dec 10: Eph 4-6
Oct 8: Matt 15-17	Nov 9: John 11-12	Dec 11: Philippians 1-4
Oct 9: Matt 18-19	Nov 10: John 13-15	Dec 12: Colossians 1-4
Oct 10: Matt 20-21	Nov 11: John 16-18	Dec 13: 1 Thess 1-5
Oct 11: Matt 22-23	Nov 12: John 19-21	Dec 14: 2 Thess 1-3
Oct 12: Matt 24-25	Nov 13: Acts 1-3	Dec 15: 1 Timothy 1-6
Oct 13: Matt 26	Nov 14: Acts 4-6	Dec 16: 2 Timothy 1-4
Oct 14: Matt 27-28	Nov 15: Acts 7-8	Dec 17: Titus-Philemon
Oct 15: Mark 1-3	Nov 16: Acts 9-10	Dec 18: Heb 1-6
Oct 16: Mark 4-5	Nov 17: Acts 11-13	Dec 19: Heb 7-10
Oct 17: Mark 6-7	Nov 18: Acts 14-15	Dec 20: Heb 11-13
Oct 18: Mark 8-9	Nov 19: Acts 16-17	Dec 21: James 1-5
Oct 19: Mark 10-11	Nov 20: Acts 18-20	Dec 22: 1 Peter 1-5
Oct 20: Mark 12-13	Nov 21: Acts 21-23	Dec 23: 2 Peter 1-3
Oct 21: Mark 14	Nov 22: Acts 24-26	Dec 24: 1 John 1-5
Oct 22: Mark 15-16	Nov 23: Acts 27-28	Dec 25: 2John-Jude
Oct 23: Luke 1	Nov 24: Rom 1-3	Dec 26: Rev 1-3
Oct 24: Luke 2-3	Nov 25: Rom 4-7	Dec 27: Rev 4-8
Oct 25: Luke 4-5	Nov 26: Rom 8-10	Dec 28: Rev 9-12
Oct 26: Luke 6-7	Nov 27: Rom 11-13	Dec 29: Rev 13-16
Oct 27: Luke 8-9	Nov 28: Rom 14-16	Dec 30: Rev 17-19
Oct 28: Luke 10-11	Nov 29: 1Cor 1-4	Dec 31: Rev 20-22
Oct 29: Luke 12-13	Nov 30: 1Cor 5-8	
Oct 30: Luke 14-16	Dec 1: 1Cor 9-11	
Oct 31: Luke 17-18	Dec 2: 1Cor 12-14	
Nov 1: Luke 19-20	Dec 3: 1Cor 15-16	
Nov 2: Luke 21-22	Dec 4: 2Cor 1-4	
Nov 3: Luke 23-24	Dec 5: 2Cor 5-9	
Nov 4: John 1-2	Dec 6: 2Cor 10-13	
Nov 5: John 3-4	Dec 7: Gal 1-3	
Nov 6: John 5-6	Dec 8: Gal 4-6	
Nov 7: John 7-8	Dec 9: Eph 1-3	

Made in the USA
Lexington, KY
01 June 2018